Something More than Human

Something More than Human

Biographies of Leaders in American Methodist Higher Education

Charles E. Cole, *editor*
with an introduction by F. Thomas Trotter

United Methodist Board of Higher Education and Ministry
Nashville, Tennessee

Cover photos from top (left to right): Willbur Fisk, Isabella Thoburn, William H. Crogman, John O. Gross

Table of Contents

Contributors

JOANNE CARLSON BROWN is assistant professor of religion at Pacific Lutheran University, Tacoma, Washington, and teaches and does research in nineteenth-century American church history, historical theology, and feminist theology in the Western tradition.

CHARLES E. COLE is the editor of *Quarterly Review: A Scholarly Journal for Reflection on Ministry* and a former staff member of the General Board of Higher Education and Ministry of the United Methodist Church, Nashville, Tenn.

ROBERT F. DURDEN is professor of history at Duke University, Durham, N.C., where he served as chair of the department, 1974–80, and has written *The Dukes of Durham* (1975), as well as some half-dozen books in U.S. history, with particular emphasis on southern history. His book, *The Self-Inflicted Wound: Nineteenth-Century Southern Politics,* is to be published in 1985. He is also doing research on a history of Duke University.

CAROLYN DE SWARTE GIFFORD is coordinator of the United Methodist Women's History Project for the General Commission on Archives and History of the United Methodist Church, Madison, N.J. She published articles on the WCTU's image of woman in the late-nineteenth century in *Women in New Worlds,* vol. 1, 1981, and *Women and Religion in America,* vol. 1, 1981.

LOUIS-CHARLES HARVEY is professor of theology and ethics, United Theological Seminary, Dayton, Ohio, and has published numerous articles on black pastors and the black churches for religious periodicals.

ROSEMARY S. KELLER is associate professor of religion and American culture, Garrett-Evangelical Theological Seminary, Evanston, Ill., and is co-editor of the *Women and Religion in America* and *Women in New Worlds* series. She is also codirector of the Institute for the Study of Women in the Church at Garrett-Evangelical and is beginning research in 1985 on personal spirituality and social responsibility.

GERALD O. MCCULLOH is retired as associate general secretary of the Division of Ordained Ministry, General Board of Higher Education and Ministry of the United Methodist Church, Nashville, Tenn. He is the author of *Ministrial Education in the American Methodist Movement,* 1980.

JAMES D. NELSON is professor of church history at United Theological Seminary, Dayton, Ohio. He wrote the article on the Moravian Church in the *Encyclopedia Brittanica* and has made a new translation of the *Life of Jacob Albright,* by George Miller, originally published in 1811 in German.

FREDERICK A. NORWOOD is retired as professor of church history at Garrett-Evangelical Theological Seminary and is the author of *The Story of American Methodism,* 1974, and the editor of *Sourcebook of American Methodism,* 1982.

MICHAEL D. RYAN is associate professor of theology at Drew University, Madison, N.J. He edited and contributed to *The Contemporary Explosion of Theology,* 1975, and *Human Responses to the Holocaust,* 1981.

EVAN SCOLE is a writer and editor in New York City who once edited a newsletter for Fisk University, has written for the Black College Fund, and has contributed numerous articles to various United Methodist publications.

NORMAN W. SPELLMANN is professor of religion and psychology at Southwestern University, Georgetown, Tex. He wrote chapters on the Christmas Conference and the division of 1844 in the *History of American Methodism*, 1964. He is co-author of *The Methodist Excitement in Texas* (1984) and wrote a history of First United Methodist Church, Wichita Falls, Tex., and *Growing a Soul*, 1979, a biography of A. Frank Smith.

ARTHUR W. WAINWRIGHT is associate professor of New Testament, Candler School of Theology, Emory University, Atlanta, Ga.

DOUGLAS J. WILLIAMSON is studying for a Ph.D. degree in church history at Boston University. He has written two articles on Willbur Fisk for *Methodist History*, the first in October, 1982, and the second in January, 1985.

CHARLES YRIGOYEN, JR., is general secretary of the General Commission on Archives and History of the United Methodist Church, Madison, N.J., and editor of *Methodist History*.

Editor's Preface

AS PART OF the celebration of the United Methodist bicentennial, 1984–88, the General Board of Higher Education and Ministry publishes this and other volumes. These books express in one form the historic commitment of the denomination to higher education. Although celebration sometimes connotes an uncritical acclamation of past accomplishments, this enterprise was conceived as a way to evaluate the past with as much regard for veracity as reverence for the tradition. Such a critical assessment means taking note of lapses and errors, and the underlying assumption of the publishers is that after two hundred years the church can reflect on its experience with maturity and some degree of self-transcendence.

To acknowledge limitations of the past does not obviate the need to recognize gratefully that both higher learning and the church's sense of mission belong to a single vision. The term *vision* seems appropriate, since those who comprehend the possibility and promise of the future are often called visionaries. Many of these seers, prophets, and wise persons have been teachers and leaders in schools and colleges of the church. The metaphor of seeing also recalls the close relation between wisdom and faith, the insight and intimate knowing that in biblical parlance characterize the lover and the beloved, the master and the disciple.

Histories of higher education typically emphasize masters and not disciples, but these books pay homage to the latter through reflections on campus ministry, the contribution of students and graduates, and the role of the church in tutoring nations and cultures. Histories often seem to be chiefly institutional, but these books will focus on individuals, ideas, and communities as well. And to speak of history sometimes implies that only the past will be considered, whereas these publications seek to stimulate the church to rethink itself into the future.

If we were to rethink who we are, we could not omit higher education. We are a church of many ethnic communities, and the church has emphasized inclusiveness through the historically black colleges and its commitment to accessibility. We are a church engaged in many theological tasks, the primary one being the attempt to understand our peculiar identity as God's called and chosen in this historical moment, and theology and higher learning have been nearly coterminous. We are also a church in mission, and that mission has always included higher education.

These bicentennial books have several purposes, then. One is to raise the consciousness of the church about the way higher education grows out of the very being of the church. The church would be a religious body without higher education, but it would not be the United Methodist Church. Another purpose is to stimulate the church to address the theological reasons for its continuing ministry in higher education. This theological task arises from the church's calling as Jesus' disciples to reflect continuously on its calling and mission. A third purpose is to initiate discussion of public policy issues related to higher education, particularly church-related higher education. Many of these policy issues involve the fundamental principles and values for which the church has fought throughout its history.

Finally, these volumes also have the purpose of opening up areas of further research into church-related higher education—what it was and what it is now—with the hope the United Methodist Church can re-envision the future. The romance of the past can enrich an appreciation for our potentiality. To know our history is to expand the future of higher learning and the church. History that interprets the past can be alluring and highly constructive; but history that impels us toward the future can be reinvigorating and even transforming.

Introduction

by F. Thomas Trotter

General Secretary
Board of Higher Education and Ministry

THE LITERATURE OF the Wesleyan movement abounds with writing about the early Methodists and their evangelistic spirit, their social concerns, and their penchant for innovative ecclesiology. Only infrequently have commentators noted the extraordinary attention paid by Wesley and his friends to education.

The fact is that the followers of John Wesley had a certain rage for learning. Wesley himself was one of the most learned men of his time. Even by modern standards, his library was impressive. His mastery of literature, classical and scientific, was extensive. He confidently expected his associates to be equally well-informed and equipped. He never described himself as a parish priest, but as a member of Oxford. The university defined his self-understanding. To this day, United Methodist preachers favor academic gowns to clerical garb, a remote but clear salute to the founder of the movement.

Our temptations to idolize John Wesley to one side, let it be noted that the Wesleyan movement arose in the remarkable eighteenth century. This was the period named by historians as the "Enlightenment." It was a time of rapid expansion of knowledge and articulation of the scientific methodology. Wesley's contemporaries were Newton and Rousseau, Faraday and Mills, Kant and Franklin. It was a period of exploding intellectual and social change. John Wesley and his friends breathed that air.

Therefore we understand something about the Wesleyan movement when we note that the Methodists were the only major post-Reformation movement to have been born in the Enlightenment. Most other Christian movements have their roots in the Reformation itself, including Presbyterianism, Roman Catholicism, and Lutheranism. Curiosity about the world and a passion for knowing the world have been with us from the beginning as Wesley's children. That curiosity and rage to know were products of the Enlightenment. The movement began in university rooms, with serious university students interrupting their classical studies to think about, of all things, the conversion of England.

This intersection of piety and care for the world introduces us to one

1

of the great achievements of the Wesleys, their ability to link learning and evangelism. Of course that has often been a missionary strategy. The history of Christian missions from earliest times has revealed the close connection between evangelism and learning. In order to learn about the gospel one must be able to read the Scriptures. Reading the Scriptures opens persons newly empowered to access to areas otherwise closed to them. That access inevitably leads to social change. Knowledge and piety are partners in empowering persons in their faith and work. Missioners have always discovered the revolutionary character of learning.

In this radical form, learning took root in British Methodism. The rage for learning took the form of the founding of schools for children of persons who would not otherwise have had any access to education in the closed aristocratic system of the time. Kingswood School, founded in 1747, was John Wesley's first. Originally located near Bristol, the school was opened for children of colliers, itinerant preachers, and friends of the connection. Curiously those three categories of students are still primary constituents for United Methodist institutions.

After Kingswood, British Methodists established more than 900 other "colleges"—precollegiate institutions by American custom—most of which were eventually to provide the foundation of Britain's free schools. Wesley's goals were clear. Piety was not enough. An educated person loving God was the goal and a nation of persons educated to fulfill God's plan for the conversion of England was the purpose.

It was no coincidence, then, that as the American Methodists organized themselves into a church in Baltimore in 1784, one of the first actions taken was the agreement to start a school at Abingdon, Maryland. The school thus became the first of more than 1,000 others to follow under Methodist auspices. Cokesbury College (1784) was the first of a line that stretched to Virginia Wesleyan (1966).

Unlike Britain, where the form of the schools remained precollegiate, in the new nation academies quickly aspired to become colleges. And as the nation moved westward, leaving behind the Colonial colleges, long since establishment institutions, English- and German-speaking Methodist laity and pastors planted colleges like saplings on the frontier. Nearly every county seat at one time or another had a church college. The family trees of these institutions reveal branches and roots involving mergers and reorganizations to create the splendid group of 128 United Methodist institutions surviving today.

Some of the most distinguished universities of the land at one time were related to the Methodist movement: Auburn University (1856), Goucher College (1885), Kansas State University (1858), Marshall University (1837), Morgan State University (1867), Northwestern University (1851), University of Southern California (1880), Vanderbilt University

(1872), Wesleyan University (1830), and Wilberforce University (1847). The complete historical record of universities and colleges related to the denomination is to be found in *To Give the Key of Knowledge: United Methodists and Education, 1784–1976* (Nashville: National Commission on United Methodist Higher Education, 1976).

One of the remarkable results of this extraordinary history is the fact that the system of church-related schools today has a combined operating budget in excess of the total operating budgets of all other units of the parent denomination itself. That gross figure was $2.6 billion in 1983 while the denomination reported a gross budget of $2.1 billion. In the aggregate, the system is approximately the size of the state university system of Indiana! It comprises 211,734 students, 12,934 faculty, and plant assets worth $3,483,831,000. Such figures would stagger the imaginations of the subjects of the following chapters.

Just as these data suggest a remarkable (if little-celebrated) chapter in our national history, so do the biographies of the subjects of this book represent "something more than human" energy and vision. These are truly remarkable people. Except for the Wesleys, Philip Otterbein, Jacob Albright, and Francis Asbury, most of the heroes and heroines of our tradition are known only to a few. The authors of this volume assume that it is important for our generation to become acquainted, belatedly, with this collection of dreamers and builders. For they were true Wesleyans. They combined learning and piety, evangelical zeal and enlightenment curiosity, practical vision and institutional imagination. We ought to know them better.

To our present generation, learning seems indifferent and available, therefore expendable. Since World War II, the expansion of the public sector has frequently overwhelmed the history of church-related independent higher education. Through most of our nation's history, however, access to learning was the church's mission. It is clear that the missionaries to Asia failed in their evangelical work until they began to establish schools of learning. Great church builders like Martin Ruter and W. W. Orwig were pastors and district superintendents. Willbur Fisk of Wesleyan was primarily a pastor. To note the curricula of those mid-century schools, one must admire the persistence of classical education and the presence of a religious ethos. The school and the church were partners in God's business.

The first characteristic of this noble company of pioneer educators is their utter confidence in their mission. They all were women and men without serious doubt about the centrality of education in the life of the church and the need to be somewhat outrageous in asserting that centrality. This certainty is especially true of the marvelous women included here: Isabella Thoburn, Mary McLeod Bethune, Belle Harris Bennett, and Lucy Rider Meyer. Colleges bear the names of two of them, and each of them was a model for women's liberation before the movement became popular. It is one of the ironies of missionary history that preaching and evangelism were considered the primary missionary enterprise and therefore teaching was left to spouses. Women, untrammelled by custom and prejudice in the mission field, seized the opportunity and began to teach, and schools were born. By the second generation of Christian missions in Asia, for example, education had become the highly successful strategy for opening a culture to Christianity. Many of the prominent Christian colleges of China and Japan identify strong women as founders and early leaders.

Bethune herself stands as one of the nation's great educators and a remarkable builder of Christian higher education. Not only did she excel in a profession dominated by men, but she exercised extraordinary national leadership for black people through her influence with Franklin and Eleanor Roosevelt and later administrations. She represented the highly personal style of college leadership of that period. Howard Thurman is but one of many national figures to have come under her care as a youth and who, from the perspective of late age, gave her honor. She has recently been honored by a postage stamp bearing her likeness and also a statue of her in the rotunda of the capital in Washington, D. C.

A second characteristic of this group of educators is their commitment to the idea of the connections between learning and faith. In the Wesleyan rage for learning lies the implicit suggestion that there is no disjunction between learning and faith. "Re-unite those two so long disjoined," wrote Charles Wesley, "knowledge and vital piety." As a movement of the Enlightenment, it was only natural for Wesleyans to believe that there was a connectedness to things that made experience important in discriminating God's will and God's way. So these pioneers did not see disconnections between piety and knowledge. In fact, they had a natural grace about the style of learning implied in faith. Lewis Davis, Fisk, Ruter, Orwig, and John M'Clintock were pastor/scholars, combining the piety and passion expected of Wesleyan preachers with the inquisitiveness and the scientific curiosity of frontier scholars. They were the true children of John Wesley, who himself was an avid student of the world, its sciences and its nostrums, its arts and its professions.

These educators were primarily traveling preachers. Their careers alternated between serving in the circuits, traveling as superintendents, and responding to the instructions of the conferences to establish and operate colleges. Their achievement had much to do with the establishment of what might be called the "Methodist ethos" in the nineteenth century in America. Ministers were the most educated persons in almost all communities of the land. They played a special role because of their education. In earlier periods, the religious were called "clerks"—a contraction of the word "clergy." Clerks they were because they were literate, and the word has come down to us in this fractured form.

It is amazing that these founders should not only have withstood the hostility that developed in the nineteenth century against religious learning, but that they should have prevailed in establishing a pattern for religious learning that survives into our period. In the mid-twentieth century, the traditional pattern of American higher education changed dramatically. Whereas before World War II, 75 percent of college students attended private, mostly church-supported colleges, after the war, 75 percent of college students attended public, state-supported colleges and universities. Thus many of the clergy completing education in the last three decades have not been nurtured in church institutions. Learning has taken on a more utilitarian shape. Rising costs have made private alternatives more problematic for United Methodist people. The usefulness of liberal learning in a church environment is called into question by the very persons for whom that was once self-evident, namely, the clergy.

It is helpful, then, to reassess the visions of these pioneers, whose worlds were perhaps less complex, but no less challenging. That they saw the ministry of learning as part of their ministry of the gospel is instructive.

An otherwise modern person may be surprised to discover how well informed and learned these pioneers were. There is a temporal conceit that too carelessly assumes that knowledge is cumulative. Live later, be smarter! Socrates helped his generation separate knowledge and wisdom. Knowledge without the gentle and ruthless exercise of judgment and experience is often demonic. So a third characteristic of this group of educators is the care and respect with which they approached academic work.

The charter of Illinois Wesleyan University (1850) recalls the founding of the school in the prairie. A handful of farmers established the school with produce for endowment. But what imagination and wisdom they had. Wherever in the charter the word *college* had been used, someone had scratched out that word and interlined the word *university*.

One's initial reaction to this can excusably be understood to be outrageous. A university in the open country? But wait. Americans were pious and religious folk in that period. Their world was understood by use of biblical and religious metaphors. They dreamed of the future. They saw the land as "promised" and "new Eden." Place-names re-

flected their eschatological vision: Salem, Shiloh, Providence, and Oxford, Cambridge, Paris. For the new world an old vision of a city of
human learning was not outrageous at all. Medieval European universities were in the open country when they were founded!

It is precisely this worldview of learning as the business of a community of persons willing to dream of the future that powered the schools
and colleges of the denomination. That meant for these women and men
a dual citizenship. They were citizens of the university where sectarianism was disability. But they were also citizens of the church. They
walked the fine line between loyalties. Yet their higher loyalty was to the
unity of piety and faith, and they lived out this unity in their lives.

There are remarkable stories about remarkable persons in this collection. Some of my teachers were students of some of these heroes of
learning. The late Ernest Cadman Colwell, my mentor, was a student of
Andrew Sledd whose story is told here. It is not unlikely that Sledd's
influence in biblical scholarship has never been fully described. His students became the leaders of critical New Testament scholarship in the
period 1935–75. In addition to the intellectual stimulation this one
teacher exerted on a generation, his students caught from Sledd a deep
piety and devotion to Christ that infused their work with remarkable
directness.

Sometimes the stresses between college and church became painful
indeed. Most educators have had to face such issues. What is reassuring
about the United Methodist system of higher education is the ability the
college and the church have had to wrestle with issues of apparent contradiction in institutional goals. One of the great moments in United
Methodist history is described in the chapter on William Preston Few. A
great university was born when Few refused to back off from support for
a faculty member whose publications challenged racist policies of a
powerful newspaper editor. William H. Crogman, the first black teacher
to come out of the freed slaves, pioneered in an equally impressive manner by espousing the ideals of W. E. B. DuBois for black empowerment.

Finally, the persons introduced to the reader in this collection were
persons of more than normal vision. That, by the way, is not a bad definition of a teacher, certainly of a builder. Given the complexities of institutional development known to us today, which of us would venture to
such bold initiatives as those of a John Dempster, who founded two great
theological schools (Boston and Garrett-Evangelical) and who, at the
time of his death, was making plans to go to the West Coast to found yet
another?

Among the heroes in this book, John Wesley Powell is probably better known outside the church. There he is considered one of the found-

ers of modern topography and mapping. He was one of the nation's experts on Indian cultures and, with students on an early "field trip," explored and mapped the Colorado River. He is generally considered to be the father of the United States Geological Survey, a work he came to after his teaching career at Illinois Wesleyan.

Another unforgettable visionary was Robert S. Maclay, whose career is inextricably linked with two universities on either side of the Pacific (Aoyama Gakuin and USC), and who also opened Methodist missionary work in the nation of Korea in 1884.

Two of the visionaries included in this volume I knew personally, but not well. Daniel L. Marsh was president of Boston University when I was a seminarian there. A person larger than life, he had the wit and the nerve to gather together a collection of loosely associated schools into a centralized campus within the shadow of the most prestigous universities in the land. That his vision has been filled by his successors is indication of the accuracy of his judgments.

John O. Gross was my predecessor once removed. He was the "builder" of the higher education system of The United Methodist Church. During his years, the denomination embarked on an extraordinary program of expansion and revitalizing institutions. He embodied the Wesleyan style of piety and learning held in uncomplicated ways and expressed in institutional gestures.

This is the bicentennial quadrennium of the United Methodist Church. This book of essays about the pioneers of church higher education is intended to recall to our consciousness the enormous contribution of education to the nation and to the church. The women and men introduced to you herein are examples of the vitality that still infects the Methodist way of seeing the world—namely with the binocular vision of piety and learning.

Other volumes in this series will explore other issues, including the theology of learning and strategies for the future and the history of the schools themselves. It is fitting that the first volume be focused on these spirits who, though flawed as all of us are, have left us a precious legacy and hope.

1

Belle Harris Bennett
(1852–1922)

Lucy Rider Meyer
(1849–1922)

by Rosemary S. Keller

R ELIGIOUS TRAINING SCHOOLS were among the most visionary Protestant educational ventures on the nineteenth-century
American religious and cultural scene. Between 1880 and 1915, educators founded nearly sixty training schools where lay people, most of
them women, prepared for professional service in churches and social
agencies. There they enrolled in brief, highly practical programs which
stressed the acquisition of biblical knowledge and skills useful in the
mission field. The training schools prepared persons for evangelism and
social service among the "heathen" of inner-city ghettos and foreign mission stations.

The schools responded to pressing conditions on the national and
world scene: first, to urbanization and the influx of immigrants in American cities, and second, to the foreign missionary movement and its call
to release millions from spiritual darkness and social degradation.
Churches like the Salvation Army came into being to address urban
need. Within established denominations, foreign and home mission
boards received increased program emphasis and funding. Inauguration
of women's missionary societies provided vigorous impetus to movements at home and abroad. Social service agencies, such as the YWCA
and the YMCA, settlement houses, and city missionary societies,
avowed religious motivation but fostered no denominational ties.

The expanding missionary enterprise depended upon trained
human resources. Because ordained ministers were unavailable in the
quantity needed, a host of laypersons were required for professional and
volunteer service. They came forward as consecrated home and foreign
missionaries, Sunday school teachers and administrators, pastors' as-

BELLE HARRIS BENNETT

Photo courtesy of Scarritt College.

LUCY RIDER MEYER

Photo courtesy of Garrett-Evangelical Theological Seminary.

sistants, evangelists, settlement workers, and secretaries of "Y"s. The turn-of-the-century became defined as an "age of laic activity in spiritual things." Within and outside denominational work, laypersons served the purpose, described by Dwight L. Moody of Moody Bible Institute trainees, as "gap men" or "irregulars" on the mission frontiers.

Religious training schools became the principle centers for preparation of lay workers, with United Methodist forerunners among the leading innovators. No women stand out more significantly for their major contributions to the Methodist Episcopal Church (MEC) and the Methodist Episcopal Church, South (MECS), than Lucy Rider Meyer and Belle Harris Bennett. They share the distinctions of being bold pioneers for laity rights for women and founders of the first and most important lay training schools in their respective denominations. Meyer founded the Chicago Training School for City, Home, and Foreign Missions in 1885. Based in part upon inspiration from Meyer, Bennett began the Scarritt Bible and Training School two years later. Instituted as training centers for women, the schools only later admitted men. Although all graduates did not become deaconesses, the schools served as official institutions for their preparation after the MEC introduced the office of deaconess in 1887 and the.MECS in 1902.

The lives of Meyer and Bennett span almost the same years, just as their personal backgrounds and contributions to the two Methodist denominations are remarkably parallel. Lucy Rider was born in 1849 and Belle Bennett three years later; both women died in 1922. Rider's heritage was grounded in old and substantial New England stock, and Bennett's represented the luxury and culture of Southern plantation life.

The fathers of both girls were farmers of means. Born in New Haven, Vermont, Rider's family traced its ancestry to early Massachusetts settlers. Bennett's ancestors migrated from Maryland to Whitehall, Kentucky, the small town of her birth. The first child of Richard Dunning Rider and his second wife, Jane Child, Lucy grew up in a family of nine children, two being younger brothers of her own, and six being older half brothers and sisters. Samuel and Elizabeth Chenault Bennett christened Belle, the younger of two daughters and the seventh among eight children, Isabel Harris after her paternal grandmother.

The homes of both families were centers of Methodist piety. The Riders read the Bible aloud together each day and sang hymns and prayed as a family. Lucy experienced personal conversion "to Jesus" at age thirteen as a direct result of a Methodist revival meeting. Her childhood appears to have been happy and secure, and she enjoyed vigorous play along with emphasis on religion and education from her early days. She attended elementary schools in her local community and was graduated with normal school preparation for teaching in 1867 from New Hampton Literary Institution in Fairfax, Vermont.

"Homelands," the plantation upon which Bennett grew up, was characterized both by its piety and gracious living. Tracing her denominational heritage to her paternal grandfather, a Methodist circuit rider, Bennett's family background also exemplified the white aristocracy of the South. Servants, financial security, political influence, and warm hospitality surrounded her from childhood. Her ancestors included Revolutionary War leaders, governors, senators, and state legislators. She received an excellent private education for a girl of her day. At age eleven, Bennett entered Dr. Robert Breck's school in nearby Richmond, Kentucky, continued her training at the Nazareth School in Bardstown, and completed her education at College Hill, Ohio.

Transitions between her own educational training and practical teaching experience marked the next several years of Lucy Rider's life. Spending a year in the South, in Greensboro, North Carolina, she instructed children in a Quaker freedmen's school. She returned to Vermont the following year with two young black women who established homes of their own in the area. In 1870 she entered Oberlin with advanced standing and was graduated two years later. While attending Oberlin, Rider became engaged to a young man who was preparing to be a medical missionary. To prepare herself to share missionary life with him, she studied two years, from 1873 until 1875, at the Woman's Medical College of Pennsylvania in Philadelphia. Her fiancé died in 1875, however, and Rider returned home to care for her parents, who were invalids. During the following three years, between 1876 and 1879, she served as principal of the Troy Conference Academy of the MEC in Poultney, Vermont; studied chemistry at Massachusetts Institute of Technology; and became a professor of chemistry at McKendree College in Lebanon, Illinois.

These experiences increased Rider's desire to serve humanity more directly. Resigning her teaching position, she became field secretary for the Illinois State Sunday School Association in 1881. She traveled extensively, working with leaders in religion, education, and social work. Another brief experience of teaching, instructing in Bible at the Northfield (Massachusetts) Seminary for Girls in 1885, preceded her marriage to Josiah Shelly Meyer, a businessman and YMCA worker in Chicago. Deeply interested in church and social work himself, their marriage became a rich relationship shared both personally and professionally. One child, a son, Shelly Rider, was born in 1887. Soon after, his mother resumed her medical training and received an M.D. degree from the Woman's College of Chicago.

Immediately after their marriage, Lucy and Josiah Meyer began their professional partnership as founders of the Chicago Training School for City, Home, and Foreign Missions. The vision originated from her long-felt need for a "Bible normal school" to train women entering religious, and particularly missionary, careers. Along with four students, the Meyers inaugurated the school in 1885, she becoming principal and he business manager. The Chicago Training School soon became a center for Methodist-related social work in the area. In the thirty-four years of the Meyers' codirection, the school graduated more than 5,000 students. Some forty philanthropic agencies, including hospitals, orphanages, and homes for the elderly, were spawned by the training school directly, or by its graduates. The deaconess movement became the most important and central work growing out of the school. The General Conference of the MEC authorized the work of deaconesses and prescribed rules for them in 1888. Commended by the Rock River Conference in 1887, the Chicago Training School became the first official deaconess training school of the denomination.

Bennett's young adulthood contrasted notably with that of Lucy Rider Meyer. Her active social life from early years was "crowned with all the graces of Southern womanhood." Until age twenty-three, she led a life of social diversion. Though many suitors presented themselves, she never chose to marry. When Bennett turned toward Christian philanthropy and church service, she always served on a voluntary basis. Her family's financial security meant that she never needed to seek paid employment, in contrast to Meyer.

Though she had long attended the local church in nearby Providence, Kentucky, with her family, Bennett did not become a member of the church until she was twenty-three, when she was motivated by a visiting Presbyterian evangelist. Such a decision, in one way, seemed a next logical step from her devout upbringing. Bennett never rebelled against the expectations set by her family. Rather, in her young adult years, she and her older sister, Sue, moved with ease into the two activities open to women in the church—teaching a Sunday school class and singing in the choir.

Spiritual growth, however, was not accomplished with such ease as is suggested on the surface. After joining the church she spent a summer attending revival meetings and religious lectures at Lake Chautauqua, New York, then returned to Kentucky where she experienced the baptism of the Holy Spirit. Deep soul-searching led to periods of depression, as well as to spiritual renewal, during her early church work. During one time of depression, in which she experienced "undefined sin" breaking her communion with God, Bennett turned to her close friend in Louisville, Harriet Thompson, who warned Belle that her immersion in Christian service had led her to neglect the nurture of her soul. Bennett then began the spiritual discipline of daily Bible study. She also recognized her need for spiritual support from others, such as that given by Harriet Thompson and her sister, Mette, who remained her close friends and spiritual companions over many years.

As was true of Meyer, Bennett's Christian commitment found primary expression in service to others. Missionary work became the central "vocation" of Bennett's life, arising in much the same way and time as did Meyer's. While attending a missionary meeting in Carlisle, Kentucky, in 1887 with her sister, Bennett experienced a deep concern over the lack of training of foreign missionaries. Learning that the Chicago Training School had originated out of the same need, Bennett wrote Meyer and received information and encouragement from her. Returning from a summer assembly at Lake Chautauqua in 1888, she responded audibly with these words to a felt call to begin a missionary training school for women: "Yes, Lord, I will do it."

Presenting her cause to the Woman's Board of Foreign Missions of the MECS, meeting in Little Rock, Arkansas, the following year, Bennett immediately received sanction by the board to raise funds for an institution of practical missionary training. Though at first she hesitated to accept the responsibility, she spoke widely in southern churches and camp meetings, drawing warm responses by her deep conviction, dignity, and sense of humor. Her effectiveness resulted in a clear sign before the end of the year to begin the project.

Nathan Scarritt of Kansas City, Missouri, offered land and $25,000 for a building, with the stipulation that the church contribute an equal amount. Bennett and Scarritt overcame opposition to establishing the school "so far west" in Kansas City and to including the training of home as well as foreign missionaries. The school was dedicated four years later in 1892, debt-free and partially furnished. The difficulties she experienced in reaching this success were formidable, as Bennett wrote: "There were days when I longed for death to relieve me of the responsibility of persuading the Church that missionaries needed training for their work. I was as literally driven of the Holy Spirit to establish the Training School as was Paul into Macedonia."

Bennett declined to serve as the first principal of Scarritt, continuing instead in the voluntary position of vice-president of the board of managers until her death. Scarritt sent more than one thousand workers during her lifetime.

Two primary questions emerge regarding the vision of the institutions and the practical application of the training given in the Chicago Training School and the Scarritt Bible and Training School by Meyer and Bennett: what were the foci of the educational programs of the schools, and how did deaconesses apply their training in the mission field after graduation?

Both schools concentrated on the training of laypersons, mostly women consecrated as deaconesses for service in the home and foreign mission fields. The most creative thrust of the institutions was preparation of students for work of evangelism and social service in inner cities, crowded by a host of European immigrants. Approximately one-third of the deaconesses graduated by Scarritt and probably a similar percentage by the Chicago Training School went to foreign mission fields. Others became nurses or wives of pastors.

Courses of study lasted two years or less. In Scarritt's first decade, only 107 of 264 students stayed the full two years. Religious zeal seems to have been the main gratification, for administrators said that no dedicated soul was left out. Students came from varied educational backgrounds, and leaders designed programs to accommodate that diversity. The 1913 bulletin of the Chicago Training School, for instance, included a "graduate division" for high school graduates, and a "special division" for persons of less academic background. Faculty measured performance more by dedication to service than by academic excellence.

Finally, lack of finances did not preclude students from admission. No tuition was charged and the cost of room and board was minimal. The schools could be run on such a basis financially because maintenance costs were low. Since most of the faculty were part-time and female, they received no salary. Until 1917, all employees of the Chicago Training School received only the allowances provided for deaconesses. Understood as an opportunity for service, their work carried no financial gain.

From her research into the training school movement, Virginia Brereton describes three main purposes in curriculum design: "to promote knowledge of the English Bible, provide a high proportion of practical subjects, and expose their students to varied forms of religious work by sending them outside the schools." Study of the Bible and its practical application provided the primary emphases of the schools. Pragmatic concerns called for use of only English texts of the Bible. Instructors feared that work in Hebrew, Greek, or Latin texts would tempt deaconesses to talk over the heads of ordinary people and take their time and energy away from direct personal service to others. Stress was put upon memory and recall of specific passages to soften the hearts and improve personal conduct of both the deaconesses and those evangelized.

Practical orientation determined methodology of the training schools in all their curriculum. Primary concern centered on how to teach the Bible and to convert the unredeemed. Instruction included bookkeeping for pastors' assistants and medicine for nurses, deaconesses, and medical missionaries. Other courses focused on the church's role in addressing poverty and crime in the inner city and methods of relating to persons in foreign mission stations.

Finally, the schools' curricula included on-site training in churches, settlement houses, slum mission centers, and hospitals comparable to modern-day field education in seminaries. The city served as a gigantic "laboratory," as stated in the Chicago Training School catalog: "A Christian training school should be in the heart of a great city for the same reason that a medical school needs to be near a hospital."

Two basic needs facing churches after the Civil War determined the mission work confronting deaconesses. First, middle-class, church-going citizens looked to deaconesses to help temper the threat of immigrants pouring into American cities. They feared this newly arrived foreign element to be "unchristian and ignorant masses," potential "revolutionary tinder." Deaconesses became key resources to evangelize and Americanize these masses, to save the cities.

Secondly, expanding work in foreign outposts necessitated single women missionaries. Most women who had served outside the United States earlier in the nineteenth century were wives of male missionaries. By 1860, general boards of denominations and women's societies called for more women in the mission field to work particularly with native women. They contended that native women had a right to education and elevation and could be of enormous influence in converting their husbands to Christianity. Juggling responsibilities as wives and mothers with church duties left wives of missionaries overburdened. Increasing the pool from among single women, notably deaconesses, provided the obvious source.

Although deaconesses ministered to all persons in the mission field, they recognized particular responsibilities for other women whose needs could not be met by male missionaries. "Woman's work for woman" in the foreign mission field took three primary forms: first, evangelistic efforts among the secluded, upper-class women of India and China and among the poor in cities and villages; second, academic, domestic, and industrial training of women and girls of all classes in mission schools; and, third, medical care of women and children often in hospitals and dispensaries built especially for females.

The work of deaconesses in America's inner cities had distinct parallels. Directed toward women and children in the slums, it focused on the same three thrusts of evangelism, education, and medical assistance. Deaconesses maintained settlement houses that provided practical, academic, and religious training. As the earliest social workers, they did house-to-house visitation to help meet individual needs of families in the neighborhoods.

"Woman's work for woman" in the inner cities was primarily directed toward personal religious conversion. Deaconesses recognized, however, that basic needs of food, work, and family had to be met for spiritual change to follow. Most secular settlement houses, such as Jane Addams's Hull House, held humanitarian uplift as their characteristic goal. The religious training schools went further, however, in teaching the Bible and in seeking religious conversions among the people of the neighborhoods.

The major justification of "woman's work for woman" was in making newly converted women agents in the evangelistic enterprise. Females became the crucial power in rehabilitating their families. "Woman's work" was often directed to mothers forced to shoulder full family responsibilities because their husbands were addicted to alcohol and their children were poorly fed and clothed. The stability of the home rested on the mother. Convert and train the women; then, the salvation of society, through their husbands and sons, would follow.

The needs for deaconesses in home and foreign mission fields during the late nineteenth century outran the available supply. Their services were welcomed and valued. Controversy regarding deaconesses arose, however, in determining whether their status was laity or clergy. James Thoburn, an MEC bishop and an advocate of the Chicago Training School, sought to dispel rumors that deaconess work would lead toward ordination. He argued that these women "speak for Jesus" and were not seeking rights for themselves. Because deaconess work constituted a sphere "for women only," its members were not crossing over the boundary line acceptable to established leaders of the church.

Meyer held the clear vision of deaconess work, however, as enlarging the boundaries for professional work of women in church and society. In an article written in the *Message and Deaconess Advocate* in 1895, she acknowledged the stereotype of the deaconess. And then she proceeded to shatter it:

> A deaconess is often pictured as a goody-goody kind of woman who goes softly up dirty back stairs, reading the Bible to poor sick women and patting the heads of dirty-faced children. But there is nothing a woman *can* do in the line of Christian work that a deaconess may not do. Her field is as large as the work of woman, and the need of that work. In deaconess ranks to-day may be found physicians, editors, stenographers, teachers, nurses, bookkeepers, superintendents of hospitals and orphanages, kitchen-gardners and kindergartners. In Omaha not only the superintending nurse, but the superintendent of the Methodist Episcopal hospital, an institution that within two years has cared for 1040 patients, are *(sic)* deaconesses.

The training school movement exemplified "woman's work for woman" in another way. Funds for the schools came primarily from the sponsoring agencies of women's missionary societies in the MEC and the MECS. The nickle-and-dime contributions of countless thousands of women in local churches in all parts of the country, along with the faith of their founders to trust the movements to God's care, brought the dreams of training schools to reality. Bennett described her experience of her early efforts to fund Scarritt:

> With the eyes of human wisdom the enterprise seemed one of childish weakness. No money, no resources . . . committed to an earthen vessel, untried and unknown, but I went out as directed in God's strength, committing my works and my ways unto Him. . . . From the old and young and rich and poor, donations have come. . . . Women have taken earrings from their ears, and watches from their bosoms, saying, "Take these, we have no money, but we want to give something for the cause of Christ."

Meyer wrote of the Nickel Fund (sic), through which women of the MEC financed the second home of the deaconess order in the 1880s, in a similar manner:

> Can a Twenty-five thousand dollar Home be built out of nickles? There are one million of women in the Methodist Episcopal church of the United States alone. Some one pleads for a penny a day from each of these women for the cause of missions. I would not ask that—365 cents every year—but five cents from each, not once a year, but *once in a life-time*—five cents, the despised nickle that we hand out so readily for a street-car fare or the daily paper—and $50,000, twice the amount asked for, would be in our hands for this building.

The returns from the Nickel Fund did not bring the desired $50,000. They did account for $3,000 the first year, however, and with other contributions, enabled construction to begin.

By such appeals, the training school staffs brought women throughout the country into sisterly alliance with the deaconess movement. The 1888 "Do-Without-Band" of the Chicago school provides a further notable example. There was no membership fee; a woman simply committed herself to the pledge: "I will look about for opportunities to do without for Jesus' sake." The school sent out fifteen hundred letters, asking each woman to contribute ten cents for an addition to the training school building and to mail copies of the letter to friends. More than $6,000 was received, along with responses such as: "I am delighted to be able to form one link of this beautiful chain of loving sisters. Inclosed (sic) find a dollar to make my part good and strong."

The Chicago Training School continued at the center of Meyer's professional and personal life until a few years before her death. With struggle, she maintained the independence of the school when the Woman's Home Missionary Society sought to assume authority over all Methodist deaconess work. Further dissension resulted from conflict with her husband over emphases of school policy. He favored concentration on biblical and religious training, while she sought a broader philanthropic approach. The conflicts led to declining enrollments from a peak of more than two hundred students in 1910. The Meyers resigned from their positions as principal and business manager in 1917.

A variety of educational concerns remained at the center of Bennett's life in later years. Much of her work focused on home missions. After the death of her sister Sue in 1892, Bennett sought to realize Sue's dream of education for children in in the mountains of southeast Kentucky. The Sue Bennett Memorial School opened in London, Kentucky, in 1897, and Bennett carried its financial burden until 1901.

As president of the Home Missionary Society of the MECS, and the Woman's Board of Home Missions of the denomination which grew out of it, Bennett worked to establish church settlement houses at the turn-of-the-century. The "Wesley Community Houses" and "Bethlehem Houses" for blacks, which together numbered more than forty, maintained a religious orientation along with a broad social program. In 1902, Bennett persuaded the General Conference to staff the houses with deaconesses. Overcoming resistance in the woman's society to work with blacks, Bennett also succeeded in establishing an industrial department for women at the Paine Institute for Negroes in Augusta, Georgia, in 1901. On the international scene, her educational interest resulted in fund-raising for the building of a woman's college in Rio de Janeiro, as well as the ecumenical Woman's Christian Medical College in Shanghai.

The training schools, however, remain the central educational contribution of Meyer and Bennett to the heritage of United Methodism. The worth of their efforts may be measured in part by evaluating the quality of education offered in the schools.

Decline of the schools in the World War I era after retirement of the founders suggests negative aspects of their legacy. Both the Chicago Training School and Scarritt had operated on meagre budgets since their founding, by means of resources donated by benevolent church women rather than money gained from endowments. This underfinancing particularly affected the ability of the schools to recruit faculty. Most faculty were training school graduates themselves, with no higher academic credentials, who taught out of dedication to the church and received only room and board for remuneration. Other teachers included clergymen, hired on a part-time basis, whose courses often modeled those of their own seminary experience of many years past. Rather than maintaining a uniform and structured curriculum, the offerings were generally determined by whoever might be available to teach in a given year.

Training schools faced crisis in the World War I period when rising educational standards necessitated institutional uniformity and new accrediting agencies for colleges and later seminaries. Agencies of the churches, such as boards of missions, also called for expanded curriculum and a more thorough preparation of candidates than training schools could accommodate. Professionalization, both for pastors and for lay workers in religious education and related areas, became the dominant goal. Proper academic credentials, which colleges and seminaries could provide, were increasingly valued over the experience and dedication of zealous deaconesses. In the process, seminaries opened doors more widely to women for training in Christian education and other practical fields, cutting into the normal supply of candidates for training schools. As enrollments dropped, training schools developed shorter-term ministerial programs open to men. They were unable to compete effectively with seminaries with expanded educational offerings and increased endowments.

Unable to attract more specialized and highly-trained faculty, to broaden curriculum, and to raise endowments, the Chicago school finally became a part of Garrett Biblical Institute in 1935. Work in Christian education remains an important part of the seminary's curriculum, however.

Unlike other training schools, Scarritt survived difficult times by adapting to the realities of the era. It raised academic standards to become a two-year college, with admission dependent upon graduation from a junior college. Scarritt also created a two-year graduate program and developed an institutional connection with Vanderbilt University. After moving from Kansas City to Nashville in 1924, it was renamed Scarritt College for Christian Workers and maintained its original purpose as a training center for laity. A central group of buildings, named after Bennett and provided through a memorial fund for her, keeps her identity before the church even today.

Despite decline and changes in the training school movement, the original vision and goals of its founders provide important legacies for United Methodism in the late twentieth century. The Chicago Training School and Scarritt were among the first Protestant institutions committed to the professional training of women for church service. Almost seventy-five years before women gained full ordination rights in the United Methodist Church, the training schools began preparing thousands of women to be Christian educators and pioneer missionaries through the world. Even though they were generally subordinate to men in the functions they performed, deaconesses forged the first female professional roles and paved the way for women who would later more forthrightly seek equal status with males.

Ministry, envisioned as the calling of laity as well as clergy, stands as a second major legacy of the Chicago Training School and Scarritt. Both founders averred that clergy could not and should not carry the full mantle of professional church leadership. The demise of many training schools came from their inability to integrate effectively lay and clergy education in the early twentieth century. In the effort to train responsibly both clergy and laity for "the ministry of all Christians" today, seminaries and conferences may gain practical insights of pitfalls to avoid from the training school movement.

A final notable legacy lies in the thrust of training school education itself. Certainly by contemporary academic standards of professional education for church service, the schools fell short. For their own day, however, they stood as bold and innovative ventures to expand religious education to previously unrecognized candidates for ministry—women and laity. Further, their effort to blend the theoretical with the practical, academics with field education, defined the training schools' purpose. The schools, as seminaries today, were not institutions for graduate study in the social sciences, but centers of preparation for professional church workers. This vision was focal. It accounted for the vitality and innovation which made religious training schools a distinctive movement one hundred years ago and a living legacy today.

A final note on Meyer and Bennett. Beyond their educational concerns, they share the further distinction of being the first laywomen seated by the general conferences of their denominations. Meyer was elected and seated at the 1904 General Conference of the MEC, after a prolonged struggle in the denomination which had begun in 1888. Bennett and other women began a drive for laity rights for women in 1906, finally achieving victory in 1918. Though the first woman to be elected to General Conference of the southern church in 1922, ill health prohibited her from attending. Bennett died of cancer later that year. After retirement in 1917, Meyer suffered prolonged illness until her death in 1922. She died at age seventy-two of Bright's disease and heart failure.

Meyer and Bennett were committed both to expanding the rights and roles of women and to strengthening the institutional church. They dedicated their lives to working within that structure. Like other notable Methodist laywomen of their day, such as Jennie Fowler Willing, a founder of the Women's Foreign Missionary Society in the MEC, and Frances Willard, organizer of the Women's Christian Temperance Union, they were "institution builders." Without their creative vision and hard work, the churches would have been less effective as an arm of evangelism and social service to the masses.

The effectiveness in expanding the roles of women lies in the ability of Meyer and Bennett to define "the practical and possible" for their day. If ordination for women was a far-off dream, development of separatist structures "for women only" proved reasonable and realizable. The power women wielded, the contribution they made, and the learning they gained from separatist organizations, can never be underestimated. Further, such structures reached countless millions of women, creating early bonds of sisterhood.

Finally, Meyer and Bennett were success models of female leadership for their day. Willard's call for "the Ballot for Home Protection" to gain suffrage for women, may be compared to Meyer's conviction that women should be professional church workers because "the world needs mothering." If such women knew how to use language acceptable to society, they also vowed to create previously unknown avenues of leadership and advocacy for women in church and society through their organizations.

In an 1895 edition of *The Message and Deaconess Advocate*, Meyer tells the story of Hilda, abbess of Whitby, England, who was born in A.D. 614. Meyer discloses the wide influence of Hilda, who founded a monastery for both monks and nuns, became the abbess, and headed the training college from which six bishops went forth. Further, she took part in the councils of the Synod of Whitby which determined the form of the Church of England. "Her counsel," Meyer quoted, "was sought even by nobles and kings."

Meyer concluded her article on this provocative note: "I closed the life of this noble Abbess of Whitby, wondering if God sent a St. Hilda to Methodism *what would we do with her.*"

Perhaps Belle Harris Bennett and Lucy Rider Meyer were something of "St. Hilda's of Methodism" for their own day.

SOURCES

Lucy Rider Meyer's *Deaconesses* (3rd ed., 1892) provides an important account of her own work. The major biographical work based on primary sources is Isabella Horton's *High Adventure: Life of Lucy Rider Meyer* (1928). An anti-Meyer treatment is given in Woman's Home Missionary Society (MEC), *Early History of Deaconess Work and Training Schools for Women in American Methodism, 1883–1885* (1913). An authoritative tribute is contained in the *Christian Advocate*, March 23, 1922.

The fullest account of Belle Harris Bennett is found in Mrs. R. W. MacDonell, *Belle Harris Bennett, Her Life Work* (1928). Also see Sara Estelle Haskin, *Women and*

Missions in the Methodist Episcopal Church, South (1920) and Mary N. Dunn, *Women and Home Missions* (1936). Memorial articles are found in *Missionary Voice*, October, 1922, and *Christian Advocate*, July 28, 1922.

Several important recent annotated articles on Rider and Bennett are included in *Women in New Worlds: Historical Perspectives on the Wesleyan Tradition*, vols. 1 & 2 (1981, 1982), edited by Rosemary Keller, Louise Queen, and Hilah Thomas. The authors include Virginia Brereton, Mary Agnes Dougherty, Catherine Prelinger, and Keller. Authoritative biographical sketches and further bibliographical resources on both women are given in *Notable American Women*, vols. 1 & 2 (1971), edited by Edward T. James, Janet Wilson James, and Paul S. Boyer.

2

Mary McLeod Bethune (1875–1955)

by Evan Scole

W HAT DID MARY McLeod Bethune contribute to church-related higher education? Although the literature on Bethune is copious, very little of it has focused on this question. And the question is important because Bethune was an unusual person, and her place in the development of church-related higher education was in some respects quite distinctive. She was a teacher, and many have written about her role as educator. She was a founder of an institution, and that too has been the legitimate subject of inquiry. She was also a national figure, a religious figure, and a cultural figure. What, though, did she contribute to church-related higher education that was unusual and different? One interpretation places her on the side of Booker T. Washington in the controversy over industrial education versus classical or liberal education for blacks. Others point out her activity in working with leaders as evidence that she believed in the philosophy of W.E.B. DuBois—that education of the elite is the path upward for blacks. Her relationship in this controversy cannot simply be relegated to one side or the other, and therein lies part of her creativity. If we consider the whole context of black education in the United States, Bethune's contribution becomes even richer to consider, because she remains the outstanding example of how a leader in church-related higher education expanded the notion of service as a vital component of higher education.

Born July 10, 1875, on a farm owned by her parents near Mayesville, South Carolina, she was the fifteenth child of Samuel and Patsy McLeod, former slaves. Mary Jane McLeod determined at an early age that she would read, when after picking up a book, oftentimes, she was rebuked by a white playmate to "put that down, you can't read." In a pattern that

MARY McLEOD BETHUNE

Photo courtesy of Bethune-Cookman College.

became second nature to her, she took up the challenge and not only learned to read but at about age twelve found herself the beneficiary of a scholarship from a white woman in faraway Denver. Consequently Mary went to Scotia Seminary, a Presbyterian school in North Carolina. From there she moved on to Moody Bible Institute in Chicago, singing at the police station and intensifying her already conservative religious consciousness under the Fundamentalism of the redoubtable Dwight L. Moody. Next in succession was Haines Normal Institute in Augusta, Georgia, where she encountered another influential mentor, Lucy Laney, under whom she taught children.[1]

Laney was born a slave in Macon, Georgia, and was graduated from the first class of Atlanta University. After teaching for several years, she accepted an invitation from the Presbyterian Board of Missions for Freedmen to start a school in Atlanta. When the church failed to provide the funds, Laney raised the money herself and started a school in 1886 in the basement of a church. She received aid from Mrs. F.E.H. Haines of Milwaukee and the school was later named for her. The Presbyterian Mission Board eventually provided both funds and land for the institution. Bethune taught the eighth grade under Haines and also worked with children in the Sunday school, which reached one thousand in attendance.

Transferred by the Presbyterian Board of Education to Kindell Institute in Sumter, South Carolina, Mary McLeod met and married Albertus Bethune, a former teacher with a fine singing voice who was working in a department store. In their second year of marriage, she gave birth to the couple's only child, Albert McLeod, who became the ninetieth grandchild born to her parents. By now Mary McLeod Bethune had begun to find the grooves for her budding career, and after starting a mission school, again under the auspices of the Presbyterian Church, in Palatka, Florida, she began to search for a place in which to plant her own institution. She chose Daytona. Among the reasons, she later said, was that it had "a fine club of white women . . . through whom I thought approach could be made."[2]

Here then, in 1904, at approximately the same time the Vanderbilts and their friends were testing their expensive cars on the beach only a few miles away, this determined black woman, still in her twenties, still with almost no money, and armed with a patchwork education and her own dreams (actual dreams of crossing rivers and receiving gifts from a man on a white horse), took $1.50 and opened a school, which at its inception had four little black girls and her son as its student body.

No matter that she knew almost no one in Daytona. No matter, either, that her driving passion for the education of blacks soon left in its wake the wreckage of her marriage. Her husband left for another town and died after a few years. And it also did not matter that 1904 was hardly a time, and the South hardly a place, for blacks, whatever their grit or their vision, to be doing anything other than surviving in an oppressive social and economic climate. Bethune seemed to take little account of the fact that American society in general, and southern society in particular, held very low expectations of the ability of black women to accomplish anything other than to be "an automatic incubator, a producer of human livestock," in her words. They were thus "doubly victimized" and "doubly invisible," according to a later writer.[3]

But Mary McLeod Bethune defied all expectations: she started a school—Daytona Literary and Industrial School for Training Negro Girls. She had in mind, she later said, to start "a new kind of school." She said, "I am going to teach my girls crafts and home-making. I am going to teach them to earn a living. They will be trained in heads, hand and heart."[4] She apparently intended to exploit the need of black families, whose men worked on the railroad being built in the area by H.M. Flagler, for basic education for their children. If her intentions soon became obvious, they corresponded to actual need, for after only two years her school had 250 pupils and 4 teachers.

She also had a patron: James M. Gamble, the soap millionaire, who spent the winter months in Daytona. Since neither she nor her constituents had any funds—tuition ran a meager 50 cents a week—she baked sweet potato pies to sell to the construction crews on the railroad and went door to door asking for contributions of money or goods. A contrast to the life-style of the white upper crust and their racing machines was Mary on her rusty bike, riding up and down Daytona streets seeking support for her school. After making forays into the white women's club, she finally approached Gamble himself. "I'm not coming to you for money," she stated, "but to ask for your personal interest in the work." He gave it, and became the chair of her board of trustees. Of course, he gave money, too, as did all of her patrons, white and black, but her success with Gamble taught her how to gain access to the philanthropy that constituted, under the circumstances, the only realistic hope of becoming a foundation for a school. Local blacks also contributed monetarily and in other ways to the school. Dr. Texas A. Adams, a prominent black physician in Daytona, established a hospital on the campus, and it served blacks in the entire community when there was no hospital for blacks in the area.

Bethune also threw her loyal students into the cause, dressing the girls in blue skirts and white blouses and taking them into the hotels where they were not only applauded but where their teacher-cum-fundraiser came into contact with even more white patrons. Before long she was traveling to the North, there to knock on more doors and tap even

more funds. By 1907 she was able to see the first actual building constructed—Faith Hall. She attracted other women to teach while she carried on her promotional efforts. By 1911 the school was accredited as a
secondary school. By 1921 it had a truck farm, seven buildings, assets
worth $250,000, and its educational program consisted of teacher prepa-
ration and training in seven industries. As an anonymous writer noted
in an understatement, "A woman such as Mrs. Bethune needs plenty of
scope for her activities."[5]

Such condensed review of the events of forty-five years may obscure
the fact that this struggle was never easy. The truth is that Bethune faced
a never-ending fight for funds to keep the school going. Her benefactors
operated out of a style of personal benevolence that, while motivated by
sincere generosity, did not place the school on a permanently sound
financial footing. So it was that in the early 1920s she began to look
around for a support system, trying first her old friends the Presbyterians, then the Episcopalians and Roman Catholics. For one reason
or another all said no. Gamble and D. H. Rutter, two of her board members, were members of the Methodist Episcopal Church (MEC), and possibly it was through them that she made contact with Garland Penn,
corresponding secretary of the Methodist Board of Education who was
responsible for Negro schools. In a letter to a colleague, Penn called the
Daytona school "a monument to Mrs. Bethune."[6] Although the written
records do not provide evidence for the party initiating the contact, circumstances suggest that Bethune sought out the Methodists, who responded with considerable interest. They had good reason, in
Jacksonville, Florida, they had an institution, Cookman Institute, that
was as desperately in need of direction as Bethune's school was in need
of money.

Cookman Institute began as a night school in 1872 with support from
the Freedmen's Aid Society of the MEC. The school was named for a
white minister interested in providing for the ex-slaves. Very soon after
its inception, the school received support from the MEC in Florida, including blacks in its membership. It also received some support from the
John F. Slater Fund, noted for its aid to black institutions. By the time of
the First World War, Cookman had some 250 male and female students
enrolled in a curriculum that was largely industrial but included teacher
training and music. Like Bethune, Cookman comprised an elementary
and high school. But Cookman had difficulty finding a permanent
leader; it faced competition in Jacksonville from another school for black
women operated by the Woman's Home Missionary Society of the MEC;
and it had financial problems. Thus the merger appealed to those in the
MEC who were responsible for overseeing black institutions.

Bethune was worried about losing control of her school. The Methodists were reassuring on that point, telling her they wanted her to continue as head of the new institution, which was renamed the Daytona-Cookman Collegiate Institute shortly after the merger. In the trade-offs, the new school became coeducational; the Jacksonville property was sold and proceeds went to the new school; the faculty of the Daytona school remained intact; and most importantly, Bethune got the financial support she had been seeking. The agreement provided that the school would receive $100,000 within a year and another $100,000 in the next year. The Methodists promised to pay an unspecified amount annually to support the school. The merger was completed in 1923. The name of the school was changed to Bethune-Cookman College in 1929 in honor of Mary McLeod Bethune.

Both sides seemed to have been rewarded beyond their expectations. Although Bethune was to complain about the slow payment of the second $100,000, she received more than the day-to-day handouts to which she had become accustomed.[7] What she achieved was technical support in managing a school. Cost accounting, content of the curriculum, faculty recruitment and development, library building, relationships with other institutions—all these tedious administrative details became the content of countless letters between Bethune and her professional counterparts in Chicago. A letter from Merrill J. Holmes, educational director in the Department of Educational Institutions of the MEC Board of Education, in 1928, illustrates the kind of expertise the MEC offered its institutions:

"I am returning your faculty list," he begins, and comments that the list "involves too heavy a financial outlay." Then he goes over the number of faculty and their salaries, as well as the figures for students: "The total value of the salaries is $26,033. Meanwhile the trend in student attendance is in the wrong direction. . . ." And as for the curriculum, "Your plan of organization is excellent in many ways. . . . You are providing both cultural and vocational training. Your program, however, is more extended than the number of students warrants." The conclusion is, "The urgent need is for more students. Lacking that, we could use fewer teachers." Holmes goes on to comment on academic courses, suggesting that they be limited more, and sums up with what he thinks is an appropriate teacher-student ratio: "Fifteen teachers for 156 students is the ratio of 1 teacher to 10 students, approximately."[8]

There is more about the construction of buildings, the kind of secretarial and clerical support needed, whom to appoint to administrative positions, and so on. The letters from Bethune demonstrate an equal attention to detail, with a ready acceptance of the numerous requests for statistics, plans, and lists. The letters are remarkable for their even tenor from a woman who might have been expected to take umbrage at the constant advice given by people far away who may never have had the responsibility of managing an institution. She seemed grateful for the chance to have a burden shared and perhaps also to learn about the many technical complexities of school administration. But she was equally as capable of making demands of the bureaucrats as they were of her. In 1931, for instance, Holmes wrote to her stating that because of the Depression, World Service contributions had declined, and the board had less money to share with its schools. Bethune wrote back asking for immediate payment of a $5,000 appropriation expected during the year, since many local creditors were pressing her for payment: "Now, Dr. Holmes, if it is possible for your Board to do this for us, please do it speedily. Four men have been into my office already this morning. The first of July has passed and they have been waiting for that day, according to our promises. Please do not fail us."[9]

The onset of the Depression brought heavy pressures on all institutions, and Bethune's school ran a deficit almost every year, but the deficits were not large. By 1937 she wrote to one of her patrons in Massachusetts: "We have worked through our financial situation in a most wonderful manner, and have been able to bring our deficit down to a figure between fifteen hundred and two thousand dollars."[10] By that time Bethune and the school had advanced in several ways. At Bethune's behest, the educational program edged into two years of junior college, then into a full-fledged four years, with elementary and high school grades being dropped as the school evolved into a genuine college. It became a two-year college in the early 1930s and was accredited as a four-year college in 1948.

One important result of the Methodist connection was that Bethune, who had already begun to be noticed in circles beyond the region, received new freedom to articulate the cause of blacks. Through her contacts with philanthropists, she had already begun to associate with the celebrities of the time, bringing Vice President Thomas R. Marshall to Daytona in the 1920s, then meeting Lady Nancy Astor and Pope Pius XI on a tour abroad in 1927. These contacts impressed her friends locally, black and white, but surprisingly it was the black women's network that brought her into the arena of real power. She became president of the National Association of Colored Women (NACW) in 1924, a group associated with the establishment in the traditional loyalty of blacks to the Republican party. The NACW established an office in Washington, D.C., and Bethune began to stay there for long periods. Calvin Coolidge invited her to a White House conference on child welfare. She was the only black person among thirty-five guests Eleanor Roosevelt, wife of the then-governor of New York, invited to a luncheon in New York City in 1927 for leaders of the National Council of Women of the U.S.A. After the ascendence of Franklin Roosevelt to the presidency, Bethune served on a planning committee of the Office of Education for a National Conference on Education, held in 1934. She met FDR for the first time in 1935 at a White House conference on the National Youth Administration (NYA), organized the year before to provide work opportunities for young Americans, white and black. That same year she received the prestigious Springarn medal from the National Association for the Advancement of Colored People. She had attained national attention, but she also lacked something—real power to affect national events.

Once again Bethune proved a ready learner. She perceived that in order to advance to a more influential position, she needed the backing of a large organization. She organized the National Council of Negro Women in 1935, the purpose of which was "to answer the need for group power and influence in pushing for social reforms in government."[11] The next year, FDR appointed her to a post in the NYA. She toured the country, identifying communities where the need was greatest and trying to break down racial barriers at every point. She rallied her own supporters: "Regardless of political ideas or religious training, we must stand together as Negroes facing the problems of Negroes."[12] And she cajoled the masters of the house, saying to FDR: "We have been taking the crumbs for a long time. We have been eating the feet and head of chicken long enough. The time has come when we want some white meat."[13] Bethune did not launch frontal assaults on the barbed wire of segregation but consistently objected to segregation within the system. At the time, even the powerful FDR did not openly support anti-lynching laws.

Bethune's characteristic modus operandi mixed personal charm with confrontation, open encouragement to blacks and their supporters with a profound understanding of the realities of the situation. Bethune's resistance to racism became legendary. In the early years of the school, the Ku Klux Klan tried to frighten her and her students, but she ignored their threats. She spoke out and verbally attacked whites who referred to her as "Mary" or even "Doctor" in public. "Now to Mr. ____ and everyone in this audience," she said on one occasion to the face of her offender, "my name is Mrs. Mary McLeod Bethune."[14] She pleaded with FDR not to segregate blacks and whites in the armed forces during the Second World War but had to be content with seeing black women in the Women's Army Auxiliary Corps receive training equal to that of whites, but in separate units, and be integrated in some hospitals where they served. Never lacking in brass, she demanded of the chair of a conference on women in policy-making that a member of the National Council of Negro Women be appointed to the continuation committee after the conference.[15] She questioned train conductors, taxi drivers, any one she encountered who seemed too ready to discriminate.

During her tenure with the NYA, which lasted into the 1940s, Bethune continued to work for the college, sometimes dovetailing trips across the country for the NYA with fund-raising efforts for the school.[16] As president of her school, she determined policies in all areas, even to the point of dismissing students or faculty whom she believed to have violated her code of morality. When asked about her imperialism by friends, she would laugh and say, "I come from a long line of despots," alluding to the family memory that the McLeods descended from African royalty. Yet at times she relied on her femininity to gain her goals, and she would admit to perplexity on occasion.

One of these occasions arose in 1937 when Bethune had been spending ever-greater lengths of time traveling around the country and fulfilling her duties in Washington. Having left the dean in charge, she returned to find faculty members upset over their cavalier treatment at his hands and those of other administrators. "They have a volume of bitter resentments and they still have swords up, fighting on all sides. I went to bed and they were still out on the campus, talking," she wrote. The best she could offer was a suggestion to improve communications. Despite the dean's hint that "you may be able as president to be away from the campus for a year or a little longer and the school may run on its own momentum, but sooner or later the wheels will begin to creak," she offered no comment on her absentee leadership. An "acting president" served until her retirement in the 1940s.[17]

Finally, though, even her mountains of energy began to run down. She retired from the presidency of Bethune-Cookman College in 1942, although she still maintained power. Her second retirement, in 1947, was more actual, yet she not only continued to be keenly interested in the school but in national events as well. She had time to attend the organizing session of the United Nations in San Francisco and to advise President Harry S. Truman to appoint Ralph Bunche to the U.S. mission to the UN. She also had time to run afoul of the right wing in 1952 when a New Jersey school board refused to let her speak because of complaints from an anticommunist league. She was an inveterate joiner of organizations and at times seemed to be both pro- and anti-labor, as well as pro-peace and pro-disarmament. About racism, however, there was no confusion about her stand.

On May 18, 1955, Chaplain Rogers Fair was about to begin an evening service in the chapel on the Bethune-Cookman campus. Just before the service started, someone entered from outside, came up to him, and whispered in his ear. He turned to the assembled students and said,

"Mary McLeod Bethune has just died." Immediately the chapel emptied. Students milled about her home, where her body lay after she died there of natural causes. The college president, Richard Moore, sat on the front porch, smoking a cigar, answering questions, and calming those who were upset. The crowds finally disappeared about 2:00 A.M., although a female student, Florence L. Roane, organized a night-long tolling of the school bell with several other women students. The next few days were filled with preparations for the funeral, responses to the media, and a slow realization on the part of those identified with the college that their founder was no more. Five days later her funeral was held in the chapel, and afterward her body was borne by school boys dressed in blue, clasping hands, as 101 young women dressed in white carried flowers to the burial site on the campus.[18]

In her "Last Will and Testament," published posthumously and now canonized by American blacks and those who cherish the Bethune legacy, she declared, "I leave you love . . . hope . . . a thirst for education . . . faith . . . racial dignity . . . a desire to live harmoniously with your fellow man . . . a responsibility to our young people."[19]

What then was Mary McLeod Bethune's distinct contribution to church-related higher education?

Bethune's religious consciousness was steeped in the conservative Protestant tradition. Her tutelage under domestic church missionaries and Moody, and her assent to her mother's deep faith, led her to follow a kind of civil religion: "I was keenly aware of the common heritage and background shared with all those loved ones," she wrote in 1950 after revisiting her old home near Sumter, South Carolina. And she added that she "was humble in the recognition that the fundamentals of a good life—cleanliness and godliness and industry—were in all of us."[20] Over and over, throughout her life, she affirmed faith in God, the fellowship of humankind, and personal virtue. These basic affirmations she saw very much confirmed in the need for education—education of the heart and hand and mind. But it was not a denominational faith, and as much as she appreciated the views she shared with Presbyterians and Methodists, she never made her school into one identified in content with a particular heritage. At Bethune-Cookman College in 1930, long enough after the merger with the Methodists to demonstrate denominational solidarity, only 87 out of 225 students were Methodists.[21]

Religious though Bethune was, and her religious convictions blended with her civic loyalty and her humanitarian outlook. She seems to have followed consciously the Booker T. Washington philosophy of education, and its practicality lent itself well to the kind of religion she espoused. Her students were to work hard, to become self-reliant, to imbibe knowledge, yes, but to do it while learning responsibility for themselves and others. Her students learned sewing, gardening, some music, but religious music, and almost all of the curriculum in the early years was devoted to "industrial training."

Yet in her activities in the NYA and on the national scene, Bethune seemed to exhibit a philosophy much closer to that of W.E.B. DuBois. Bethune demonstrated, in the years after the 1923 merger, particularly, nothing more nor less than the necessity of operating at the highest levels of society in order to achieve broad gains for all. Within the confines of the existing racism and segregation, she managed to put the condition of blacks squarely on the agenda of the president of the United States. Through her "boring from within" in the Washington bureacracy, she got attention for the needs and problems of blacks in the conferences, policies, and legislation of the 1930s and 1940s. As a leader in the "Black Cabinet," she influenced the selection of blacks to participate in the national administration, and in so doing, she prepared numerous blacks for later leadership in the judiciary, politics, and the military. One of those she encountered in Washington, Robert Weaver, who went on to become secretary of the U.S. Department of Housing and Urban Development, said of her, "Mrs. Bethune . . . was a complete human being. However, what is more important is that she was extremely effective."[22]

Part of her effectiveness lay in her ability to cooperate with other black leaders of the time. In Washington in the early 1920s she came into contact with Mary Church Terrell, Nannie Helen Burroughs, Josephine St. Pierre Ruffin, Hallie Q. Brown, and other black women who had come into prominence through political contacts in the Republican administrations.[23] Charlotte Hawkins Brown at Palmer Memorial Institute, a Presbyterian school in Sedalia, North Carolina, very much resembled her in temperament and function, and the two were friends. The "Black Cabinet" included not only Weaver but also Robert L. Vann, Eugene Kinckle Jones, Frank S. Horne, William J. Trent, William H. Hastie, and other young blacks beginning to exert leadership in the black struggle for rights.[24] But there is no doubt that Bethune played a peculiarly significant role, a role that others could not match in exerting pressure inside and outside to open the doors for equality and justice.

Service has traditionally been a part of higher education, along with teaching and research. In her case the servant role extended the vision of education with which she began. Although her educational views were conservative, her visions of what followed from education were expansive. Since she believed in a kind of holism in which the individual is to exhibit virtue in all of life, she demonstrated how such integrity could take on flesh and blood in the midst of very limited opportunities for blacks. We are familiar with this model from its recent expression in black culture, religion, and education, in which black role models can often provide a motivating lure and power that help the individual to overcome tremendous handicaps in skills or knowledge. Bethune pioneered in creating this model, and her continued adulation by blacks provides evidence that it was sincerely felt. The statue of Bethune erected in Lincoln Park in Washington, D.C. in 1974 reflects this adulation and emphasizes her contribution to later generations by showing two children with her, stretching out their hands.

For all that, the kind of service that Bethune exhibited belongs not merely to blacks or even her own American society, but to humankind. She showed that human beings can change for the better, and what is more important, that the struggle against malicious powers and principalities can actually be a successful one. This belief has been severely shaken in our own day, and the recollection of her deeds and her life story might do much to encourage us to place higher learning in the context of service. It is hard to think of an individual in church-related higher education—certainly not a black, certainly not a woman, or even of a white male—who was able to exert the influence that Bethune did on national policy. She thus stands as an example of that rare leader who understands how to operate within the realities of power relationships in order to make gains for her own time and that of succeeding generations. And she did much to lay the groundwork for the age of desegregation. Her ability to integrate religious beliefs into action, her example for what blacks and women can achieve, and her accomplishments in service in higher education make her a unique figure in church-related higher education.

NOTES

1. Details on the early years of Bethune come chiefly from Rackham Holt, *Mary McLeod Bethune: A Biography* (New York: Doubleday, 1964), pp. 8–48. Although flawed by omissions and dubious direct quotations, the Holt book remains the best biography of Bethune. For the history of Florida and Daytona, see Pleasant Daniel Gold, *History of Volusia County Florida* (E.O. Painter Printing, DeLand, Fla., 1927) and T.E. Fitzgerald, *Volusia County: Past and Present* (Observer Press: Daytona Beach, Fla., 1937).

2. Interview with Bethune by Charles Johnson, unpaged typescript, 1947, Bethune papers, Bethune-Cookman College, Daytona Beach, Florida.

3. The "incubator" quote comes from a speech Bethune delivered on June 30, 1933, to the Chicago Women's Federation, "A Century of Progress of Negro Women." Quoted in Barbara Grant Blackwell, "The Advocacies and Ideological Commitments of a Black Educator: Mary McLeod Bethune 1875–1955" (Ph.D. diss., University of Connecticut, 1975), p. 95. The second quote comes from

Bethune, "Notes Before the Women's Club," undated typescript in the Amistad Research Center, New Orleans, cited by Gerda Lerner, ed., *Black Women in White America: A Documentary History* (New York: Pantheon, 1972), p. xvii.

4. Walter Russell Bowie, *Women of Light* (New York: Harper, 1963), p. 123; quoted by Blackwell, p. 53.

5. *Crisis* 26 (September 1923):222.

6. Letter from Penn to P.J. Maveety, Feb. 13, 1923, quoted in James P. Brawley, *Two Centuries of Methodist Concern: Bondage, Freedom and Education of Black People* (New York: Vantage Press, 1974), p. 186.

7. In a letter to Holmes, Jan. 2, 1929, Bethune wrote: "When this school was taken over by the Board of Education of the Methodist Episcopal Church, it was with the distinct understanding that we were to receive from said Board two hundred thousand dollars, according to our written agreement. Of this amount one hundred thousand dollars have been paid. Repeatedly, Drs. Maveety and Penn assured our Board that this money would be paid us as soon as your Board could sell some property." Bethune was not favorably inclined toward a proposal from the board that the college undertake an endowment campaign of $200,000 because "it would be difficult to make clear to contributors to the Institution who are not Methodist that the Board of Education had fulfilled its pledge to the Institution." Bethune Papers, Bethune-Cookman College.

8. Letter from Holmes to Bethune, June 16, 1928, Bethune Papers, Bethune-Cookman College.

9. Bethune letter to Holmes, July 3, 1931, Bethune Papers, Bethune-Cookman College.

10. Letter from Bethune to H. M. Fillebrown, Bass River, Mass., Sept. 8, 1937. Bethune Papers, Bethune-Cookman College.

11. The words are that of Blackwell, p. 7.

12. Holt, p. 200.

13. Holt, p. 193. In this case the statement was made in a public meeting, but Bethune did have some tete-a-tetes with FDR. Bethune was criticized for language about blacks that some interpreted as meaning she catered to whites. The fact that she did not resist segregation more openly and forcefully was also criticized. See B. Joyce Ross, "Mary McLeod Bethune and the National Youth Administration: A Case Study of Power Relationships in the Black Cabinet of Franklin D. Roosevelt," *Journal of Negro History* 60 (January 1975): 1–28. But these criticisms have not been treated seriously in this essay for two reasons. One is that they pertain mostly to her work in the NYA, not in higher education. The

other is that Ross ignores the total context in which Bethune worked, in which she did take initiatives when she believed they had some chance of success and would not interfere with other goals. It is all too easy to ignore the terrible economic suffering in the Depression, and the relief of that suffering seems to have weighed heavily in Bethune's thinking about policies and programs.

14. Her foster son, Edward R. Rodriguez, described this incident in Daytona. "Founder's Day Address," Oct. 3, 1977. Bethune Papers, Bethune-Cookman College. Holt gives several other examples.

15. Bethune was rebuked by the conference organizer, Charl Ormond Williams, director of field service for the National Education Association, who wrote rather condescendingly to Bethune on Sept. 22, 1944, "As I remember, you were not present in the morning when the set-up of the conference was fully explained." Williams insisted that no additional members could be named to the continuation committee, since it was elected by the full conference, the White House Conference on How Women May Share in Post-War Policy Making, held June 14, 1944. But it is revealing that one of the committee members, Minnie L. Moffett of Dallas, wrote to Williams on Sept. 4, suggesting that another woman serve in her place on the continuation committee. Williams did not suggest one of Bethune's black women as a replacement, when it would have been easy to do so. Charl Ormond Williams Papers, Manuscript Division, Library of Congress.

16. One example is a letter from Bethune, on NYA letterhead, to Dr. Rose Franzblau, Cincinnati, Ohio, on Oct. 27, 1942, in which Bethune wrote, "We need money so badly," apparently about contributions to the college. Franzblau Manuscript Collection, Columbia University Rare Book and Manuscript Library.

17. The faculty dispute is described in notes that were apparently made by Bethune and now appear in a six-page carbon of a typescript dated May 26, 1937, "Statements of President Bethune, in conference with Dean Bond and Mr. Taylor." Bethune Papers, Bethune-Cookman College.

18. Someone in Bethune's household wrote an account of the death and funeral, "Days of Death and Mourning for MARY MCLEOD BETHUNE," five-page photocopy of a carbon in typescript, Bethune Papers, Bethune-Cookman College. Information about the interruption of the chapel service and the students tolling the bell came from an interview by the author with Rogers Fair, Bethune-Cookman College, in Daytona, April 29, 1986.

19. "My Last Will and Testament," was first published in *Ebony* 10 (August, 1955), pp. 105–110. It has been reprinted many times, including in the Holt biography.

20. Bethune in her column in the *Chicago Defender*, June 20, 1950. Quoted by Blackwell, p. 42.

21. Form filled out Nov. 6, 1930, unsigned, from Bethune-Cookman College to Joseph P. MacMillan, assistant secretary, Division of Educational Institutions, MEC Board of Education. Bethune Papers, Bethune-Cookman College.

22. "Mary McLeod Bethune 1875–1955," a *Time* pamphlet, 1974. Cited by Blackwell, p. 136.

23. Bethune corresponded frequently with Terrell and Burroughs, and they met often in the councils of the black women's network as well as at public conferences. Mary Church Terrell and Nannie Helen Burroughs Papers, Library of Congress Manuscript Division. Terrell was the first president of the National Association of Colored Women, which had Ruffin as its organizing force. Brown formed what has been called the first national organization for Negro women in the 1890s, the Colored Women's League of Washington. See John P. Davis, ed., *The American Negro Reference Book* (Englewood Cliffs, N.J.: Prentice-Hall, 1966), pp. 542–543.

24. Vann was the editor of the *Pittsburgh Courier;* he became a special assistant to the attorney general. Jones was executive secretary of the National Urban League and was an adviser on Negro affairs in the Department of Commerce. Horne was a poet and teacher who served in several federal housing programs. Trent worked in both the Department of the Interior and the Federal Works Agency. Hastie was dean of the Howard University School of Law when he was appointed as an assistant solicitor in the Department of the Interior; later he served as a civilian aide to Secretary of War Henry Stimson. Davis, p. 628; John Hope Franklin, *From Slavery to Freedom: A History of the Negro American,* 4th ed. (New York: Knopf, 1974), pp. 402–03, 408.

3

William H. Crogman
(1841–1931)

by Louis-Charles Harvey

ONE OF THE more obscure figures in the history of the education of black people is William H. Crogman. He lived during the time of such intellectual giants as W. E. B. Dubois, Alexander Crummell, and Booker T. Washington. Consequently, his contribution to higher education specifically for black people is often overlooked. This chapter will discuss the life and contribution of this master teacher and advocate for the education of black people.

William Henry Crogman was born on the island of Saint Martin in the West Indies on May 5, 1841. He was orphaned at the age of twelve and became a mariner two years later. The ship upon which he traveled had a mate named B. L. Boomer. Boomer came from a family of sea captains and young Crogman sailed with him for eleven years. During this time he visited ports in Asia, Europe, Australia, and South America. At the conclusion of this experience Crogman went to Boston, Massachusetts, to live with Boomer.

For the first twenty-five years of his life Crogman had received no formal education but had gained a good knowledge of people and places. Boomer persuaded the young Crogman that an education would make him more useful, and Crogman worked and saved money for two years. In 1868 at the age of twenty-seven he entered Pierce Academy in Middleboro, Massachusetts, and pursued work in English and French, distinguishing himself as a student.

After graduation in 1870 Crogman accepted a position as an English instructor at Claflin University in Orangeburg, South Carolina. While at Claflin he became aware of the need for a knowledge of Greek and Latin and began to study the latter by himself. His tenure at Claflin lasted

WILLIAM H. CROGMAN
Photo courtesy of Clark College.

three years; subsequently, he enrolled at Atlanta University for a four-year study of the classics, which he finished in three years. Crogman received his bachelor's degree in 1876 and his master of science degree in 1879 from the same school. Honorary degrees were bestowed upon him by Atlanta University and Clark University in 1901.

His service to Clark University, today known as Clark College, began in 1880 and lasted forty-five years; thirty-eight years as teacher of classical languages and seven as president. Crogman's involvement in the life of the school went even further. He was also one of the petitioners for a charter for the school, a charter member of the board of trustees, and the first secretary of the board, serving 1877–1923. James Brawley in *The Clark College Legacy* (1977) notes that the minutes of the board are valued highly by Clark University because of Crogman's Spencerian penmanship and clarity of writing. In 1903 he became the first black president of Clark. When he retired from the presidency in 1910 Crogman went back to the classroom, where he remained until 1921.

Little is known about Crogman's family. He was married to Lavinia C. Mott of Charlotte, North Carolina, who was also a graduate of Atlanta University. She was described as a queenly woman who was refined and cultured. To this marriage seven children were born. One of their daughters, Edith, became the wife of Bishop Robert N. Brooks (1888–1952) of the Methodist Episcopal Church (MEC).

Crogman's activities were not limited to Clark University. He was an active layman in the MEC and was elected a lay delegate to the General Conference in 1880, 1884, and 1888. In the last two conferences he was elected as assistant secretary. In 1892 he was again recognized by the MEC when he was appointed to the University Senate, whose purpose it was to determine the minimum requirements for the baccalaureate degree in all Methodist colleges and universities.

In 1895 another honor was bestowed upon him in recognition of his reputation as an educator. The cotton-producing states of the South decided to have an International Exposition in Atlanta in this same year. Crogman was chosen as chief exposition commissioner for the black people of Georgia, the cotton states, and the International Exposition. His responsibility was to visit the leading cities of the South and enlist black people to participate by developing an exhibition on black life. Partly because of his leadership the exposition was a success, and Crogman was made permanent chairman of the board of chief commissioners. He was a man who contributed significantly to the life of the community and the country in which he lived.

Crogman made his greatest contribution in education, however. This contribution has two foci: Crogman's roll as a master teacher and as an advocate for higher education for black people. But his achievement cannot be understood apart from the context in which he lived and worked.

In the last decades of the nineteenth century black people in this country were just beginning to experience the pains of true freedom. Although the Civil War had ended and blacks had enjoyed some successes during Reconstruction, these gains were short-lived. The thirteenth, fourteenth, and fifteenth amendments to the Constitution prohibited slavery and bestowed civil lights on the newly freed slaves, including their right to vote. But reactionary state legislatures in the South undermined these federal acts and threatened to disenfranchise blacks. In fact, many blacks were disenfranchised by both legal and extralegal means, with the Ku Klux Klan playing a role in the latter as a terrorist organization.

Realizing the importance of education, black leaders in the North and South began to address this problem. When William Crogman came to national prominence, the education of black people was being influenced by the philosophies of Washington and Dubois. Washington had been born a slave but had managed to gain his freedom. He was educated at Hampton Institute. After teaching for a while, he founded Tuskegee Institute in 1881. Washington's view of education for black people was one of self-help, implemented through industrial training. This self-help philosophy was reflected in his famous speech in 1895 at the International Exposition in Atlanta. (It is not known whether Crogman heard the speech but he was, as indicated earlier, chief exposition commissioner.) In the speech Washington espoused technical and industrial education programs even at the expense of cultivating other intellectual and cultural values. Furthermore Washington believed that the best way to pursue civil rights in the South was to leave the situation alone and allow it to settle itself. These positions turned black intellectuals against him.

Prominent among Washington's critics was Dubois, a Harvard-educated scholar and Atlanta University professor who as an outstanding critic, editor, scholar, author, and civil rights leader, and one of the founders of the National Association for the Advancement of Colored People. Dubois's enormous literary output reveals his view that education for black people must allow them to cultivate their own aesthetic and cultural values. This view was a direct contradiction to Washington's belief that education for blacks should concentrate on technical and mechanical skills. Central to Dubois's theory of education was the importance of the "talented tenth" of black people, who would become leaders and improve the plight of their less-educated brothers and sisters.

In 1897 a group of black intellectuals who disagreed with Washington's exclusive focus on industrial education founded the American Negro Academy. This academy was initiated by the Reverend Alexander Crummell, a noted theologian and educator. The academy had five stated objectives: the defense of black people against vicious assaults; the publication of scholarly work; the fostering of higher education among black people; the formulation of intellectual tastes; and the promotion of literature, science, and art. Herbert Aptheker remarked in *A Documentary History of the Negro People in the United States* (1951):

> Anticipatory of Dubois' concept of Negro liberation as the work of the "talented tenth" of an intellectual elite fully propounded by him in the 1900's was the founding in March, 1897, of the American Negro Academy . . . prominent in it were three other ministers, F. J. Grimke, L. B. Moore and J. Albert Johnson and four professors, W. E. B. Dubois, W. H. Crogman, W. S. Scarborough and Kelley Miller (p. 765).

In the midst of the philosophical struggle between Washington and the American Negro Academy, Crogman developed his idea of education for black people. He opposed Washington's exclusive emphasis on industrial education. Instead, he preferred Dubois's theory of educating the talented one-tenth of black students in the liberal arts. Despite his accord with Dubois he did not reject the importance of vocational training for some black people. His presidency of Clark University revealed that he attempted to combine both of these perspectives in a balanced manner.

A very important aspect of Crogman's contribution to higher education is his teaching. Apparently he loved teaching and took it very seriously. For nearly forty years he influenced hundreds of students by exposing them to the arts and humanities. In his classes he also taught his students about the broader ideas of life and culture. Crogman's views on education and the role of blacks are contained in *Talk for the Times*, a book of his speeches and writings published by Clark University in 1896.

On May 5, 1891, the fiftieth anniversary of his birth, friends and former students honored him with letters. One of his students, The Rev. Prof. J. M. Cox, who was professor of Latin and Greek at Philander Smith College in Little Rock, Arkansas, poignantly described this master teacher:

> Under no other teacher could six years of my life have been more pleasantly spent. . . . I often think of the many excellent qualities that characterize him both as a man and as a teacher. . . . I take pleasure in saying that I found him ever accurate in general knowledge, thorough in classroom preparation, positive in demands and forceful in every utterance.

Cox went on to say that system and method marked Crogman's instruction and that he had the ability to motivate even the dullest student. These factors impressed Cox, who concluded that "he is certainly a master of his very high calling, teaching." Crogman's contribution as a master teacher was perhaps his greatest legacy to Clark College. However, in a more general manner his contribution to higher education was that of an advocate for the education of black people. In this sense he was important in shaping the philosophy of education for blacks in the early decades of this century.

Crogman was called upon many times, mostly by northern white audiences, to speak on behalf of education for black people. His speeches as an advocate have three major themes: the black person is educable; the need is to combine education for black people with Christian principles; education for black people should be balanced—it should train the hands, but should also expose students to aesthetic and cultural values.

In a speech delivered before the National Education Association at Madison, Wisconsin, in July, 1884, Crogman spoke forthrightly to the first of the themes. He was concerned that many hindrances were being created by white southerners to prevent the progress of blacks. One such hindrance was the view held by some southerners, and articulated by a U.S. senator from Alabama, that black people, even with the help of Congress, the Freedman's Bureau, and the civil rights statutes, simply had not grown stronger as a race. Crogman's response is typical of his outrage at such perspectives:

> I say this is a remarkable passage; remarkable because coming from a United States Senator, who ought to be better informed with regard to a race in whose midst he lives. He cannot see that we are stronger as a race . . . than we were fifteen years ago and that, too, in the face of the facts which were collected, not by black, but by white men.

He went on to indicate that black people had nearly one million children in school, published more than eighty newspapers, and had about fifteen thousand students in high school and colleges. Such ideas, in Crogman's opinion, failed to account for the condition black people were in after the war. The reason for this condition was the lack of educational opportunities provided by the South.

Others simply assumed that the black person could not be educated. Crogman told the story of a white man from Ohio who had spent time in the South teaching black people. In an article chronicling this experience, the man concluded that black children could not learn as fast as white children in Ohio and by implication could not be fully educated. Crogman's response was emotional:

> Well, when I read that I said to myself, if black children down on Southern plantations and white children up in Ohio are expected to move [at the same

pace] along the lines of education, it is high time for our Anglo-Saxon friends to begin a thorough revision of philosophy.

He continued his discussion of this incident by saying that such notions leave out the fact that black children lacked the same advantages in life, such as an educated mother and father and a stable home environment that promoted learning. Given the same opportunities black children could be educated. This theme is repeated numerous times in other speeches as well.

Another example is found in the speech, "The Negro's Needs." In this speech Crogman discussed the view of James Lenfestey, who traveled from Michigan to Georgia to assess the condition of the black person. Lenfestey, a white man, described black people in a very negative manner, implying they could not be educated. In this article he asked, What becomes of the young graduates? He answered they were to be found as waiters in hotels and as servants to gamblers. He concluded that in order to attempt to educate the young black children, an army of teachers was needed. Crogman called this a wholesale slander of black people that failed to recognize that at the close of the war these people owned nothing, represented nothing. However, soon they had become teachers, doctors, and property-owners and were progressing.

The main hindrance to the education of black people, Crogman suggested, was the counter-education which was continually occurring in society. By counter-education he meant that black people were taught one thing in church or school and another by society. For example, they were instructed that God made them, that Christ redeemed them, and that the Holy Spirit sanctified them. In society they were taught that although God made them, there was a vast difference between a white person and a black person. This reality made the education of black people in this country a very difficult enterprise, but not impossible. For Crogman the idea that black people could not be educated was a fallacy. Black people were not inherently inferior to white people intellectually. Given the same opportunities as whites, black people could become educated members of society who would contribute greatly to it.

Another theme of Crogman's thought was the importance of Christianity in the education of black people. In an address delivered at the anniversary of Freedmen's Aid Society in Ocean Grove, New Jersey, August 13, 1883, he talked about the beneficial effects of the principles of the Christian faith for the education of blacks. Crogman acknowledged the pioneering work by the Christian churches of the North in leading the "New Crusade" for black education in the southern field. Using the Bible and the spelling book, these crusaders had to accomplish their task in the midst of hostile white southerners and of the prevailing negative sentiment that the Negro could not be educated.

A very important aspect of Crogman's advocacy on behalf of black education was his appeal to white northerners on the grounds of their moral responsibility to aid the education of blacks. One memorable address was given in Plymouth Church, Brooklyn, New York, previously pastored by Henry Ward Beecher, an ardent advocate of social rights. Crogman pointed out the fundamental need of black people for educational opportunities. He asserted that the South was too poor and weak to help. It would take the good will of the people of the North to help. He appealed to the North for specific aids (such as endowments) to strengthen the various departments of the schools, for help to purchase textbooks, and for scholarship aids: "For it is to the Christian people of the North that the Negro for many years must look for help and sympathy and cooperation. . . . The burden of Negro education has fallen upon you in the past and as Christians and patriots must for many years yet to be to you."

The importance of education combined with Christian principles was that it helped instill moral principles within individuals. Crogman did not deny that certain vices existed among black people. He deplored them and suggested, "Wherever in the South Christian education has reached the freed man, it has awakened in them *(sic)* a taste for the true and beautiful. This may be seen in the changed manner of living of many of them . . . Christian homes, the strength of any nation, are being built up." Crogman rejoiced that the schools established by the Freedman's Bureau were Christian schools. In them all teaching was seasoned with the teaching of God. Loyalty to God and to one's convictions were crucial aspects of the education of black people at these institutions. This same trend was continued in an address delivered on the occasion of the laying of the cornerstone of the library of Gammon Theological Seminary, an institution of which he was trustee. In this speech Crogman remarked, "The cornerstone of the New South is to be no longer human slavery, but Christian education. In this and nothing else lies the solution of the so-called Negro problem." This speech also called for the necessity of an educated clergy because of the stature of the preacher in the black community.

Christian education would not only benefit black people, but it would also benefit the entire South. In this he was addressing those who were trying to regain the glory of the old South through repression. Crogman stated firmly that the welfare of the South and the peaceful solution of the race problem must not be sought in the curtailment of human rights but in the widest possible promulgation of Christian education.

The third major theme of Crogman's advocacy of education for black people was the notion of a program that combined both industrial training with the arts and humanities. He recognized that the schools founded by the Freedmen's Aid Society were exemplary in combining these principles:

> . . . there seems to be at present a fair prospect of inaugurating a different order of things in these newly founded schools of the South . . . a place where the hand shall be trained along with the head, a place from which a young man is graduated, he will not feel compelled to teach or preach or to be an editor when he might serve God and his country better by being a machinist or a woodworker.

He continued by noting that not everyone could be a teacher, preacher, lawyer or doctor. Education for blacks must be so conceived that there was someone to push the saw, drive the plane, operate the plow. While these people were necessary, Crogman concluded that there must be among black people "an intelligent virtuous middle class, the salt of all ages." This last point seems to point back to Dubois's concept of the talented tenth whose responsibility it would be to lead the race and uplift it through the promotion of high cultural ideals. Crogman stated: "There are many intelligent Negroes who would have long since sought for themselves a more congenial home . . . had it not been for the conviction that they have work to do, that their energies, their influence, their intelligence are needed by their weak and ignorant brethren."

This educational philosophy was also implemented during the time Crogman was president of Clark University. As James Brawley in *Clark College Legacy* explains:

> Not only did he advance the work in agriculture which was a young department when he became President. But he also did much to raise the standards in all the academic departments. At the end of Dr. Crogman's presidency much emphasis was still being placed upon industrial work and also upon culture (p. 52).

Clark University celebrated its fortieth anniversary in 1910. This was the end of Crogman's administration as president. The celebration turned out to be not only for Clark University but also for the recognition of Crogman, a master teacher and advocate for the education of black people. This joyous event did not end his career at the school. Crogman returned to the classroom and taught twelve more years. On May 10, 1922, at the age of eighty, he retired from teaching, thus ending a career of nearly a half century of continuous service to Clark.

William H. Crogman was an effective advocate for his people and for the cause of education. In addition to his gifts of teaching and advocacy he was a brilliant orator whose speeches reflect a vast knowledge of philosophy and classical literature. Crogman also coauthored two books on the history and progress of black people, *Progress of a Race: The Remarkable Advancement of The Afro-American,* in 1899, and *The Colored American: From Slavery to Honorable Citizenship,* in 1905. Following a long and successful career he died in 1931 at the age of ninety.

SOURCES

Aptheker, Herbert. *A Documentary History of the Negro People in the United States.* New York: Citadel Press, 1951.

Brawley, James. *The Clark College Legacy.* Atlanta: Clark College, 1977.

Crogman, William H. and Kletzim, H. F. *Progress of a Race.* Atlanta: J. L. Nichols, 1899.

_____ and Gibson, J. W. *The Colored American: From Slavery to Honorable Citizenship.* Atlanta: Hertel Jenkins, 1905.

_____. *Talks For The Times.* Atlanta: Clark University, 1896, including the following speeches:

"Negro Education: Its Helps and Hindrances"

"The Negro's Needs"

"Beneficent Effects of Christian Education"

"Laying of the Cornerstone: Library of Gammon Theological Seminary"

"The Negro Problem"

"Christian Scholars for Negro Pulpits"

"Importance of Correct Ideals"

"Twenty-Sixth Anniversary of Emancipation Proclamation"

Simmons, William J. *Men of Mark.* Chicago: Johnson Publishing, 1970. Ebony Classics Reprint.

Wesley, Charles H. *International Library of Negro Life and History.* Vol. 3. *Historical Negro Biographies.* New York: Publishers Company, 1968.

4

Lewis Davis
(1814–1890)

by James D. Nelson

T HE BEST THING our Church ever thought of is the Christian College."[1] This statement was made in 1886 by Lewis Davis, just then
concluding a career of service to higher education that extended over
four decades, in spite of the fact that his only education had been eighteen months spent in the academy at New Castle, in the mountains of
western Virginina. In our late twentieth century, higher education has
become so universally available that it is generally assumed that anyone
who has not enjoyed it is therefore opposed to it. This was far from the
situation with the "Father of higher education" in the United Brethren in
Christ branch of present United Methodism. True, Doctor Davis, as he
came to be called universally, was almost entirely self-taught. But he
was, apparently for that very reason, strongly impressed with the advantages of schooling, a major factor in his choice of a vocation in Christian ministry dedicated to "the Christian College."

Davis ranks with no contest as *the* pioneer of higher education in the
United Brethren Church. He served as actual founder and for eighteen
years president of Otterbein College (or university as it was then called)
of Westerville, Ohio—that denomination's first institution of higher education. He also spent fourteen years as "Senior Professor" or chief academic officer of Union Biblical Seminary in Dayton, Ohio (later to
become Bonebrake, and still later, United Theological Seminary)—that
church's only theological seminary. His illustrious career of leadership
was carried out despite a lack of formal schooling and in the face of
strong, if largely unorganized, hostility toward higher education in the
culture at large and in the denomination in particular. This antagonism
was focused especially against the idea of an educated ministry. Davis

51

LEWIS DAVIS

Photo courtesy of Otterbein College Archives.

chose to educate himself and spend his life educating others rather than make a virtue of his own personal necessity and join the antagonists to formal schooling. That he did these things in ministry must in large measure remain a mystery of grace. To trace this effect of his vocation as educator in the church known as United Methodist is the undertaking of the present essay.

Davis drank early of the unique populist wisdom and prejudices of the southern American highlands exhibited during the Jacksonian Era. He was born February 14, 1814, on a small farm in Craig County, one of the western tier of counties in Virginia and in the midst of the Appalachian Mountains. His father, William Davis, was a veteran of the War of 1812, and a Welsh by national inheritance. The father was by inclination a sportsman and rather an indolent farmer; he loved good horses, liked to hunt, and was in considerable demand as a fiddler. Although a man of high moral standards who appreciated the value of Christian culture, he was not what passed in churchly circles of the time as a Christian. His wife and the mother of their six children, of whom Lewis was the fourth born, was of Scot descent. With the assistance of her uncle who lived nearby and the efforts of her children, she kept the home economically afloat.

> The father was a large man, weighing about 200 pounds, and in build very much like his son Lewis. The mother, on the contrary, was small, active and very industrious. She was a gentle, loving woman of warm heart and pure life; one of the old type of "new lights" then somewhat prevalent in her neighborhood. The first and most lasting religious impressions ever made upon the son were made by the tender teaching and most faithful example of this devoted Christian mother.[2]

From an early age Davis learned habits of strict personal discipline. His father, despite his lack of attention to farming, was a man of authority and strict adherence to the frontier code of truth-telling. The son seems at no time to have fancied the career of a mountain farmer, and as a youth of eighteen he determined to take up a trade. Since blacksmiths from time to time had visited the farm and exposed him to their work and life, Davis decided to learn that trade. Thus he committed himself as an apprentice to a blacksmith, Jacob Hammond of nearby New Castle, Virginia, who was a prosperous and pious maker of edged tools. Davis stayed for three years with the Hammond family, years which were to prove a major turning point of his life.

Hammond was a devout Methodist, and he regularly gave shelter to itinerant Methodist preachers. The master took a deep personal interest in his apprentice, observing Davis to be bright and quick to learn. Hammond lent Davis books to read and encouraged him to think about going to school. It was he who first discerned, or in any case mentioned, Davis's great promise. He predicted that Davis would never become a blacksmith, instead visualizing a broader field of influence. During the several years of Davis's stay there, the home was frequently visited by the Rev. Jeremiah Cullum, a Methodist preacher who encouraged Davis to go to school and prepare himself for a future quite other than black-smithing. On one visit, on inquiring for "Lute" and learning he was already in bed,

> Mr. Cullum went to his chamber and, kneeling by his bed, began to talk in a most earnest and sympathetic way of what he believed to be the call of God to young Davis to go to school and equip himself for a great work, at last breaking forth in an impassioned prayer which so profoundly stirred the youth lying upon his bed that he solemnly resolved then and there to consecrate his life and devote himself to study as a preparation for anything that God had for him to do.[3]

Carrying out this resolve was no easy matter, but Davis's mother was quick to sympathize with his commitment. Armed with fifty dollars which she obtained from her uncle—and which she could hardly spare—Davis entered with great hopes the academy at New Castle. He was able to stretch his stay in this institution to cover eighteen months, the sum total of his formal education. During this time, now in his early twenties, Davis made very rapid progress in learning. At the end of this period, now twenty-three years of age, he still had no clear direction for his life. He had experienced a religious conversion early in his stay with the Hammonds—while still eighteen—but had declined to join the Methodist Episcopal Church according to his own testimony because of its stance on matters he considered of great moral significance:[4] he regarded with concern its failure to take a stand against slavery and secret societies, both issues which took rise in populist sentiments of early nineteenth-century mountain culture. And as we shall see, these remained central issues for him to the end of his life.

While in this state of mind Davis undertook an apparently aimless ramble into the territory to the west. He and two other travelers, probably also blacksmiths, went as far as Charleston, now West Virginia, and on their return tour Davis stopped with a Mr. Hurless, a family acquaintance. There he was asked if he could teach school. On his affirmative response, he was retained for three months as teacher of the local school, and at its conclusion he was hired for another six months. This became an important interlude in his life, since the Hurless family was of the United Brethren persuasion and was visited by a traveling preacher on missionary assignment from the Scioto Conference of that denomination, the Rev. William W. Davis. While there Lewis Davis worshipped with the family and taught a Sunday school class. Hoping to attract this promising young man to the communion, William Davis, the traveling preacher, gave Lewis Davis the United Brethren *Discipline* to read.

It was just the thing he had been waiting to find. It seemed to him, to use his own language, "that God had made him for these sentiments and this discipline." Simple, unostentatious and reformatory, all attracted him.[5]

While still a student at New Castle Academy, Davis had become an active member in a debating society. As a teacher and neophyte member of the United Brethren Society, he was encouraged and became engaged in exhorting and preaching. In the year that followed—1838—Davis received a quarterly conference license to preach.[6] Whether this took place in present West Virginia or in Ohio is not known for certain, but in the spring of 1839 he was examined and admitted as a member of the Scioto Conference of the United Brethren Church at Pleasant Run, Ohio. Ordained on May 5, 1842, his itinerant career lasted eight years, the last as a presiding elder. As his first assignment he joined another preacher on Bush Creek Circuit, "a circuit which embraced a large part of the counties of Ross, Pike, Adams, Brown and Highland, and was three-hundred and sixty miles around. Twenty-eight regular appointments were filled on each round."[7] His second appointment was to Burlington Circuit, from which he went to Circleville Station where he also served, in 1843–44, as a solicitor for the publishing house. The following year he was once again a circuit preacher, and in 1845 he became a presiding elder.

It was during his career as a circuit preacher that Davis met and married his lifetime partner. He and Miss Rebecca Bartels were united in marriage by their friend, the Rev. David Edwards, later to become a bishop. Rebecca Davis, who was known affectionately by generations of students as Aunt Becky, survived her husband by five years.[8] Early in their stay at Westerville they added to the household Mary Englehart, a German girl who became a helper in the home and remained for forty-two years a mainstay in its orderly working. She became the third in the team of "Dr. Davis, Aunt Becky, and Aunt Mary."

The life of an itinerant preacher is far from conducive to a studious ministry. However, already as an apprentice Davis had demonstrated his ability to commit lengthy texts to memory. Now he gained a widespread reputation as a man who sought to develop himself through the careful study of books rather than reading as such. As an example, in studying Watson's *Institutes* (later to become his standard text for systematic theology) he first spent six weeks on reading, followed by a period of taking notes on certain sections which resulted in the memorization of certain passages. Then he and Bishop Edwards would discuss and compare their ideas.[9]

Such studious endeavor was not always eagerly welcomed, or even understood, by the layfolk who hosted Davis on his rounds. His eager hosts usually expected a gregarious preacher and were often disappointed by his need to spend most of his time in study. On one occasion his host, a Mr. Chapman, kept seeking him out to talk until finally Davis had to say, "'Mr. Chapman, I can't stand this.' 'Stand what, Mr. Davis?' was the courteous reply." Realizing he had seemed rude, Davis explained his lack of education and facilities for learning and how he had obligations to keep on learning, and in that household from then on "he was allowed to study when he chose, without being subjected to any interruptions." When another particularly talkative host indicated to him that as a preacher, he was being paid to talk, Davis replied this way:

"Brother Wood, I can't talk all the time, and if you won't allow me to study some while in your house I must go elsewhere, where I can study." The result was the men soon understood each other, Davis studied as he wished thereafter, and while on that circuit never had a warmer friend than Mr. Wood.[10]

A reputation as a lover of learning soon developed around Davis throughout Scioto Conference, which was to make him an obvious champion and leader in the impending initiative into the field of higher education. There seemed a natural transition from learner to teacher, as his passion for education, in such a large measure frustrated by the circumstances of his early life, lent him the motivation to be an academic pioneer. Thus his conference turned to him when it went about the establishment of a college.

Enabled by action of the General Conference of 1845 the Scioto Conference took steps to establish a college. Because of the establishment of Ohio Wesleyan University at nearby Delaware, Ohio, the Blendon Young Men's Seminary of Westerville, Ohio, was rendered defunct, and its facilities became available to the conference at the bargain price of $1,300—the amount of its debt.[11] Davis was involved in each step of the transition of Blendon Seminary into Otterbein University of Ohio, the first college of the United Brethren Church. At the end of his academic career, some forty years later, Davis described his earliest experiences as "general agent" and board of trustees member, at a meeting of the alumni and teachers of the school:

We visited it [Blendon Seminary] and looked the grounds all over. We concluded that it was good and cheap, and so reported to Scioto Conference, just forty years ago last fall. They bought it, with Jonathan Dresbach, William Hanby, and L. Davis, trustees. Then we began to think of a name. Otterbein University of Ohio was suggested. We thought of college. We did not just know the difference between a college and a university. We thought, somehow, that a university meant more than a college; so we took it all in and called it Otterbein University. . . .

I wrote a subscription, the first of the Church for this educational work. I subscribed and paid the first dollar for higher education in this Church. . . . Great as he was . . . Otterbein did nothing for higher education, neither did his immediate successors. But we went into it. . . . Shall I tell you the amount I subscribed? Fifteen dollars; no more, no less.[12]

Having made his own modest subscription, Davis went out to seek other contributors to this cause:

I went to a man . . . known all over the Church—for his subscription. . . . I began to press him some, but I got only ten dollars. I went to another man, and he said he would give me ten dollars if I would take it in books. . . . Brother Hanby gave me twenty-five dollars—grand, good man! I went to Jonathan Dresbach; he was worth $100,000. He gave me fifty dollars. From another I got twenty-five dollars and from another fifty dollars, and so the work began. Now I had the cream. I must start out elsewhere; so I started for Sandusky Conference, way on the Maumee. . . . I got to conference a little late. I had heard the bishop would antagonize the work. Bishop Russel was then presiding bishop. He was a strong man—strong in intellect, with a mighty brain well stored, and strong in prejudices. I met him tremblingly. "I have made up my mind to oppose this," he said. I told him I had come to represent the work. "You be still, you be still," was his reply. I told him I could not be still, and if they gave me an advisory seat I would advocate it. I got a chance, but he managed to rule me out of order. I said something, but I was always too early or I was too late, or something was wrong, so that he ruled me out of order. He did oppose it in a characteristic speech of half an hour, and then put the question; but they voted for the college, but by a small majority. It was a victory, but a dear one. I felt that a few more such victories would defeat me.[13]

At the Muskingum Conference Davis once more faced Bishop Russel, who managed this time to defeat the proposal of a college. Davis reflected:

Bishop Russel was a typical man. He was a gentleman—grand, noble, manly, intelligent. He was a representative of the Church of that time as to the educational work. The fathers of the Church were well represented in him. They were not opposed to education, but they did not believe it the business of the Church to educate. This sentiment I met through the entire Church. Other churches had the same view largely. They were getting rid of it faster than we were. Perhaps Otterbein held it; Newcomer and Geeting held it; I know Asbury held it. This we had to combat.[14]

The school opened in 1847 with Prof. William R. Griffith as the main teacher. The first graduates ten years later were two women. In 1871 when Davis left Otterbein, there had been one hundred and forty-four graduates.

The strong-willed and highly energetic Davis was set in motion in what was to be his life work when he was elected by the Otterbein trustees to be general agent, on December 5, 1846.[15] At the meeting of the full board on April 26, 1847—which is generally regarded as the foundation date of the institution—the task of preparing the campus and buildings for classes to begin fell also to Davis. And when it came time to provide for the nutritional needs of the students in a boarding establishment, this too was his responsibility for the better part of a decade. Schools were supported by a rather complex structure of persons who were called "agents." There were usually a "general agent," a "resident agent" and a body of "traveling agents" in various areas of the constituency of the school. To these persons fell the finance and management of the college. At the head of this structure, as well as of the instructional staff and faculty, was the president.

Although Griffith, son of a United Brethren minister and graduate of DePauw University, was retained as principal of the "university" and served ably in that capacity, Davis was in fact its chief administrative officer. Conflict between the two led to the withdrawal of Griffith in August of 1849.[16] In that year William Davis of Cincinnati was elected president and was the first person to hold this title, but he failed to move to Westerville and to take the office seriously. He was thus in the following year, 1850, replaced by Lewis Davis, who had continued to manage the affairs of the institution through all these changes. In 1853 Lewis Davis was surprisingly elected a bishop of the church, and during the quadrennium that followed, he combined episcopal and presidential duties, to the general neglect of the former. When re-elected to the episcopacy in 1857, he resigned from the presidency of the "university" to give full time to his work as a bishop. His successor at Otterbein, Alexander Owen, stepped down in 1860 because of failing health, so Davis resigned from the episcopacy to assume the office of college president once more. He remained in this office until the autumn of 1871 when he moved to Dayton, Ohio, to be senior professor (effectively president) of the newly founded theological seminary of his denomination, Union Biblical Seminary. Meanwhile, in 1868 he was granted the honorary degree of doctor of divinity by Washington and Jefferson College in Pennsylvania.

As suggested by his later reminiscences, Davis had a great deal to learn about the care and development of an institution of higher education. His aim was to promote learning in his church by means of a high-quality school conceived and developed in the spirit of that communion. Bare survival was, at least during those early years at Otterbein, a matter of primary concern. From the very beginning the institution was plagued both by debt and by inadequate facilities and staffing.

A school like Otterbein had the character of an extended family, and in that family—at least in this case—the president stood as the strict and authoritative patriarch. Even a casual review of the minutes of the faculty, the executive committee (or prudential committee), and the board of trustees shows how Davis fulfilled this august role.[17] To him fell the task of official reprimand, both public and private, of students or staff members who had been found guilty of some misdemeanor or crime against the rather strict regulations that governed the common life of the "family." If there was a musical instrument to be procured, he procured it. If a stove was to be moved, it was he who made the arrangements. If an agent was to be dismissed, the task fell to him. If the fund-raising traveling agents needed motivation, Davis laid down the law. And along with all this, he was instrumental in shaping the educational work of the school.

Davis was a teaching president. He taught a wide range of subjects, from physiology to logic. Fortunately, from his hand we have an extensive essay on his theory of education from the year 1852[18] in which he proposed what he called the education of the "whole man"—physical, mental, and moral. In the essay he dealt with these three factors in just that order. He presented a strong case for the importance of healthful diet and habits of rest and physical exercise, regarding this area as most often neglected in institutions of higher education and thus of special concern. Under mental education fell a concern for the whole human psyche: intellect, will, and emotion. The acquisition of trust in the form of knowledge was given a leading role, but just as important was the exercise of the will, which today would fall more or less under the heading of ethics. Finally, this section contained the transition to Davis's category of moral education. The human feelings or affections provided a pivot from the mental (in a sense the psychological) to the moral (in the strictest sense, the religious) education. The whole concern in moral education was with religious development and the pious and charitable behavior that correlated with its inner affective states of feelings. The institutions of learning with which Davis was associated embodied the theory of education and of humanity as set forth in this essay. This embodiment can be seen generally in the stress on religious experience and habits of piety, but his theories are most evident in the schools' emphasis on what would today be called "health," including regular habits of eating, bathing, and exercising.[19]

Along with the day-to-day administration of the college several special issues occupied Davis during his tenure at Otterbein. The first of these was a personal sentiment against slavery, which became a national issue during his presidency. During his time at Otterbein these antislavery sentiments became a preoccupation, and he was a part of the underground railway involved in conducting fugitive slaves from the South to Canada. Among several anecdotes stands one from his wife which is particularly reflective of Davis's attitude:

> A young man from the South found his way to the college, and also found a home in the family of the president. He was polite and courteous, a moderate student, but indoctrinated with southern ideas, and of course believed that slavery was the natural condition of the black man. Mr. Davis was anxious to correct his erroneous views, and took occasion at meal time as the most opportune period, to put his opinions before the student . . . [who] bore it all patiently. The end came one day when a fugitive slave, on his way north, stopped at the president's, and he [the president] insisted he should be brought out to the table to eat with the family, including the young man. This was the straw that broke the camel's back. . . . By permission he left the table and went to the hotel to get his dinner. . . . Some parties anxious to know the trouble inquired if he did not have a pleasant boarding place. The young man answered it was all pleasant and good except one thing: "It was niggah at breakfast, and niggah at dinner and niggah at supper: it was just niggah all the time."[20]

Davis was a man of strong and overt convictions. In southern Ohio he found no difficulty in encountering a heated confrontation regarding his views on the rights of black folk. After a confrontation with railroad officials over the removal of a black man from a train, Davis stated: "I have sought to treat all men without guile. I do not cover up my convictions. If I have a sentiment which men ought to know, I must assert it. It is both a pleasure and a duty."[21] In the course of the war that followed—during this period of Davis's presidency—he had many opportunities to express his sentiments. A man capable of an abrasive style, one of his favorite statements was, "First pure, then peaceable."[22] Another anecdote illustrates his straightforward approach to the conflict of views:

> While residing in Westerville one of the old citizens, Mr. Westervelt, saw him on his way to the polls on election day and said to him, "President, you are going to vote with the abolitionists, of course." "Yes." "Well, you and the preachers like you have done all they could to bring on the war." "Yes, I did all I could," was the cool reply. "Well, I don't want anything more to do with you," said the astonished citizen. Davis said, "Let me explain: the Saviour said, 'I came not to send peace on earth, but a sword.' I advocate the truth, and if that brought on the war, then I am guilty. This was made the occasion of war. I was willing to take the consequences of telling the truth."[23]

The first problem faced in his work at Otterbein was antagonism to the very idea of a United Brethren college. Of this period we read:

> The friends of these early schools were compelled to fight their way at every step. The general sentiment to all appearances was irreconcilably opposed to any advance in this direction. A large majority of the ministers shared this opposition. It was not an unusual thing for some of them in their pulpits to thank God they had never rubbed their backs against college walls.[24]

On the other side of the issue, Westerville could not even boast of the presence of a United Brethren class or society at the time the college was moved there. Davis developed the idea that the town should become a haven of that denomination, and early urged a numerous migration of those people to Westerville. In this context, he found it necessary to defend his own vocation as well as that of his school:

> I feel, dear brethren, that I am engaged in the cause of Christ: if I did not I should at once desist. When we remember that we, as a people are laboring, not to build an institution to "manufacture ministers" (let this be the work of God) but to train the juvenile mind to think—to teach the youth how to act so as to be useful in time and ready for eternity: I say, when we think of the great blessings we may thus confer upon our race, I feel willing to endure with patience all the opposition I may meet with.[25]

A few months later he wrote: "I labor in all this with all the seriousness and religious conscientiousness and trust in God, that I do in preaching:-—for this plain reason: it is as much *the work of God*."[26]

Associated with this antagonism on the part of many were the problems Davis faced in regard to two matters related to the school. The first of these was the effort to implement a manual labor system at Otterbein, and the second the effort to raise an endowment to support the school by the sale of scholarships. One of the prejudices against higher education on the part of the common people who made up the United Brethren Church was that it would render those who enjoyed its privileges unfit for hard work—in short, that educated folk were idlers. The manual labor idea was that all persons in the school would be involved daily in physical labor—students, staff, and faculty. How this fitted into Davis's theory of physical education is easy to see, and at the very start, he seemed to favor the system.[27] But Davis was a practical man and apparently learned what other schools that had tried similar plans had learned—that it simply does not work to mix studies with the agricultural labor which was available: The time and effort demands contradict each other too directly. Yet it was necessary to deal with the demands and expectations of the constituency as represented on the board of trustees. A comparison of the minutes of the various bodies of the college reflects the flow of interest. The implementation of this program was a major concern to the board in the early to middle 1850s and finds a more subdued interest in the executive or prudential committee in the middle to later 1850s, while in the minutes of the faculty one would hardly know there was such a program.[28] The plan was doomed by its impracticability and allowed to die of benign neglect, but this failure was to play a fateful role in the endowment scholarship program.

At several points in its early history Otterbein and its governors devised, proposed, and sought to implement a program to raise an adequate endowment for the school by selling scholarships. Various terms were proposed, but in none of them did inevitable inflation play a role. The most favorable incentive in the program to raise $75,000 was a perpetual and transferrable scholarship for one student's tuition, which was sold for $100. Under these terms the holder of the scholarship, and that person's successors, could keep one student designated by them in the college as long as the institution survived. Fortunately, a majority of the subscribers refused to pay for the scholarships because of their disappointment over the failure of the manual labor program. Those who did pay were a source of financial loss to the school for years to come, until the last of the scholarships were finally bought back by the school.

One crisis which could hardly be anticipated, but which precipitated the collapse of more than one such college was—fire! About 2 A.M. on January 26, 1870, the uncompleted main building of the college was discovered to be on fire. The building containing chapel, library, recitation rooms, laboratory, and three well-finished literary society rooms was gutted by flames. By 4 A.M. Davis had convened a meeting of the faculty in his home just across the street from the burning main hall. Plans were there made for the uninterrupted continuation of the work of the school,[29] and in a sense, this and the year that followed were to prove Davis's finest hour. The insurance money from the fire was applied to pay the debt of the school. Davis himself was central in raising $35,000, which went for the construction of a much more satisfactory building than the one which had been destroyed.

The building of the new main hall was his last undertaking as president. In the fall of the following year, 1871, Davis and his household moved to Dayton, where he was to continue his career as an educator at Union Biblical Seminary and spend the rest of his life. His departure from Westerville marks the end of what has been called the pioneer period of Otterbein College. He had seen the village grow from a backwoods crossroad to a thriving little town, and the college grow from no more than a secondary or preparatory school to a firmly established college with a well-ordered and solidly constructed campus.[30] During this period, Lewis Davis *was* Otterbein University.

Davis brought with him to Dayton his experience as a teacher, a high reputation in the United Brethren Church (especially with important lay and clergy leaders in the city of Dayton) and perhaps most important, eighteen years of experience as an academic administrator. In the final analysis, he played much the same role at Union Biblical Seminary as he had played at Otterbein. He assumed a similar role in the management of the school, except that there he was much more teacher than administrator. In the early years he became a member of and dominated the executive or prudential committee. He knew how to make the system of agents work, and his experience was relied upon by all. He had full knowledge of how students were to be handled, and at the seminary, too, Davis assumed the role of the patriarch. No doubt because he was here dealing with mature students, matters that at Otterbein were handled by public reprimand at the morning prayer service, or in a classroom, were handled person to person in privacy. All efforts were taken to avoid any public humiliation of students and to avoid open conflict among the faculty. For Davis, teaching meant going back to Watson's *Institutes* as the standard handbook in systematic theology.[31] At the seminary he had a strong sense of his academic responsibility, and he carefully avoided involvement with other concerns. He declined most of his many invitations to preach or speak or dedicate churches as a distraction from his specific calling.[32]

Davis continued as senior professor and professor of systematic theology until his retirement at the end of the 1884–85 school year, when he stepped down as "president" of the school at age seventy-one. He remained as emeritus professor with some teaching responsibilities for one more year. During this time he was active and effective in faculty meetings, but at its end he retired from the work.[33]

The years that followed his retirement were marked by inner grief and outward conflict. Between the General Conference of 1885 and that of 1889, it became increasingly clear to all that the constitution and confession of faith of the United Brethren Church would be amended, and most important for Davis, that the rule against membership in secret societies would be repealed.[34] When the inevitable came to pass in 1889, Davis and a substantial number of other important members seceded from the denomination. We find the tragic note in the standard denominational history that Davis withdrew "irregularly" from the Scioto Conference, whose meetings he had faithfully attended during the period of his academic career. He did not, however, withdraw from his local class in the Summit Street United Brethren Church in West Dayton.[35]

After a brief illness, Lewis Davis died in his home on March 23, 1890, at age seventy-six. His final words were those of the Shepherd's Psalm.[36] Although he had made thorough plans for his funeral in his own meticulous and methodical way, it was held in the Summit Street Church rather than as he had planned, in his home, so that all the seminarians could attend. There are strong indications that the church split which marked his last year was an occasion of deep grief for him, and that he looked forward to his death.[37] That the dispute caused self-doubt is clear from his reminiscences. Again from 1886 we read:

> I have sometimes feared lest my life might in some sense be considered a failure. But when I see this gathering [alumni and teachers of Otterbein], and look at the fruits of this toil, I am greatly cheered.
> . . . .
> If there is anything of which I am proud it is of this work. As Cotton Mather said of that grand institution, Harvard, "It is the best thing the fathers of the country thought of." So I would say, the best thing our church ever thought of is the Christian college. God bless it and bless you all.[38]

NOTES

1. H. A. Thompson, *Our Bishops* (Dayton, Ohio: United Brethren Publishing House, 1904), 405.

2. Thompson, *Our Bishops*, 389.

3. Henry Garst, *Otterbein University 1847–1907* (Dayton, Ohio: U. B. Publishing House, 1907), 38–39.

4. Thompson, *Our Bishops*, 395; Garst, *Otterbein University*, 40.

5. Thompson, *Our Bishops*, 395.

6. A. W. Drury, *History of the Church of the United Brethren in Christ* (Dayton, Ohio: Otterbein Press, 1953), 442.

7. John Lawrence, *The History of the Church of the United Brethren in Christ* (Dayton, Ohio: U. B. Printing Establishment, 1861), 2:254.

8. P. R. Koontz and W. E. Roush, *The Bishops*, 2 vols. (Dayton, Ohio: The Otterbein Press, 1950), 1:392–93. There is no indication that there were any children born to this marriage.

9. Thompson, *Our Bishops*, 397.

10. Thompson, *Our Bishops*, 397–98.

11. Garst, *Otterbein University*, 21–25.

12. The meeting was held in the Davis home in Dayton, Ohio, Dec. 31, 1886. Thompson, *Our Bishops*, 401–02.

13. Thompson, *Our Bishops*, 402–04.

14. Thompson, *Our Bishops*, 404.

15. *Religious Telescope* (16 Dec. 1846): 163.

16. William W. Bartlett, *Education for Humanity: The Story of Otterbein College* (Westerville, Ohio: Otterbein College, 1934), 24.

17. A thorough study has been made of the manuscript minutes of the faculty, the executive committee, and the board of trustees in the process of preparing this essay. All of these items are to be found in the Otterbein Room of the Otterbein College Library, Westerville, Ohio.

18. L. Davis, *Essay on Education* (Circleville, Ohio: Conference Office of the United Brethren in Christ, 1852).

19. These emphases can be observed both in the curriculum and in the rules regulating student behavior at Otterbein University and at Union Biblical Seminary.

20. Thompson, *Our Bishops*, 420–21.

21. Thompson, *Our Bishops*, 419.

22. Drury, *History of UBC*, 444.

23. Thompson, *Our Bishops*, 420.

24. *Religious Telescope* (18 July 1866): 182.

25. *Religious Telescope* (30 Dec. 1846): 180.

26. *Religious Telescope* (20 Jan. 1847): 204.

27. *Religious Telescope* (23 June 1847): 377.

28. The present author found only one clear and indisputable reference to the manual labor program in faculty minutes during the period under scrutiny.

29. Bartlett, *Education for Humanity,* 45; Garst, *Otterbein University,* 181–82.

30. Harold Hancock, *The History of Westerville, Ohio* (Westerville, Ohio: The Author, 1974), 1–78.

31. A careful study has been made of the manuscript faculty minutes of Union Biblical Seminary during this period as a basis for this reconstruction.

32. George Funkhouser's funeral oration for Davis in *Religious Telescope* (9 Apr. 1890): 226.

33. The first marks of a sabbatical program for the seminary faculty are contained in a motion by Davis in faculty minutes of the Union Biblical Seminary for March 9, 1886.

34. For a discussion of this complex controversy, see Drury, *History of UBC,* 491–504, 513–18.

35. Drury, *History of UBC,* 711; Thompson, *Our Bishops,* 425.

36. *Religious Telescope* (9 Apr. 1890): 226.

37. "Let me give an incident concerning the late Dr. Davis. While a student in Union Biblical Seminary I called on him one evening with a copy of the Life of Bishop Edwards [written by Lewis Davis] which I owned, and requested that he write something with his signature, on one of its blank pages. The old father seemed pleased with my request, and cheerfully consented to comply with it if I would leave the book and call again. This I did and found he had written the following:

'Dayton, Ohio, January 6, 1889

As I am now seventy-five years old, I hope soon to pass from this life.

Yours truly,

L. Davis'"

from J. F. Leffler, "West Nebraska Conference Items" in *Religious Telescope* (16 Apr. 1890): 247.

38. Thompson, *Our Bishops,* 401, 405.

5

John Dempster
(1794–1863)

by Frederick A. Norwood

FRANCES WILLARD, FAMOUS resident of Evanston, Illinois, was a sharp and penetrating observer. Of her cocitizen John Dempster she had this to say:

> I can see that first president of Garrett Biblical Institute: tall, attenuated in figure and physically past his prime, not more by reason of age than of relentless mental grip and unmitigated toil; stately in bearing as a prince, and gallant as a courtier in manner; with square jaw, corrugated brow, beaked nose that nothing sublunary ever balked; mouth firm but kind and eyes blue and dominant as an eagle's, glowing with primeval fire.[1]

She was well acquainted with this formidable person for the crucial last ten years of his active and productive career, during which he presided over his proudest creation, Garrett Biblical Institute, a theological seminary in "the great American valley" near Chicago, which he called "the future London of the New World."

He had come fresh from the nurture of another theological seminary, the Methodist General Biblical Institute, in Concord, New Hampshire, and his work was not yet done. In the year he died he was full of dreams and plans for a third institute of theological learning to be located in California, that ultimate goal of the restless pioneers of the westward movement. John Dempster was one of those restless pioneers. But his dreams were concerned not with land and gold but with raising up a new generation of educated ministers in the Methodist Episcopal Church (MEC) which he loved so dearly.

Therefore, as a figure in the history of Methodist higher education,

JOHN DEMPSTER

Photo courtesy of Garrett-Evangelical Theological Seminary.

the primary significance of this forceful man lies in the area of theological education. But theological education rests firmly on the broader foundation of liberal arts, which found expression in church-related colleges and universities. Although Dempster does not figure largely in the development of colleges and universities as such, his life-work in building theological schools, while at times confronted with fierce opposition, is a direct consequence of the rise of higher education. Self-educated, he was at once both an exemplar of the educated minister and a creator of the special institution for their training.

Willard encountered him late in life, when he was scarred and worn from unremitting work and struggle. He had been born fifty-nine years before, in 1794, in Montgomery County, New York, near Amsterdam. His father, James Dempster, a native of Scotland, broke with his family when he joined the Wesleyan movement and became a circuit-riding preacher. He was one of the ministers sent by John Wesley to serve Methodists in America before formation of the MEC. Later he reverted to his Calvinist background and became a Presbyterian minister in Florida, where he died when his son John was nine years old.

Because of his father's early death John had few educational opportunities. But nevertheless he managed to train himself in basic skills. As an adult he pursued avidly those areas of knowledge most important for Christian witness. He developed an extensive and sophisticated, although stilted, literary and theological vocabulary. He mastered both Latin and Greek, read the Greek New Testament, and made progress in Hebrew. He was mildly criticized for overindulgence in words of classical derivation to the neglect of plain Anglo-Saxon.

By the time he was eighteen he had become a seller of tinware. In September, 1812, he attended a Methodist camp meeting in Deerfield, Herkimer County. Legend has it that in his youthful drive for status he made his mother sew him a ruffled shirt and lend him her gold watch for the occasion. In spite of all this finery, God won out and John was converted. George Peck, his ministerial contemporary in New York State and a noted editor and writer, commented: "He soon began to report himself to the meetings within his reach, and it was not long before it was evident that his occupation was gone, and he was likely to have other wares to offer to the people besides his dishes."[2]

He proceeded through the normal stages of Methodist ministry and was admitted to the Genesee Conference. Except for one appointment in Canada, he itinerated for about twenty years in New York State, including service as presiding elder. Along the way he met and married Lydia Clancey, daughter of a wealthy Methodist farmer, William Clancey. They had four children: Sara (McKee), Orrea (Lansingh), Mary [?] (Goodfellow), and Clancey John Dempster. Even at this early stage of his career he demonstrated concern for an educated ministry. When Genesee Wesleyan Seminary was founded in Lima, New York, in 1832, he became its president.

But a major change was coming. In 1836 Dempster accepted an appointment as missionary in Argentina, where he and his wife spent six years. Although he was far from home, his service in Buenos Aires was a measure of his potential, similar to the apprenticeship of John Wesley's missionary assignment in Georgia. Dempster's was considerably more successful. He founded the first Methodist church in Argentina, began a school, and set about constructing its first building. Already he was showing great skill as a minister, educator, and organizer. Unfortunately Lydia suffered a breakdown of health in South America, and she remained an invalid most of the rest of her life.

Shortly after they returned to the United States John Dempster was appointed president (or financial agent) of the infant Methodist Biblical Institute in Newbury, Vermont, succeeding Osman C. Baker, who had led the enterprise since its beginning. Soon this fledgling school moved to Concord, New Hampshire. There, as Thomas M. Eddy observed in a funeral address on Dempster's death, he and two faculty colleagues opened the school in a private house "without money, without endowment, without lands, without popular favor, but with strong faith in God, and confidence in the future approval of the church."[3]

Suspicion of seminaries was widespread. Through his entire life Dempster had to contend with powerful elements in the church which opposed any kind of formal theological education. Such lively and influential ministers as Peter Cartwright and Alfred Brunson combined ridicule of book-learned preachers with romantic affirmation of "brush college"—the on-the-field training young men had in company with experienced elders. Both of these lived to accept not only college education but also theological seminaries. But the early days in Concord were not easy. One young student who studied there under Dempster commented:

> It was believed by many that they would foster a formal, unsimple, unheroic, and inefficient ministry. These opinions were not only cherished by the greater proportion of the layity [sic] and ministry, but they also exerted a strong influence over the minds of the Bishops. Some of the Bishops looked with positive disfavor upon the new departure in the Church, while all put it upon a rigid probation.[4]

But Puritan leaders in New England, the land of Harvard and Yale, advocated an educated ministry. Rising to their persistent challenge, Methodists responded with the Newbury Project. The Newbury Biblical

Institute, whose founding date has been traditionally given as 1829 (with little substantial evidence), was actually a secondary or preparatory school, far removed from the "higher education" associated with theological education in the twentieth century. Richard Cameron describes the early institutional form as "about as sharply defined as the morning mist." In 1847, this school joined the Methodist Biblical Institute in Concord, bringing three professors and perhaps a dozen students. While some unanswered questions surround the actual historical connection between the two schools, it is known the enterprise enjoyed the title Methodist General Biblical Institute. Many Methodists of the day, including the few college-educated, would have gagged at the term "theological seminary."

So they persevered. Dempster had responsibility for the fields of theology, church history, and moral science.[5] Already his abstruse vocabulary was beginning to sap strength from his preaching. Although students sometimes failed to follow his metaphysical explanations, they nevertheless flocked to hear him teach and preach. He remained as president of Methodist General Biblical Institute for some seven years, until another Macedonian call took him to Evanston, Illinois. The school continued to grow, moved again to become Boston Theological Seminary, and in 1871 was organized as the school of theology in newly formed Boston University. Hence Dempster's roots, originally in New York State, were planted firmly in New England. His adult ministry was educational rather than pastoral; but it certainly was itinerant.

He bade a reluctant farewell to his colleagues and students in 1854, and moved with his family to Evanston. The reason was an irresistible call to take his dream of theological education to the immense middle part of the continent, the Mississippi watershed, which he, like others in those times, called "the West." He became rhapsodic in an address to the students he was leaving behind.[6] "This future garden of the New World" stood in need of a strong school for training Methodist ministers for service in what he was convinced would become the powerful and populous heartland of the nation. Moreover, the school would be located in or near Chicago, "the miracle of the New World," "the future London of the New World."

Heady stuff! It's a wonder that the young men under his instruction in isolated Concord did not migrate en masse.

He had already heard of a plan to establish a theological school in Illinois. He made a trip of exploration and met with John Clark, Grant Goodrich, Philo Judson, Orrington Lunt, and John Evans (after whom the town was named) at the Clark Street MEC in Chicago on the day after Christmas, 1853. They were all men, but they worked under the shadow of a woman who made the project possible; Eliza Garrett, widow of a former mayor of Chicago. She pledged the major part of her estate to the new school, which got under way with a first building the following year. Dempster moved with his family toward the end of 1854, to be president at the institute. Garrett Biblical Institute with its three faculty opened to four students on January 1, 1855.

For the next ten years Dempster labored hard and long to nourish his new theological child. In 1856 it had a sister, Northwestern University, on the same campus in Evanston. Nurtured by a common parent, the MEC, the two institutions grew together symbiotically. According to *Northwestern University, a History*, their boards of trustees constituted "an interlocking directorate."[7] This sibling relationship continued until well into the twentieth century. The seminary survived several dire financial crises, grew to maturity as an important constituent of the Chicago complex of theological education, almost perished in the Great Depression (and was saved at the last moment by its then much-larger sister), and through merger in the 1970s became Garrett-Evangelical Theological Seminary.

One decade, however, proved the limit for John Dempster, educational itinerant circuit rider. As the clouds of controversy over slavery and the union exploded in the Civil War, he expanded his life-long dream and planned still another seminary, this time in the far West near the shores of the Pacific Ocean. Some of his children were already in San Francisco: one of them, Sara, had recently been married there. The parents were naturally eager to meet their new son-in-law.[8] Dempster was prepared to leave Evanston, as ten years before he had left Concord, when calamity stopped him short. As a result of surgery he died in Chicago on November 28, 1863. Lydia continued to live in Evanston for ten more years.

Such was the vigorous and eventful life of the man who best personifies that segment of higher education concerned with the theological training of ministers. How did he view that kind of education? What did it have to do with the liberal arts and church-related colleges? What kind of minister did he envisage as its product?

We can make a beginning by assessing his attitude towards the goals of Northwestern University. Like his successors, he maintained very close relations with the university, which presently outgrew the seminary. His "Charge to Rev. Dr. Foster," delivered at the inauguration of Randolph S. Foster as university president in 1856, sets the foundation. The central purpose of higher education he defined as "a systematical development of man's faculties which best adapts him to the utmost activities of life, and fits him for life's close."[9] Several points should be emphasized: first, *systematical*, according to rational purpose and plan, nothing optional or fortuitous or "elective"; second, *adaptation* for the strenuous life, no levity, no sport, no shilly-shallying; third, *preparation* for dying. Dempster wholeheartedly supported the principle that the purpose of life is learning how to die well. This lay behind what he called the "disciplining process." He stood firmly on the basis of liberal arts understood in the context of Christianity. As he charged President Foster (a man who was sympathetic with the holiness movement of the times and later became a bishop), the university should continue its pursuit of broadly based Christian liberal arts, free from both the "bondage of the Church" and the "despotism of the State." It should follow a middle course between a preparatory school and an advanced professional university, it should be willing to accept advantaged and disadvantaged students, and it should promote a Christian viewpoint: "The Church, through all the ages of her history, has been the grand educator of the race."[10]

This approach to higher education fit perfectly his understanding of the theological training of ministers. Let us return to his "systematical" principle. "Though Providence has never ceased to aim at training the human intellect and affections for a nobler future," he averred, "that aim is now more direct, and the moral forces employed are now more powerful."[11] In this age, he insisted in another address, "intellectual wealth" is needed for effective proclamation of truth. "A well-stored mind" is important—but not with indiscriminate facts and desultory knowledge. Rather the crucial factor is "systems."[12]

By this Dempster meant the ability to organize knowledge by mental discipline in the interest of one overriding purpose. That purpose is for ministers "to make known God the Trinity to man the sinner."[13] In order to bring the educational process to bear on this purpose, "the power of patient, fixed, and protracted attention must be his."[14] Hence the study of modern science is important, in order that these disciplines may demonstrate the universal reign of God's providence. Repeatedly in his addresses and sermons to the students in Concord and Evanston he dwelt on the central necessity of a "unity of pursuit," an "entire singleness." The minister "combines and lays under contribution all events to his purpose." All geniuses in all fields have exhibited the indispensable characteristic of single and exclusive concentration on one object of effort.

Dempster's notion of concentration in one direction, specialization if you will, is not to be confused with narrow-mindedness. On the contrary, all knowledge, the whole world, is the proper area of study, provided it is unremittingly devoted to one purpose for ministers: saving souls. This view of theological education is remarkably close to that of John Wesley, who, although a highly educated man of the university, trained in the liberal and scientific arts, considered himself to be "a man of one Book." His preachers had only one task in their calling, to preach the gospel and save sinners. But in the process they must study widely and diligently. So John Dempster. Theological education is a lens which directs all knowledge in focus on the single object in view. His concept of ministry included personal religious experience, piety, and a call to preach, combined with a disciplined broad education and training designed to bring all together in singleness of purpose, unwavering attention to one goal.

Dempster exemplified this process in his own ministry, both on the early preaching circuits and later in educational leadership. His day was thoroughly organized, including ample time for study. Each area of study had its designated time in which no extraneous thoughts or considerations were allowed to interfere. One can only imagine the severity with which he would have met interruptions. Unity of pursuit—entire singleness of purpose. In his self-directed curricula all was directed to God's ways with men. But the searching of those ways led him far.

For Dempster ministry was not only personal, in individuals, but social, in institutions. Hence he was in the forefront of the struggle against slavery, both before and during the Civil War. He stood forth strongly at the General Conference in 1856 and 1860. He and another minister, W. W. Paton, were designated by their fellow ministers in Chicago to present directly to Pres. Abraham Lincoln in September, 1862, their conviction that he should emancipate the slaves. He welcomed modern science, provided it was cleansed of the secularism and materialism with which it was frequently burdened. He yearned for the great future which he believed was dawning. He was a man of his times and rooted in them. But his educational understanding freed him to encompass a higher vision of a new day.

Hence one is not surprised to learn that his understanding of ministry included a strong missionary motive. This motive covered both domestic missions, aimed at native Americans who already had suffered grievously at the hands of westward-moving pioneers and blacks who though emancipated would continue to be oppressed, and foreign missions of all kinds. The compulsion to proclaim the gospel in all the world was a major part of Dempster's message to fledgling ministers as they strove with singleness of purpose to bring all knowledge to the service of their calling.

As his one extant portrait shows, John Dempster faced life with a certain grim intensity. That same quality is found in his educational program. Although little in the modern world should be outside the purview of the educated minister, all knowledge must fall into focus, with "unity of pursuit" and "entire singleness," on that overriding goal to which John Wesley himself called his followers.

NOTES

1. Frances Willard, *A Classic Town* (Chicago: Women's Temperance Publishing Association, 1891), 229.

2. Anon., "Recollections of Rev. John Dempster, D. D." Manuscript biography in Dempster papers, Garrett-Evangelical Theological Seminary, 30 pp. The quote is on p. 5. This is a prime source on Dempster, written by an early student in the Concord seminary, who met him in 1849. He was a member of the second graduating class of 1851.

3. Thomas M. Eddy, "Funeral Sermon," in John Dempster, *Lectures and Addresses* (Cincinnati: Poe & Hitchcock, 1864, ed. D. W. Clark), appendix, 14. See also Richard M. Cameron, *Boston University School of Theology, 1839–1968* (Boston: BUST, 1968); and *Nexus*, 11 (May 1968).

4. "Recollections," 6.

5. *Zion's Herald*, 21 (4 Sept. 1850): 141. Several other references may be found in early issues.

6. "On the Importance of Locating a Biblical Institute in the West," in *Lectures and Addresses*, 190, 194.

7. Harold F. Williamson and Payson S. Wild, *Northwestern University, A History, 1850–1975* (Evanston: Northwestern University, 1976), 10. Compare Frederick A. Norwood, *From Dawn to Midday at Garrett* (Evanston: Garrett-Evangelical Theological Seminary, 1978).

8. See letters by Sara in Dempster papers.

9. Dempster, "Charge to Rev. Dr. Foster," in *Lectures and Addresses*, 242–43.

10. Dempster, "Charge to Rev. Dr. Foster," 250.

11. Dempster, "The Characteristics of the Age in Their Demands on the Ministry," in *Lectures and Addresses*, 45.

12. Dempster, "Truth," in *Lectures and Addresses*, 144.

13. Dempster, "Characteristics," 65.

14. Dempster, "Truth," 146.

6

William Preston Few
1867–1940

by Robert F. Durden

I N THE CASE of a large and complex American university, to apply the aphorism that as an institution it is but the lengthened shadow of one person would be an oversimplification. In the case of Duke University, however, the person coming closest to meriting the accolade is surely William Preston Few. It is true that he inherited from others the idea of organizing a new university around an already established liberal arts college, and the funds for achieving the goal came primarily from James Buchanan Duke. The fact remains that it was Few, a soft-spoken Shakespearean scholar and teacher turned first a dean and then a college president, who transformed an inherited and vague dream into a concrete plan, persuaded Duke to underwrite it, and presided over the new university from its launching late in 1924 until his death in 1940. Deficient as an orator and in what a later, image-oriented generation would call charisma, he managed, to use one of his own favorite phrases about others, to "do some permanent good upon the earth." This contribution was made possible by his profound belief in certain religious and philosophical truths and his ability to inspire and lead through his wisdom, his powerful pen, and his unfaltering and unselfish dedication.

Born as the second son on December 29, 1867, to Benjamin Franklin Few and Rachael Kendrick Few, "Billy" Few grew up in the rural communities of first Sandy Flat and then Greer in Greenville County, South Carolina. His father was a medical doctor and druggist who managed to send all five children to college, and the family was one of moderate means. Baptized in the Jackson Grove Methodist Church in 1871, Few joined the same church as a teenager. Speaking in 1932 at the centennial celebration of the church his grandfather had helped to establish, Few

WILLIAM PRESTON FEW

Photo courtesy of Duke University Archives.

testified: "When a boy I walked down the aisle of this church . . . to commit my life to the service of God and humanity, and I have never failed to follow the gleam from that day to this."

Precarious health afflicted him from childhood on, but he managed to attend high school in Greer and to enter the Methodist college of Wofford in nearby Spartanburg in 1885. Studious and introspective, he distinguished himself academically but, as he wrote his mother at the end of his first year, he felt that he needed to "build up socially and physically." He believed he was "undoubtedly weakest at these two points" and one "ought to try to be as symmetrical in character as he can."

Electing to become a teacher after graduation from Wofford in 1889, he took his first post at an academy in Darlington, South Carolina. "I am simply and surely the hardest worked man you ever saw," he soon wrote his sister. "I sometimes thought I had been hard-worked while a student, but I have six things to do now where I had one to do then. Rushing into a school like this with no experience and with no technical training was a risky thing." Few added that he had just attended services at the Presbyterian church, and the preacher was "slow till it hurts. . . . But I do have to be very dignified and look wise like an owl. Here is a great objection to the school-master's work: He must pretend to know everything. This keeps me on my tiptoe, for I lack a heap of knowing it all. Indeed I never have been so burdened with my insignificance as of late."

Despite his misgivings about his work and his continuing anxiety about learning "the art of living with others," Few must have performed creditably, for Wofford invited him in 1890 to become an instructor of English and Latin in its preparatory school. One who knew him then later recalled "a tall, thin, shy, timid man" with scholarly attributes. After two years in that post, Few entered Harvard in 1892, and despite serious health problems, including a long bout with what he described as "inflammatory rheumatism" that seriously affected one of his eyes, he received his Ph.D. degree in English in 1896.

As is so often the case, accident next played a large role. It happened that Trinity College, a small and struggling but ambitious Methodist college in Durham, North Carolina, needed a one-year replacement for its professor of English in the fall of 1896. Having moved to Durham only four years earlier, Trinity in 1894 had acquired as its president John Carlisle Kilgo, a Methodist preacher and educator from South Carolina. While serving as a part-time professor and traveling agent for Wofford College, which he had attended for the one year of his formal collegiate training, Kilgo had known Few and thus came to employ him on a temporary basis.

That the one year turned into a lifetime was due not only to Few's abilities and character but also to the fact that Kilgo, more than any other single individual, rekindled the interest of the wealthy Duke family in Trinity College. Washington Duke, who had launched his family in the tobacco industry after the Civil War, was so inspired by Kilgo's powerful sermons and dynamic leadership of Trinity that he offered an endowment of $100,000 in 1896 if the college would admit women students "on an equal footing with men," a policy which Kilgo and the trustees promptly and happily accepted. As for Few, Kilgo reported to the trustees that though everyone had been impressed by the "superior ability" of the young professor and wished to retain him, the college's budget would not allow it. "I placed the matter before Mr. B. N. Duke [son of Washington Duke]," Kilgo added, "and through his munificence the College has been given a new chair in English, making this department in Trinity the strongest in the state, if not in the entire South."

Although Few's character and personality were shaped long before he arrived at Trinity College at the age of twenty-eight, Kilgo had a marked influence on the younger man's educational philosophy and career. The two were totally different in temperament and style, Kilgo being a spellbinding orator and combat-loving controversialist while Few was a quiet teacher-scholar and irenic mediator. Yet the two men grew to work remarkably smoothly as a team after Few became the first dean of the college in 1902.

Aside from certain ideals and policies which he inherited from his predecessor at Trinity, John F. Crowell, Kilgo had experiences in South Carolina that led him to hold, passionately and outspokenly, a number of ideas about education and the church. A champion of loftier, more rigorous educational standards for the South, an idea which Trinity College had already embraced and continuously advanced—often in the face of complacency and even opposition—Kilgo believed in Christian higher education, that is, in voluntary and church-supported rather than tax-supported, state-run colleges. He argued, moreover, that "a great college could not be built in the South upon popular subscription" because the average southerner could not "visualize the large amount of money needed for higher education." The necessity, therefore, of finding sources of private wealth to provide an endowment for a voluntarily supported college was obvious. Highly critical of the educational chaos in the South and what he described as educational frauds arising from "money-conceived plans," he shunned narrow sectionalism as well as sectarianism. "If Trinity College were a sectarian college," Kilgo asserted, "if its chief aim was to advance the denominational interests of the Methodist Episcopal Church, South, then I would not waste my time and labors upon such an unworthy project." Unlike Few, Kilgo had no claim to high scholarship, yet he apparently understood, respected, and won enthusiastic loyalty from the small band of excellent young professors at Trinity.

Few would later de-emphasize the element of opposition to the state-supported colleges that was part of Kilgo's crusade for Christian higher education. But aside from that, Few's favorite educational themes—excellence and high standards rather than mere size, a close relationship for Trinity College with Methodism but without sectarianism, a national rather than sectional outlook, and a sympathetic but critical approach to the South and its myriad problems—all had been advanced by Kilgo and Trinity College long before Few became president. Few never claimed to be an innovator; he proved to be, nevertheless, a creative and far-sighted educational leader whose feet were firmly planted on certain educational and religious principles.

Within a few years of his coming to Trinity, Few apparently felt that he wished to cast his lot with the institution and spend his life in service to it and through it to North Carolina, the South, and the nation. In 1900, after only four years at Trinity, he confessed as much in a letter to Kilgo:

I can say without a tinge of cant that my chief ambition now is to help on in my little way the great work we have begun at the College. You, of course, know that already, but perhaps it won't hurt for me to say it again at this time, and to assure you that the treatment I have received during the dark year [of recurring eye trouble?] from the College and from my personal friends in and at the College has bound me to the College with a love that is one of the passions of my life. I hope to spend a good part of my days in attempting to pay the debt of gratitude I owe and I shall be happiest when I am set to do unpleasant tasks for the College.

These were high-sounding words, but for the following four decades Few demonstrated through his deeds—in fact, his life—that he meant exactly what he had said.

A crisis that erupted in 1903, the year after Few had been named as Trinity's first dean, tied him more closely than ever to the college. Around the turn of the century Trinity seemed to be almost chronically in the center of a public furor of one sort or another. There were numerous, complicated reasons for this but a few leading factors may be identified. In the first place, Kilgo's flamboyant style and zest for controversy earned him many enemies, some of them being among the most powerful leaders of the Tar Heel Democratic partly. Second, the Dukes, closely involved with Trinity from 1890 on, were not only already rich and growing richer from the American Tobacco Company—the "tobacco trust," headed by James B. Duke—but they dared openly to be Republicans. This was at a time when the Democrats in North Carolina, as in much of the rest of the South, were intent upon guaranteeing the permanent primacy of the "white man's party." This they set out to accomplish by disfranchising black voters (who were generally Republican after gaining the franchise during Reconstruction) and by erecting an elaborate, legalized system of racial segregation to protect "the Southern way of life" and prevent the "social equality" of the races. Challenged and frightened by angry farmers in the Populist revote of the 1890s, southern Democrats around 1900 used every known political device from terrorist tactics first learned during Reconstruction to rabidly racist appeals in order to gain and keep hegemony.

By the standards of their time and place, Few, Kilgo, and the Dukes were unorthodox in racial matters, yet none of them directly challenged segregation. They genuinely favored trying to help blacks rather than stirring up white racial passions against them. Although the Dukes, as Republicans, had a partisan interest in opposing black disfranchisement, they also had a long record of friendly actions toward the minority race. As for Trinity College, when Kilgo invited Booker T. Washington to speak there in 1896 it was the black leader's first address at a white college in the South, and the students cheered him. All of this, and more, set the stage for the crisis of 1903 in which Few played an off-stage but leading part and which gave Trinity College a pivotal role in the establishment of academic freedom in the United States.

John Spencer Bassett, professor of history at Trinity, launched the *South Atlantic Quarterly* in 1902 as a vehicle for the sort of scholarly and critical essays which he, Few, and their colleagues believed that the South sorely needed. A native Tar Heel and alumnus of Trinity with a doctorate from Johns Hopkins, Bassett did pioneering research in the history of slavery and antislavery leaders in North Carolina and watched unhappily as the Tar Heel Democrats successfully waged their virulent "white supremacy" campaigns of 1898 and 1900. When white racism continued at fever pitch even after disfranchisement was accomplished, Bassett decided to declare his views publicly and in the fall of 1903 published in the *South Atlantic Quarterly* an essay-editorial entitled "Stirring Up the Fires of Race Antipathy." By later standards it was tame indeed, even mildly racist; yet Bassett openly criticized the Democratic party for its time-worn tactics, predicted that some day blacks would win equality, and urged that whites should replace oppression with conciliation.

The storm of vituperation that greeted Bassett's article—and Trinity College itself—eventually reached huge proportions. Josephus Daniels, editor-publisher of the *Raleigh News and Observer* and one of the most powerful Democratic leaders in the state, led the attack by declaring in his newspaper that if Bassett's ideas became widespread, "then the civilization of the South is destroyed." The Trinity historian, Daniels proclaimed, had "committed the only unpardonable sin"—that is, he had criticized the white South's prevailing racial arrangements and attitudes. Lesser Democratic papers, taking their cue from Daniels, joined in the fray with one declaring that "Duke's money has made it possible for Trinity's teacher of history to fling defiance in the face of Southern ideals and call on the young men of the South to forsake the faith of their fathers and worship at the shrine of a negro." Another commented: "But since Trinity has been tobacconized, Kilgoized and republicanized with a Duke for a ruler we can probably look on the jabberings of this idiot [Bassett] with less contempt. He is the product of the theory of his own institution."

Even many alumni and friends of Trinity became alarmed at the widespread criticism of Bassett's "heresy." It was, after all, a time when colleges, rather than having the luxury of picking and choosing among applicants, had to work hard at recruiting students. Trinity, like other colleges, had to heed public opinion, at least to a degree, if it were to survive and play the role it envisioned for itself. In a similar incident a year earlier, Emory College in Georgia had sacrificed one of its professors who had aroused opposition by expressing unorthodox racial views. Kilgo thought it shameful, for he discerned, as he wrote Bishop Warren A. Candler, "a fixed design on the part of the lower elements of politicians in the South to either run the church out of education, or force our colleges to serve their vile ends of social bondage." Kilgo declared that the "supreme question in the South is, shall we be a free people or shall we be the slaves of a vile partizanship?" *(sic)*

Little did Kilgo realize when he wrote those words that a year later they would face a harsh test at Trinity. Because of the great outcry Bassett's article had provoked, and for the sake of the college, the young historian offered his resignation. The crucial question was, as the trustees assembled on December 1, 1903, would they accept it?

By a vote of eighteen to seven the trustees refused to allow the Trinity professor to be sacrificed. Moreover, they adopted a statement prepared by Few and an old friend of his, William Garrott Brown, which has become one of the landmark documents not only of Trinity College and Duke Unviversity but of academic freedom in the nation. These were among the key sentences in the eloquent declaration:

A reasonable freedom of opinion is to a college the very breath of life; and any official throttling of the private judgment of its teachers would destroy their influence, and place upon the college an enduring stigma. . . . Great as is our hope in this College, high and noble as are the services which under God we believe that it is fit to render, it were better that Trinity should suffer than that it should enter upon a policy of coercion and intolerance.

At the time, the public never knew of Few's role in what Trinity-Duke came to remember proudly as the Bassett Affair. One important trustee who did appreciate Few's contribution and who also played a decisive if quiet role in the outcome was Benjamin N. Duke, son of Washington Duke and older brother of James B. Duke. Having become a trustee of Trinity in 1889 and a key influence in the college's move to Durham in 1892, Ben Duke served as the family's principal philanthropic agent. From Few's arrival in Durham in 1896 the two men, alike in their quiet ways and neither in robust health, became close associates in the service of Trinity and the Main Street Methodist Church (which later became Duke Memorial). Long before Washington Duke's death in 1905, Ben Duke had become the family's foremost, ever-reliable supporter of the college. As early as 1902, he asserted, perhaps a bit prematurely, that "Trinity College has reached that point of capacity and efficiency to warrant the claim that it is the best institution of learning in the South." Like Kilgo and Few, Ben Duke took pride in the fact that, as he put it, the college stood "for the new forces working now very rapidly for the up-building of the whole South and tending to break up the sectional isolation and make the South a part of our common country."

Breaking up sectional isolation was a goal as much sought by Few as by Ben Duke. Expressing ideas that shaped his own career as well as the later tone and mission of Trinity-Duke, Few wrote in 1905 that the South, once the spawning ground for the likes of Washington and Jefferson, had known since the 1830s "a long day of small things, of men of local, narrow, sectional outlook . . . to whom truth is not free and universal, but limited and of special application." On the defensive first about slavery and then about treatment of the freed blacks, southerners had been too much shut in to themselves and had "lived apart from the general movement of contemporary life, cut off from the liberalizing and nationalizing tendencies that have been so strong for a hundred years." More oblique in his approach to the race question than Bassett, Few nevertheless asserted that white southerners had "at times forgotten that we must do justly and love mercy, or else we shall be more injured than are those we oppress; for as Emerson says the slave is forever owner and the victim is forever victor."

In this same essay published in the *South Atlantic Quarterly*, Few noted that religion in the South had become "somewhat different from the prevailing type now found elsewhere among men of English blood," for southerners tended to cling to "a religion that is emotional, given to profession, and sometimes froward in its retention of outworn forms, rather than conservative of the simple, essential spirit of Christianity." Concerning the paucity of first-rate literature produced in the South, Few observed that, "We in democratic America constantly need to be reminded that excellence dwells high among the rocks and to attain it we must wear out our very souls." More specifically focusing on southern conditions, he suggested that great literature "comes to a civilization that is strong and healthy and not in the miasmatic intellectual regions where we have lived for three quarters of a century."

Few did much of his most creative thinking and writing during his years as dean, and other essays of his appeared regularly in the *South Atlantic Quarterly*. Most were on educational matters, for although he had proven his capacity for literary scholarship—through his dissertation at Harvard as well as published articles—his mind had clearly turned after about 1900 in an administrative direction. His thesis in one essay, "The Excessive Devotion to Athletics," was apparent from the title, and in "The Standardizing of Southern Colleges" in 1908 he emphasized ideas that were seminal in his career as an educational leader and as a lay statesman of Methodism. After noting at the outset that the South's "whole scheme of education is in what seems to be, in certain of one's moods, a hopelessly disorganized state," Few went on to call, first of all, for "high standards and right ideals." He then traced the standardizing process that was "slowly but surely going on" through various agencies, including, among others, the Educational Commission of the Methodist Episcopal Church, South, a board on which Few served from 1898 until his death. Few recognized some of the perils involved in introducing standards: "A college must be at least in part the product of development and not a forced growth; and it should follow the lines of its own development and not be made to form itself on some wholly extraneous model."

A staunch believer in the type of permanent and self-perpetuating board of trustees that Trinity had developed, Few cherished the ties that Trinity (and later Duke) maintained with the two Methodist conferences in North Carolina. (Each conference ratified or confirmed one-third of the trustees and the alumni confirmed the other third, while the board itself submitted the names to all three groups.) Yet he also maintained the view that close ties should not mean church control. "In the long run of years," he argued, "there can be no security for a college which in its actual control is too close to the untrained mass of people, whether this mass is represented by a state government subject to popular will or represented by a church organization that reflects too immediately the changing moods of the multitude." Putting the matter another way, Few noted that to "believe in the future of America at all, or for that matter to contemplate human life with any degree of patience, one must believe that the people wish to do right and in the long run and in the main will do right; but this does not mean that they have the expert knowledge to manage a college any more than it means they are competent to argue a point of law before the Supreme Court of the United States, or to treat an acute case of pneumonia."

The double occasion of Charles W. Eliot's retirement from Harvard in 1909 and the publication of his book, *University Administration*, afforded Few an opportunity not only to pay tribute to one of the nation's foremost educators, but to indicate in remarkably prophetic words some of his own ideas about university-building. Noting the need in the South for "colleges that are strong enough to lead public opinion and that are not content merely to follow it," Few cautioned that they could not be made to order but must grow slowly. It had taken Eliot "forty years to change a provincial New England college into a true American university," Few said. After suggesting that Johns Hopkins University's "attempt to transplant to American soil a full grown German university" had not been altogether successful, Few described an attitude and a policy that would come to fruition in future years:

> An attempt in the South to imitate a university like Harvard would be equally foolish and prove equally unsuccessful. We cannot transplant. We must build for ourselves in the light, of course, of our own experience and in the light of what has been done elsewhere. This cannot be done by clinging blindly to the past and resisting all change, but must be done by patient and wise experimentation. This method is slow, but is the only sure method; and impatience of human progress finds its just reproof in President Eliot's own memorable saying that "nature's patient ways shame hasty little man."

Although not the sort of man consciously to groom himself for high office, Few clearly had developed into an obvious choice as the successor to Kilgo when the latter resigned in 1910 to become a Methodist bishop. Although some observers speculated that with the end of Kilgo's presidency, the crucial support of the Dukes would be lost to Trinity, that proved emphatically not to be the case. Ben Duke, in fact, soon informed a friend that Few was "making a rousing good college president" and that Trinity was booming as never before. Financial support from Ben Duke kept growing, and through his efforts important benefactions came occasionally from his younger brother in New York, J. B. Duke.

In the summer of 1911, soon after his inauguration, Few married Mary Reamey Thomas of Martinsville, Virginia, a graduate of Trinity (1906). When, subsequently, five sons—William, Lyne Starling, Kendrick Sheffield, Randolph Reamey, and Yancey Preston—were born to the Fews, his family took a place alongside the Methodist Church and Trinity College as things that mattered most to him.

By the time of the United States entry into World War I, Trinity had developed into one of the stronger liberal arts colleges in the South, but in choosing national rather than regional measuring rods, the college was far from complacent. Few had inherited ambitions and hopes for a wider service to be rendered by Trinity. As Ben Duke became increasingly ill after about 1915, Few, with the older brother's blessings and constant help, turned more and more, through rare interviews and frequent, graceful letters, to James B. Duke.

Constantly and happily preoccupied with the building of the electric power industry in the Piedmont region of the two Carolinas, J. B. Duke began around 1914 or 1915 to contemplate a vast philanthropic project for the Carolinas based in large part on a substantial portion of his stock in the power company. In a meeting with Few, Duke referred vaguely to this as early as 1916, and in 1919 the two men held a more substantive conference. J. B. Duke's gifts to Trinity and, through Trinity, to the Methodist Church for aid to superannuated ministers and the building of rural churches grew larger after 1915, but he would not be hurried about his larger philanthropic plans.

Convalescing from an illness in the spring of 1921, Few had a veritable brainstorm, and for the first time worked out in his own mind— and then in a memorandum for J. B. Duke—a practical plan for organizing a new university around Trinity College. The notion that the best American universities "have at their heart a great college of arts and sciences" was an idea in which Few passionately believed and had repeated many times. Because there were already several Trinity Colleges as well as a Trinity University (in Texas), Few suggested that the expanded institution be named Duke University as a memorial to Washington Duke, whose gifts had brought Trinity to Durham. The university should include "Trinity College, a coordinate College for Women, a Law School, a School of Business Administration, a School of Engineering (emphasizing chemical and electric engineering), a Graduate School of Arts and Sciences, and, when adequate funds are available, a Medical School."

J. B. Duke was not ready in 1921 to act on Few's proposal but by December, 1924, he was. The Duke endowment and Duke University were both born at that time, and the new university was designated as the recipient of approximately one-third of the annual income of the endowment, for which Duke initially provided securities worth $40 million, and to which he later added $67 million through his will. In addition, J. B. Duke provided about $19 million for the conversion of the old Trinity campus into a new Woman's College of Duke University and for the building of the Tudor Gothic stone structures on the new, several-thousand-acre campus a mile or so to the west.

"Then after all, my dream and your dream is to be realized in full," Few exulted to Ben Duke at Christmas, 1924. "Isn't it glorious?" Indeed, the South had never known philanthropy on the scale of J. B. Duke's, and many educational institutions could only envy the good luck of Duke University. It was far from being, however, the "richest endowed university in the world," as popular journals kept repeating in the late 1920s and in the 1930s. Few went to great and laborious lengths attempting to set the record straight but finally and wearily declared, "Nobody in America should become excited by anything in a newspaper until he makes sure that he has the bottom facts."

For all of Duke University's good fortune and spectacular blessings, Few privately had to face some painful facts in the late 1920s. He had sold an exceedingly ambitious plan to J. B. Duke, but just as the vast new building program was being launched Duke died, after a relatively short illness, in October, 1925. (Ben Duke, almost a recluse in his last years, died in January, 1929.) Few could hardly publicize his dilemma but he confessed to one close associate in 1927:

> I am frankly worried. It was just as clear to me the day Mr. [J. B.] Duke died as it is now that we do not have either in hand or in sight sufficient resources to develop the other departments of the University as Mr. Duke expected us to develop them and also support the sort of medical school and hospital that the public expects of us and that all of us want to see here.

Cuts were quietly made in some of the plans for the new Gothic campus, however, and Few persevered hopefully. "The routine at times may be dull and gray," he wrote to an associate, "but the vision of the future is always golden and infinitely inspiring." By 1930 as the tall stone chapel in the center of the new campus began to climb upward among the pine trees—the last of the original Gothic buildings to be erected—Few declared in a letter, "I feel that we have now hit the open sea and that a long journey is ahead of Duke University."

The last decade of his life brought many laurels for him, including ten honorary degrees, and growing recognition for Duke University. Aside from the pleasure he took in his family and in the patient building of a university, he derived much satisfaction from the reunification of the Methodist Church in 1939, a cause for which he had worked long before becoming a member of the commission that prepared the way for the Uniting Conference. He died of a coronary thrombosis on October 16, 1940, and his body was the first to be placed in the crypt of the Duke chapel. In an essay he published in 1905 he provided, unintentionally to be sure, a fitting epitaph for himself: "The happiest men have always been those who have worked under a great inspiration, and it is a happy privilege to spend oneself in the service of an undying cause in which one believes with the whole heart."

SOURCES

The papers of William P. Few are in the University Archives of Duke University. Principal printed sources are: Robert H. Woody, ed., *The Papers and Addresses of William Preston Few* (1951), which includes a substantial biographical sketch; Earl Porter, *Trinity and Duke, 1892–1924: Foundations of Duke University* (1964); and Robert F. Durden, *The Dukes of Durham, 1865–1929* (1975).

7

Willbur Fisk
(1792–1839)

by Douglas J. Williamson

I N THE SUMMER of 1818, Willbur Fisk, a twenty-six-year-old graduate of Brown University, was "admitted on trial" to the New England Conference of the Methodist Episcopal Church (MEC). Twenty-seven years had passed since Jesse Lee had initiated the Methodist mission to New England, but Fisk was nevertheless the first member of the New England Methodist ministry to have earned a college degree. Perhaps predictably, Fisk came to dominate New England Methodist educational endeavors for the ensuing twenty years. Less predictably, but perhaps just as importantly, in those twenty years Fisk became one of the most important American Methodist theologians, the most influential member of the New England Conference, and an ardent advocate of temperance, missionary, and colonization societies.

Born in Brattleborough, Vermont, on August 31, 1792, to Isaiah and Hannah Bacon Fisk, Fisk was nurtured in a deeply religious setting, and at the age of twelve had already joined the local Methodist class. His formal education prior to college consisted of two to three years at the local grammar school, but his personal reading and writing occupied almost all of the time he did not spend working in his father's farm fields. Fisk was accepted as a member of the sophomore class at Vermont University in August, 1812. His tenure there was brief, since all students were forced to leave when the American army assumed control of the school's physical facilities during the summer of 1813 as a part of an effort to secure the northern states against the British army.

It was not until the summer of 1814, when he enrolled at Brown University, that Fisk resumed his education. He was graduated in August,

WILLBUR FISK

Photo of painting of Willbur Fisk courtesy of United Methodist Commission on Archives and History.

1815, and in pursuit of a profession he turned first to the study of law. Fisk soon found himself to be unhappy with law, and although he had not been a "professor of religion" while in college, he came to believe that the profession for which he was best suited was that of preaching the gospel. Despite this belief, he could not acknowledge having received a "divine call" to preach, and he was therefore hesitant to pursue a ministerial vocation immediately.

Early in 1816 Fisk left his legal studies to accept a position as tutor to the children of a wealthy Maryland family. He made this decision for two basic reasons: first, his health, never very good throughout his entire life, was particularly poor at this time, and a respite in a southern climate was thought to be the proper remedy; and second, Fisk had accumulated large debts to finance his education, and he needed some form of employment to eliminate those debts. Fisk's health ultimately became worse during his time in Maryland, he became increasingly unhappy with his environment, and he returned home to Lyndon, Vermont, in June, 1817.

Shortly after returning home, the "divine calling" for which Fisk had so deeply longed pressed itself upon him:

> On returning to Lyndon a new scene of things awaited him. The place was at that period favoured, under the ministry of the Rev. Phinehas Peck, of the Methodist Church, with a remarkable outpouring of the Holy Spirit. . . . Mr. Fisk had not been long at home before his mind was deeply affected, and all the associations of his early days returned with greatly augmented power. . . . And now the Lord healed his backslidings, and loved him freely.[1]

Throughout the next year, Fisk became a diligent member of the Methodist class at Lyndon and committed himself to the duty of entering the Methodist ministry. After being "accepted on trial" in 1818, he was assigned to the Craftsbury, Vermont, Circuit, where he lived the rugged life of a Methodist circuit rider.

Fisk's life changed dramatically at the New England Conference of 1819, when his preaching talents were called for in Charlestown, Massachusetts. Fisk's charge at Charlestown was a feeble and impoverished parish, but the young and dynamic preacher needed only a little time to alter that state of affairs:

> Mr. Fisk's labors at Charlestown were very successful. His congregations were quite large and respectable, but this, with his usual modesty, he ascribed to the unhappy state of the other churches, which were at variance with their ministers, and whose members therefore came in crowds to hear him.[2]

In the midst of a smoldering controversy between Unitarians and orthodox Calvinists, Fisk built a stable Methodist congregation in Charlestown. His ministry there was prematurely concluded by his poor health in 1821, but by then he had firmly established a pocket of Arminian theology in the midst of a bastion of Calvinism.

One of the most significant single incidents in Fisk's first thirty years of life occurred in the Cape Cod town of Wellfleet, where in August, 1819, he attended a camp meeting conducted by Timothy Merritt, a fellow Methodist preacher. Merritt's sermon dealing with the Wesleyan doctrine of Christian perfection not only strengthened Fisk's personal piety ("his religious emotions now acquired a wonderful intensity and elevation"),[3] but it also marked the beginning of an intimate personal and professional relationship between Fisk and Merritt. The latter had been intensely involved in a theological controversy with several New England Calvinist ministers, and he was responsible for drawing Fisk into that controversy by publishing Fisk's first public discourse on the doctrine of future punishments. Between 1822 and 1833, when Merritt transferred to the New York Conference, Fisk and Merritt worked closely on several Methodist educational and theological ventures.

From the New England Conference of 1823 until his death in 1839, Willbur Fisk was regarded, both within and without the Methodist connection, as one of the most important and influential leaders of both New England and American Methodism. In June, 1823, he married Ruth Peck of Providence, Rhode Island, following a courtship of seven years, and his new wife accompanied him as he left that same month to become presiding elder of the Methodist work in the state of Vermont. He left Vermont after his election as principal of the Wesleyan Academy in Wilbraham, Massachusetts, in 1826, a post he held until September, 1831, when he assumed the first presidency of Wesleyan University in Middletown, Connecticut. Fisk served as Wesleyan's leader until his death, though he took an extended sabbatical from August, 1835, until November, 1836, during which he traveled throughout Europe and served as the American General Conference delegate to the 1836 British Wesleyan Conference. The high esteem in which Fisk was held by his fellow Methodists was also signified by his election to the episcopacy, once in 1829 by the Methodist Church of Canada, and again in 1836 by the General Conference in the United States (Fisk declined the office on both occasions).

The final sixteen years of Fisk's life were marked by an unceasing involvement in the theological, temperance, antislavery, missionary, and of course, educational concerns of New England Methodism. Fisk was among a small group of the most important Methodist theologians of the first half of the nineteenth century. Unlike many other Methodists, Fisk was concerned with establishing the doctrinal integrity of Methodism, particularly in his native New England. This meant that he was forced to consider and write specifically on such concepts as predestination and election, moral agency, regeneration, and personal holiness. There was little in Fisk's theological writings that was not Wesleyan in origin. Still, Fisk made a major contribution to American Methodism by formulating contemporary expressions of Wesleyan theological doctrines and defending those doctrines against the criticisms of nineteenth-century American Calvinists, Unitarians, and Universalists. And as Leland Scott has noted in *The History of American Methodism,* Fisk was the first American Methodist theologian capable of carrying on extended disputations with theologians of Calvinist or Unitarian background.[4]

Fisk's first major doctrinal sermon, "On the Doctrine of Future Punishments," was delivered before the New England Conference in 1823. A unanimous vote of the conference called for its publication in the *Methodist Magazine.* A public response from a Reverend Pickering of the Providence Universalist Society occasioned Fisk's additional publication of ten articles in *Zion's Herald.* From this point forward, at least until his intense involvement in abolitionist controversies, Fisk was acknowledged as the foremost spokesman for Methodist theological positions in New England. His 1831 "Discourse on Predestination and Election" represents his most capable effort, but other major works include *Calvinistic Controversy* and two discourses in Timothy Merritt's book, *Anti-Universalism.*

Beginning in 1827, Fisk also became an active supporter of the temperance movement then taking shape within New England Methodism.[5] Among American Methodists Fisk was one of the earliest supporters of nondenominational temperance societies. His support was manifested not only by his writings, but also by his service, beginning in 1828, as an agent for the Springfield (Massachusetts) Temperance Society. It is also probable that Fisk was the person most responsible for gaining the support of Nathan Bangs, then the editor of the *Christian Advocate and Journal,* for such temperance societies. And Fisk's "Address to the Members of the Methodist Episcopal Church, on the Subject of Temperance" (1832) received widespread endorsement from American Methodist leaders. In that address Fisk advocated entire abstinence from all alcoholic beverages by all persons at all times and implicitly recommended the adoption by Congress of legislation that would banish intoxicating beverages from the nation. The address led to the formation of a General Conference Temperance Committee for the first time in 1832 and a renewed church-wide zeal for temperance reform, as well as to the

adoption by the New England Conference, in 1835, of an "entire abstinence" position concerning alcoholic beverages.

In matters related to the temperance cause, Fisk exhibited little toler-
ance for his adversaries. Although generally characterized by both his
contemporaries and later historians as a charitable and ecumenically
minded leader, Fisk often cast aside all kind words when referring, in
public addresses, to opponents of the temperance movement:

> On Wednesday evening at the Methodist Chapel in Bromfield Street, Rev-
> erend Dr. Fisk . . . delivered an eloquent discourse on the causes and evils of
> intemperance. . . . The doctor commenced by observing that there are some
> things in which men cannot be neutral. . . . His main proposition was this—
> "Those who manufacture, traffic in, and use ardent spirits are answerable for
> the evils which follow. . . . Why will they say, a temperate glass does me
> good? It is not so; rum does no one any good; at least, none worth naming.
> Rum, even if it did them some good, as the custom of using it is fraught with
> so much evil, as this custom is the fountain of all the evils that flow from
> intemperance, it should be given up."[6]

Fisk often objected to the tendency of his contemporaries to stumble
into "ultraism"—an excessive, careless zeal in advocating a particular
cause. Although later in his career Fisk warned temperance advocates
against such ultraism, he was perhaps guilty of such zeal in his own
early days of temperance advocacy. On one occasion he was heard to
thunder, "If the Church stand on rum, let it go."[7]

Fisk has also been called "the most respected and outstanding colo-
nizationist in the Methodist Episcopal Church."[8] The colonization movement was an antebellum attempt by white Americans to free black slaves
and ultimately eradicate slavery in the United States by assisting slaves
in leaving the country and settling in Africa. Like many other residents
of northern states, Fisk endorsed colonization enterprises because he
sincerely believed that they would be effective in eliminating slavery and
simultaneously restoring dignity to those who had been unjustly bound
as slaves.

In 1817 Fisk wrote: "Slavery is the curse of our country and will one
day prove its ruin."[9] He expressed a similar view eighteen years later:
"In my opinion slavery is evil—only evil—and that continually."[10] Still,
he would never support abolitionism, the movement which sought an
unconditional and immediate liberation of all slaves in the United States
and its territories. Fisk feared that abolitionism would shatter the unity
of the nation and the MEC and would alienate slaveholders, causing
them to tighten, rather than loosen, the bonds of the slaves.

Fisk's support of the colonization cause became public in 1835 when he engaged in a heated controversy over the issue with such New England Conference leaders as Orange Scott, LaRoy Sunderland, and Shipley Willson, all of whom were passionate abolitionists. The conflict between Fisk and New England Conference abolitionists continued until Fisk's death. The conflict belongs to a "painful portion"[11] of Fisk's life, for it was responsible for a serious decline in Fisk's influence in New England Methodism and even brought Fisk into an intense disagreement with his old and cherished friend, Timothy Merritt, who became an abolitionist in the middle years of the 1830s.[12]

Fisk's prominence in the Methodist temperance movement and in the colonization-abolitionism controversy occurred during the time that he served as the first principal of Wesleyan Academy and as the first president of Wesleyan University. That fact is significant, because Fisk understood his particular ministry to be that of raising up and serving Methodist institutions of higher education. Highly respected as a speaker, writer, and theologian, Fisk was seemingly always being offered positions—agent for a temperance or colonization or missions society, or bishop, or university president (at the University of Alabama, among others)—which would have removed him from Wesleyan Academy and Wesleyan University. Fisk declined all of these offers. Likewise, he never allowed his involvement in any particular cause or movement to obscure his priority in life—establishing American Methodist higher education on a firm foundation. After her husband's death, Ruth Peck Fisk recalled the words he used (in 1823) in describing this commitment to Methodist educational endeavors: "If the Lord spare my life and will give me influence, with His blessing the Methodist Church shall not want for academies nor colleges."[13]

Fisk spoke those words to his wife following an incident, in a session of the 1823 New England Annual Conference, which altered the course of Methodist higher education in New England. The incident stemmed from Fisk's refusal to raise funds for the Newmarket (New Hampshire) Academy, a preparatory school that had been founded by the New England Conference in 1817. Throughout its entire six-year existence, the academy had struggled to meet its financial obligations. Fisk believed, with some justification, that the New England Conference had not fully committed itself to sustaining, improving, and promoting the academy. As a result, he balked at complying with an assignment, given to him in 1822, to raise funds for it. Fisk's unwillingness to raise funds precipitated his celebrated exchange with the presiding bishop of the 1823 Conference:

"Why," said the Bishop, "have you not solicited funds for the Academy?"
"Because, sir, my conscience would not let me."
"Must the conference, then, be governed by your conscience?"
"No, sir, I do not wish the conference to be governed by my conscience, but I must be: neither do I wish to control the conference in any way; but if, after examining the school for themselves, the conference sees fit to place it on a different footing, it shall have my utmost exertion."[14]

Fisk's statement did precipitate the formation of a New England Conference committee to examine Newmarket Academy and make recommendations concerning its future. The committee decided to close Newmarket, which it did in December, 1823, and began making plans for opening a new school under the auspices of the New England Conference. On February 7, 1824, the conference secured a charter from the Commonwealth of Massachusetts for a school to be located in Wilbraham, Massachusetts, and to be called Wesleyan Academy. At the 1824 conference session Fisk was chosen as one of the trustees for the new institution, and he was active in planning and soliciting funds for the school. After extensive planning and preparation, Wesleyan Academy opened its doors to students on November 8, 1825. Fisk, who had been elected principal by the trustees on September 28, delivered the opening address.

Because he was obligated to serve out his term as presiding elder in Vermont, Fisk did not move to Wilbraham until May, 1826. Under Fisk's direction, however, the school prospered and grew: in July, 1826, Fisk reported to *Zion's Herald* that enrollment had increased to 75 students (50 boys, 25 girls) from the initial total of 44 students who had enrolled for the first full term in the preceding December. By the fall term of 1827 the academy had enrolled 118 students—82 boys and 36 girls. One assumes that all of those students met the criteria that Fisk had established for admission to the school: "Prerequisites for admission: Ten years of age, a capacity to improve, and an ability to read and spell with tolerable correctness."[15]

Wesleyan Academy continued to prosper under Fisk's leadership, although Fisk was unsuccessful in attempts to secure any support at all—not in finances, or faculty, or even a visiting committee—from the New York Conference. The academy also survived a colossal financial blunder by Fisk and the New England Conference, who decided in September, 1827, that *Zion's Herald* would be purchased jointly by the academy and the New England Conference and would be administered by the academy. After a single year of this arrangement, the *Herald* was sold to the Methodist Book Concern in New York. The prestige of the academy was considerably enhanced, however, when Fisk was awarded an honorary degree from Augusta College in 1829, and an ever-increasing enrollment allowed the academy to stay financially healthy.

According to Ruth Peck Fisk, it had been her husband's intention that Wesleyan Academy would some day become a Methodist college: "the brethren of the New England Conference and the trustees of the Wilbraham Academy had long looked forward with the expectation of seeing that institution enlarged to a college and that was Mr. Fisk's first desire."[16] A chain of events was set in motion in 1827, however, that would lead to the establishment of the first Methodist college in New England at Middletown, Connecticut, and to Willbur Fisk's election as that college's first president. It was in 1827 that the American Literary, Scientific, and Military Academy vacated its campus in Middletown and moved to Norwich, Vermont. Coincidentally, Fisk went to Middletown in that same year to preach the dedication sermon at a newly erected Methodist church.

A short time later, Fisk was visited at Wilbraham by a Mr. Gould, who had heard Fisk's sermon and told Fisk that the Methodists would be offered the military academy buildings at minimal cost for use as a college campus. Fisk informed Gould that he (Fisk) objected to the site as a location for a college, but that such an offer should be seriously considered by the MEC. Fisk also felt that American Methodists were not yet ready to establish a college "for the whole connection," since many conferences had yet to sponsor or develop academies, or preparatory schools. Fisk elaborated upon that viewpoint in the 1828 report of the General Conference Committee on Education (Fisk chaired the committee and wrote the report):

> 1. Our people are not sufficiently awake as yet to establish a university for the whole connection.
>
> 2. Not half the conferences are yet provided with academies under their own patronage and we think it more congenial with our religion, our civil government, and the good of society to make provision for the common instruction of the many before we exert ourselves to endow and establish a university for the few. . . . Single conferences, or groups of two or three conferences should establish seminaries that shall promote literature, morality, industry, and a practical knowledge of the arts of useful life.[17]

Members of the New York Conference, however, evidently felt that by 1829 Methodism was ready to support a college, for in that year they appointed an investigative committee composed of John Emory, Samuel Luckey, and Heman Bangs to lay the groundwork for establishing a college. The New England Conference voted to join in this endeavor and appointed Fisk, Timothy Merritt, and Stephen Martindale to work with the New York committee. The land of the military academy at Middletown was ultimately offered to the two conferences at no cost, with the stipulation that it be used in perpetuity for a college or university. In turn the joint committee recommended to both conferences that Middletown be chosen over Troy, New York, and Bridgeport, Connecticut, as the site for a new Methodist college. The recommendation was adopted by the New York Conference in May, 1830, and by the New England Conference several weeks later.

Evidently there was little or no doubt in the minds of the members of the two conferences concerning who would be the first president of the soon-to-be-opened Wesleyan University. At a meeting of the trustees in August, 1830, Willbur Fisk was elected president, and a decision was made to open the university in the third week of August, 1831. Fisk accepted the appointment, though in his letter of acceptance he expressed doubt as to whether or not he was qualified for the position: "I have a deep conviction of my own inability to perform the important and responsible duties connected with this appointment."[18] Fisk, who did not move to Middletown until December, 1831, also expressed trepidation over the prospects of the university and concern for the continued health of the academy:

> I have fears respecting my removal to Middletown. I know not how the university will prosper: I know not how my removal will affect this institution. We have as yet fixed upon no principal—Bro. Weeks too leaves us at the end of this term and we have engaged no Steward. All these things are against us but we hope for the best.[19]

In spite of his apprehension, Fisk did indeed become president of Wesleyan University, which actually opened, with 48 students enrolled, on September 21, 1831. Fisk's tenure as president lasted until his death in February, 1839. The hallmarks of that tenure were Fisk's assembling of an outstanding faculty and the development of a nationwide reputation as a quality institution of higher learning. That reputation was enhanced in general by Fisk's abilities as a writer and speaker, and specifically by Fisk's travels in Europe (between September, 1835, and November, 1836). The Wesleyan trustees had voted to send Fisk to Europe for the benefit of his poor health, but Fisk also used the trip to secure "scientific apparatus" and classical literary works which enhanced the educational resources of the university.

Although Wesleyan University was an educational success, much of Fisk's time as president was occupied with raising funds to keep the new institution afloat financially. This was not a task that he often enjoyed, as he conveyed in a letter written to his wife in 1832 during a trip to New York, on which he had already raised between $300 to $400 during a stop at New Haven:

> This begging business is bad enough at any rate and worst of all in such extreme cold weather. If any body covets the office I will give it up most cheerfully. But who will do it? And unless it is done, how shall we succeed? . . . Since I have been here [New York] business goes on slowly. It will take about as long to get the people warmed up as it did last winter and by that time I shall have to leave. I shall do what I can.[20]

When Fisk was elected president he asked the Wesleyan trustees for an additional year to do fund-raising for the new university. This request was not approved, and Fisk was thus reduced to seeking the $22,000 that Wesleyan needed to open by writing appeals to be published in Methodist newspapers.[21] The New Hampshire and Vermont conferences also undertook support of the university, but raising money was an ongoing struggle for Fisk. Wesleyan's original charter called for $200,000 in holdings, but when Fisk took over the reins Wesleyan had property and endowment totaling only $70,000. Fisk was able to increase that total to $100,000 in his nine-year stint as president, but the financial panic of 1837 and 1838 severely hampered his fund-raising endeavors.

Through all of these financial difficulties Fisk persevered, though he occasionally went without his own salary for extended periods of time. One anecdote from the notes of Ruth Peck Fisk indicates the sacrifices that the Fisks made for the life of the new university:

> When the college was new and it was difficult to obtain funds to meet their [the faculty's] expense I have known him to see that the professors were paid and though his own salary was due, to have in his own pocket none but borrowed money for three months at a time even for his charities. If I requested anything not absolutely necessary he would refer to it and on my mentioning that the Professors had been paid, he would say, "O the Professors must have their pay, if they don't get it, they will be discouraged." I generally answered, "Don't you think, Mr. Fisk, I shall be discouraged?" "O no you want to sustain me."[22]

Because of Willbur Fisk's abilities as a fund-raiser, his willingness to work tirelessly and make personal sacrifices on behalf of Wesleyan University, Wesleyan survived the many financial crises that occurred during Fisk's presidency and was solidly established as a quality educational institution at the time of Fisk's death in 1839.

Willbur Fisk contributed far more to Wesleyan Academy and Wesleyan University, and ultimately to Methodist higher education, than his fund-raising abilities. He was an outstanding and progressive educator who was constantly analyzing the processes by which people learn, and developing ideas about what should be the underlying values, the central focii of the curriculum, the physical environment, and the methodology of a high-quality education. As a result, he was never hesitant to introduce a new program of study or teaching method at the academy or the university when such a program or method would, in his estimation, improve the quality of education offered to students.

Underlying all of Fisk's work on behalf of Methodist higher education was his staunch belief that education performs a dual role in society; that is, that education ought to be concerned with the growth and development of the individual, and the improvement of the quality of life for the world as a whole. As Fisk put it:

> Education should be directed in reference to two objects,—the good of the individual educated, and the good of the world. . . . In establishing an institution of learning, and especially one of a high order, reference should be had, chiefly, to the condition and general interests of the great family of man.[23]

Fisk also contended, contrary to the thinking of most Americans of his day, that a "liberal education" could be of great value to persons for all walks of life and not only to persons planning to enter the "learned professions." Such an education should be designed to better equip an individual to serve his or her fellow human beings. Fisk wrote:

> It has been supposed, that there are too many in the learned professions already, and that, therefore, there are too many who obtain a liberal education. But this opinion is founded upon two errors. One is that every liberally educated man must be above manual labor, and must therefore enter one of the learned professions; and the other is, that all who enter those professions, with the exception of the Gospel ministry, do it, and have a right to do it, from personal or family interests, and not for the public good. Whereas, a liberal education ought not to unfit a man, either in his *physical constitution*, or his feelings, for active business in any honest employment; and neither ought men, who enter *any* of the learned professions, to excuse themselves from labour and privation for the good of the world. There is a great and pernicious error on this subject.[24]

Fisk's understanding of a liberal education as preparation for serving one's brothers and sisters is reflected nowhere more clearly than in his linking of higher education and mission work. Writing in the report of the Joint Committee on Education and Missions of the 1834 New England Conference, Fisk stated that

> the two subjects of Missionary Labor and Education are nearly related to each other. . . . We have already commenced in the foreign missionary enterprise, and calls are made upon us for the enlargement of these operations in places where an acquaintance with other languages and some of the sciences and other professions, especially the science of medicine is indispensible *(sic)*. To suit these peculiarities, it is necessary that an education should be given of an appropriate character. . . . Another peculiarity in the missionary work is its identity with the cause of education. . . . The missionary himself must be prepared for the work of instruction and in many cases must have associated with him missionary teachers—all of whom need to be educated for the purpose. The question is, where shall we get the men with the appropriate qualifications for this all important enterprise.[25]

Largely because of Fisk's heavy emphasis on the interrelationship of mission work and higher education, Wesleyan Academy and Wesleyan University became centers for the education of missionaries. During Fisk's tenure at the academy, he encouraged students to form an auxiliary of the Missionary Society of the Methodist Episcopal Church. That auxiliary raised money for Methodist missions. A member of that auxiliary, Jason Lee, after being encouraged by Fisk in the early 1830s, became the first Methodist missionary to work with the Flathead and Nez Perce Indians of Oregon. And as a result of Fisk's work on the New England Conference's joint committee on education and missions, education societies began to be formed throughout the churches in the conference. These societies raised funds to endow scholarships at Wesleyan University for the education of prospective missionaries. Fisk introduced a course of study at the university that was specifically designed to prepare men to be missionaries, and this lead was followed at the academy, where a course of study was designed to train women as missionary teachers.[26]

Fisk initiated two other specific educational policies at Wesleyan University that require special mention in this context. First, Fisk initiated the awarding of an alternative diploma (other than the bachelor of arts degree) to those students who wished to pursue a college education but did not desire to study the ancient classics. Fisk believed that ancient literature ought always to be taught at colleges and universities, with ancient languages being important "if only to preserve the purity of the Holy Scriptures, and secure a correct translation of them into other languages."[27] But, thought Fisk, not all students needed to have a knowledge of the ancient classics, and he thus instituted a degree that could be earned by students who chose to study only modern literature and sciences. This "modified diploma" became the bachelor of science degree, the first such degree to be awarded by any college in the nation.

The second policy instituted by Fisk was a program in which a student could advance toward a degree as rapidly as his abilities would permit, instead of following the traditional ranking by classes. Fisk helped the faculty of the university to develop a system of "advanced placement" examinations to be given to all incoming students, as well as a system of examinations to measure the progress of already matriculated students. There is little doubt that this innovative placement system emerged from Fisk's own frustration, after leaving the University of Vermont, with being refused advanced standing at Middlebury College (which precipitated his entrance to Brown).

Another intriguing plan developed by Fisk was put into effect for a short time at Wesleyan Academy and not at all at Wesleyan University. At neither institution was the plan, which required all students to spend time in "manual labor," greeted with much enthusiasm. Fisk earnestly believed that all students should be required to participate in manual labor in order that no one educated at his institutions would ever "look down upon the labouring classes of society"[28] and that on the other hand, all "learned" persons would be able to make a living with their hands when "professions are full" or times are tough economically. If all students were required to work a few hours each week, thought Fisk, then farmers and mechanics would not think their children "spoiled" by a college education: "Thus the reproach of learning on the one hand— and the contempt of labour on the other, would be wiped away; since it would be seen, that neither is uncongenial with the other."[29]

Before bringing this chapter to conclusion, a few more of Fisk's ideas about higher education ought to be mentioned, if only in passing. Fisk was not a proponent of the founding of separate educational institutions for the training of teachers or ministers. He opposed the founding of "normal schools" but advocated extensive teacher training in the context of a "liberal education." Normal schools, thought Fisk, would not afford teachers a broad enough education to allow them to teach their charges well. Similarly, Fisk was not necessarily opposed to theological education, but he was most concerned with establishing Methodist colleges of the highest possible quality and he worried that establishing "a separate theological school would be a financial burden upon the denomination which would be greater than it could bear."[30] There is no doubt, however, that Fisk believed wholeheartedly that Methodism must have an educated ministry. And while he saw separate theological schools as a future development, he formed "theological classes" at Wesleyan University, as he had done while serving as principal at Wilbraham and as presiding elder in Vermont, in order that future Methodist ministers would receive the specialized training they would need to serve effectively in the pastorate.

Among Fisk's emphases while president of Wesleyan University was his insistence that the faculty share in all decisions regarding curriculum, the selection of new faculty members, and the dismissal of "uncomfortable associates." In advocating an early version of "merit pay" for teachers, Fisk further insisted that faculty were to be paid according to services rendered:

> If an officer should exert himself beyond his associates, or has health and mental energies which enable him to tower above the rest, he has [at present in most institutions] not only no adequate compensation for his services, but he often has the mortification of seeing others, in comparative idleness, living upon the credit of his labours.[31]

And while Fisk contended that his administration of Wesleyan University was "patriarchal" and not democratic, he remained respected and much loved by the university faculty until his death.

Still another of Fisk's ideas about higher education was that all persons should have access to it. He strove diligently to provide financial resources for young men from poor families to attend Wesleyan University. He also helped to overturn, in 1834, a regulation (that had been established by the trustees) that barred black men from becoming Wesleyan students. Women, however, were not accepted as students at the university during the period of Fisk's presidency. To Fisk's credit, however, he actively sought women students for Wesleyan Academy and insisted that both male and female students at Wilbraham be taught the discipline of scholarship. Fisk condemned the notion that women were frivolous and unconcerned with scholarly pursuits, and while at the academy he pledged himself to ensuring that female students received the same intensity and quality of education as their male counterparts.[32]

Perhaps the most important of Fisk's ideas about higher education was his strong belief that colleges and universities ought to be administered by religious denominations. Fisk endorsed some state control over private colleges in order to assure that basic educational standards were being maintained, and he felt that state government had an obligation to provide financial aid to private colleges (Wesleyan University received grants from the Connecticut Legislature in 1834 and 1838 totaling $25,000),[33] but he condemned state-run universities as places

where political partisans and sectarian bigots [create constant] conflict. . . .
Better, perhaps, that the different religious denominations manage these institutions, subject to a visitation of a commission of that state, if need be, to
prevent abuses and making their annual report the basis for granting or with-
holding such an annual stipend as may, when granted, make the incorporated
institutions successful and efficient in the cause of education.[34]

   Fisk continually asserted that a college education must have a spiritual, or religious, dimension: "Education and the Christian religion always have been and always should be intimately connected."[35] Fisk did
not think that Wesleyan University should require a particular profession
of faith for admission, and he did not understand religion in education
to mean crass proselytism, mandatory denominational instruction, or
teaching of prayers and hymns. Fisk did believe that the Bible should be
used as a textbook in university courses and that it was appropriate for
distinctive Christian morals and principles to be taught in classes and
used in setting university policies and standards. While Fisk did not
institute compulsory chapel at Wesleyan University and did not condone
"forcing" religion upon students (for fear that students might revolt
against such indoctrination), he looked favorably upon the frequent re-
vivals that took place at both the academy and the university.
   For Willbur Fisk, the development of Methodist institutions of higher
education was an integral part of the ministry of the gospel that involved
"sanctifying the literature of the day, and the mental discipline of the
young, by the influence of our holy religion [Methodism]." He added
that "when the ministers and members of the M.E. Church can satisfy
themselves that the education of the young is not appropriately a religious work, then let them as a Church, engage in it no farther."[36] Fisk
remained convinced throughout all his days that his work on behalf of
Methodist higher education, particularly in his leadership roles at
Wesleyan Academy and Wesleyan University, was a genuine ministry of
the gospel of Jesus Christ. Because of that conviction, one of American
Methodism's most intelligent and articulate leaders devoted the final sixteen years of his life to ensuring the success of Methodist higher education in New England. For that devotion Willbur Fisk will long be
remembered by those who have been and will be the beneficiaries of his
work on behalf of higher education in American Methodism.

NOTES

1. Joseph Holdich, *The Life of Willbur Fisk, D.D.* (New York: Harper and Brothers,
1842), 45.

2. Holdich, *Life of Fisk*, 74.

3. Holdich, *Life of Fisk,* 72.

4. Emory Stevens Bucke, ed., *The History of American Methodism,* 3 vols. (New York: Abingdon Press, 1964), 1:349.

5. See Douglas J. Williamson, "The Rise of the New England Methodist Temperance Movement, 1823–1836," *Methodist History* 21 (October 1982): 3–28.

6. *Zion's Herald* (ZH), 12 June 1833.

7. Holdich, *Life of Fisk,* 210.

8. Donald G. Mathews, *Slavery and Methodism* (Princeton, N.J.: Princeton University Press, 1965), 106.

9. Willbur Fisk, "Letter to Mr. H.," 5 Feb. 1817, Fisk Papers, Wesleyan University Archives, Middletown, Connecticut.

10. *Christian Advocate and Journal* (CAJ), 16 Sept. 1835.

11. Holdich, *Life of Fisk,* 234.

12. See Douglas J. Williamson, "Willbur Fisk and African Colonization," *Methodist History* 23 (January 1985): 79–98.

13. Ruth Peck Fisk, Notes, Fisk papers.

14. Holdich, *Life of Fisk,* 131.

15. ZH, 7 Dec. 1827.

16. Ruth Peck Fisk, Notes, Fisk Papers.

17. CAJ, 13 June 1828.

18. Willbur Fisk, "Letters to Trustees of Wesleyan University" (undated), Fisk Papers.

19. Willbur Fisk, "Letter to John Lindsey" (8 Oct. 1830), Fisk Papers.

20. Willbur Fisk, "Letter to Ruth Peck Fisk" (27 Jan. 1832), Fisk Papers.

21. For an example, see CAJ and ZH, 17 Sept. 1830.

22. Ruth Peck Fisk, Notes, Fisk Papers.

23. Willbur Fisk, *Inaugural Address, Delivered at the Opening of the Wesleyan University* (New York: McElrath and Bangs, 1832), 3–4.

24. Fisk, *Inaugural Address*, 7.

25. *Minutes of the New England Conference of the Methodist Episcopal Church* (Boston: David H. Ela, 1834).

26. Fisk also played a significant role in the translation of the Bible into the Mohawk language. He prevailed upon the Young Men's Bible Society of New York to begin the translation in 1831. Completed in 1839, that translation was used extensively in mission work in Canada and northern New York.

27. Fisk, *Inaugural Address*, 14.

28. Willbur Fisk, *An Introductory Address Delivered at the Opening of Wesleyan Academy in Wilbraham, Mass.* (Boston: T.R. Marvin, 1826), 14.

29. Fisk, *Introductory Address*, 14.

30. David H. Markle, "Willbur Fisk, Pioneer Methodist Educator" (Ph.D. dissertation, Yale University, 1935), 264.

31. Fisk, *Inaugural Address*, 16–17.

32. Fisk, *Introductory Address*, 5.

33. See Willbur Fisk, *An Appeal to the Citizens of Connecticut in Behalf of the Wesleyan University* (Middletown, Conn.: William D. Starr, 1839), for the detailed arguments used by Fisk to attempt to convince the Connecticut Legislature to provide much-needed financial assistance to Wesleyan University.

34. Willbur Fisk, *Travels in Europe* (New York: Harper and Brothers, 1838), 64–65.

35. *Minutes of the New England Conference of the Methodist Episcopal Church* (Boston: David H. Ela, 1835), 11.

36. CAJ, 13 Feb. 1835.

8

John O. Gross
(1894–1971)

by Gerald O. McCulloh

FOURTEEN YEARS AFTER his death, his colleagues remembered a man in motion: John O. Gross, walking rapidly, carrying a briefcase stuffed with papers, his head tilted forward and to one side, as if he were about to fall over. Fairly short, with a rotund body and a knobby nose protruding from behind old-fashioned glasses, Gross's unimpressive appearance and folksy ways belied a seemingly endless energy, phenomenal memory, and shrewd mastery of church politics. He admired men who had risen from humble beginnings to greatness—Abraham Lincoln, William Jennings Bryan, George Washington Carver, Alvin York. He spoke easily in public, sometimes in cliches, but usually quoting favorite authors such as John Wesley, Willbur Fisk, Gandhi, and William Allen White. He was forceful and persuasive, though afflicted in middle age with partial deafness. He would sometimes turn down his hearing aid when subjected to boring speeches; he would rather talk than be talked to. When he retired, a Methodist bishop saluted his "purposeful indefatigability," his "love of the church," and his "ability to see the interests of all segments of Methodism."

This colorful individual rose to a pre-eminent position in the Methodist Church. For an entire generation he served as an executive of the denominational agency charged with the care and oversight of higher education in the church. As much as any single person, he created the agency for higher education in the Methodist Church that emerged from the union of three denominations in 1939. Because of his work in building and maintaining the Methodist "empire" of higher education, *Time* magazine once hailed him as Methodism's "Mr. College," and "the man who sparked the renaissance of Methodist higher education." Gross left

JOHN O. GROSS

Photo by Henry Schofield Studio, Nashville, Tenn.

an indelible mark on the national board that he served and on the relationship of Methodist institutions of higher learning to the church. How
he did these things is the subject of this essay.

John Owen Gross was born at Folsom, Kentucky, on July 9, 1894, and
was raised in Covington, across the Ohio River from Cincinnati. He was
always proud of being a Kentuckian, doted on writers like Jesse Stuart,
and admired Lincoln as a native Kentuckian. His mother, Anna Chris-
man Gross, brought him up in the Methodist Episcopal Church (MEC),
the northern branch of Methodism. The local schools were poor, and yet
Gross determined to gain an education. He worked during the day and
attended classes at night to complete high school. With the help of Chris-
tine Dykes, a family friend, he attended Asbury College in Wilmore,
Kentucky, and received an A.B. in 1918. He then studied at Lane Seminary, Cincinnati, and the University of Kentucky, but went to Boston
University School of Theology for his theological degree, an S.T.B. he
received in 1921. (His thesis was titled, "The Problem of Suffering in the
Book of Job.")

Gross received the call to preach while he was a college student. He
became a probationary member of the Kentucky Conference of the MEC
and in 1918 became a full member of the conference. In 1920 he married
Harriet Bletzer, also an Asbury College graduate. He received his first
appointment to the MEC church at Barbourville, Kentucky, on graduation from seminary. In the year before he joined his new community,
Gross subscribed to the local newspaper to become acquainted with
names and local events. His interest seems to have been more than passing, since he and his wife lived in Barbourville long enough for all three
of their children—George, Birney, and Lucille—to be born there.

Gross's energy and enthusiasm registered. After only five years as a
pastor, all of it at Barbourville, he was appointed superintendent of the
Barbourville District. Gross later reminisced about his travels during this
period, since he had to traverse backroads by mule or on foot and visited
churches with such alluring names as "Stinking Creek" and "Trace
Branch."

Once again his work recommended him for a higher position, and
Union College, an MEC school located in Barbourville, elected him president in 1929. Despite the fact he took office in the first of the Great Depression years, Gross reduced the college debt, launched a $200,000
financial campaign in the conference, and built a faculty of promising
young scholars. The college became accredited during his tenure. The
town fathers appreciated his work so much they gave him a parade.
Myron Wicke wrote that the Gross administration "saw Union College
emerge from obscurity to regional excellence." And a history of the col-

lege included the statement that Gross was determined "to lift the mountain students from the mountains to a panoramic world beyond, never doubting his conviction of Union's place as a church school."

The Union record brought him to the attention of Simpson College, another MEC school in Indianola, Iowa. In 1938 Gross became its president. Tackling his new task with characteristic vigor, Gross again built the institution academically and financially. But his stay at Simpson proved to be short. The three branches of Methodism united in 1939. On unification, the new national denomination created new structures for its work. Among them was a Board of Education, to be located at Nashville and to comprise three divisions—local church, editorial, and higher education. The board was not given a single head, thus allowing the division executives to exercise more than normal power. Harry Wright McPherson was elected executive secretary, the top position, of the Division of Higher Education. This division had responsibility for the care of more schools than any other Protestant denomination, and it had no equivalent in any of the three former Methodist denominations. The first director of the Department of Educational Institutions, one of the division departments, died, and in 1941 Gross became the director. By 1948 he had become head of the division itself, and he remained there until he retired in 1965.

The new board faced formidable tasks. The institutions that had previously identified with only one branch of Methodism now had to adjust to being a part of a single national denomination. This new unity inspired both anxiety and hope and provided an opportunity for strong leaders to assert themselves. The relations of the higher education institutions to the church varied widely. Some remained eager to be known as church schools, others feared the stigma of sectarianism. The academic quality of the schools also varied: many were not even accredited although others were held in high regard nationally. Another part of the board's work was that of overseeing the ministry to students. Wesley Foundations, the student ministries on the campuses of state-controlled schools, and campus ministries on church-related college campuses faced an almost crisis situation as the nation entered World War II. Finally, the twelve black colleges of Methodism entered the new denomination with an uncertain status. Financially poor, culturally and religiously rich, seemingly a leftover from a by-gone era, these schools were all located in the South, although virtually all had historic ties with northern Methodism.

These and other challenges brought out the best in Gross. He used two instruments to resolve the thorny issue of church relationship. One was the University Senate, a body formed by the MEC in 1892 to establish accreditation and maintain quality in Methodist schools. Gross dominated the senate, filled it with presidents and other powerful individuals he knew, and used it to force institutions to meet high standards. Failure to meet these standards carried a severe penalty—loss of Methodist status, which could mean death in the severe economic conditions of the time. The other instrument was Gross's own personal influence. He established personal relationships with the presidents, visited them at their schools, and could recite them all by name and call them all by their first names. This informal and traditional way of exercising power fitted Gross's background and personal style well.

Beginning with World War II, Methodist colleges entered a famine-and-feast cycle. The entry of college students into the armed forces led to a 15 percent enrollment reduction in Methodist colleges in 1942, according to a report written by Gross. Gross made a statement to the House Military Affairs Committee on Feb. 4, 1943, asking that small colleges be considered for military training to offset their loss of tuition. This shortage of students reversed itself after the war and Gross had the job of helping colleges understand the G.I. Bill of Rights and find ways of coping with large numbers of veterans as students.

In the early 1950s, the church colleges had to face the question of whether to accept Reserved Officer Training Corps on campus, even though they had rarely allowed them before. Gross observed in a *Christian Century* article in 1951 that "most schools offered units will nevertheless accept them because the exigencies in which they are caught leave no satisfactory alternative." College growth began in earnest, and the Methodist Church actually founded several new schools: North Carolina Wesleyan College at Rocky Mount, and Methodist College, Fayetteville, North Carolina, in 1956; Alaska Methodist University in 1957; Hawaii Loa College in 1963; and Virginia Wesleyan College, approved in 1961 although not chartered until 1966. Another school, California Western in San Diego, came under the sponsorship of the Methodist Church in 1956, although it later disaffiliated with the church. The initiative for these new schools came mostly from sources outside the board, but Gross saw they were established in ways that satisfied high standards and made for clear relations with the church.

The tide did not always run in the church's favor. Some schools, such as the University of Southern California and Northwestern University, severed their ties with the Methodist Church during this period. Gross resisted these withdrawals but could not stop them. In addition, some Methodist schools transferred to other denominations, and some merged for practical reasons. One of Gross's strategies was to seek ecumenical support wherever possible. Hawaii Loa, supported by four Protestant denominations, is an example. Despite some losses, the assets of Methodist schools rose dramatically during the Gross years—from less than a half-million dollars in 1940 to more than $1.3 billion in 1964. The connection between the schools and the denomination generally remained strong, and virtually all Methodist schools and colleges became accredited.

Another turn of events proved more problematic for Gross. The status of students in the Methodist system had been the traditional one in the 1940s. They were considered "youth" and "tomorrow's leaders." Students suddenly turned into "men and women" as they fought and sometimes died for their country, but this wartime experience was considered temporary and the establishment attitude reverted to its previous paternalism after the war. Other forces were at work to change the status of students, however. One of these forces was the Methodist Student Movement, organized in 1941. The MSM gave rise to *motive* magazine, published monthly during the school year. The pages of the earliest issues of *motive* carry the protests, the questions, and the affirmations of students facing draft registration and military service. This forcible entry of students into national and world affairs presaged later developments.

Gross had little to do with the founding of *motive* but he contributed greatly to its success by leaving it alone. However much he may have anguished over some of the articles and art published in *motive*, he never interfered with its editorial policies, and during his years the magazine reached the pinnacle of its influence. Gross wrote several articles for *motive*, although one wonders how he must have felt about the art by Giorgia de Chirico that editor Roger Ortmayer chose to accompany Gross's essay, "Secularism and Education," in a 1952 issue. Gross's relation to students remained remote and enigmatic, however, and as campus unrest began to develop in the 1960s, Gross did not seem to comprehend its dynamics.

Gross made a more substantial contribution to students through his strengthening of the student loan and scholarship fund. The annual Student Day Offering raised only $55,000 in 1939. Furthermore, loan collections lagged badly through the 1940s. Gross reorganized the office, appointed an able director for it, and then saw collections rise greatly. By 1963 the fund had reached a more respectable level of $265,000, although its size remained very small in comparison to the needs of students and the schools.

Gross took a special interest in the black colleges. The only denomination-wide support for these twelve schools at the time of union was the Race Relations Day Offering. It produced a meagre $27,000 in 1940–41. Gross worked with Matthew S. Davage, a capable black educator on the Board of Education staff, to raise the level of giving. In 1952, when Davage retired, Gross appointed James S. Thomas to his position, and Thomas and others helped the fund rise to almost $500,000 by 1963. Gross also recommended a proposal to the 1960 General Conference to raise $1 milion in capital improvements for the black schools, a proposal that passed and succeeded in its goal.

One of Gross's accomplishments was to validate the need for black colleges. The 1954 Supreme Court decision on school desegregaton raised the question for many whites of whether black schools were still needed. Gross spoke out clearly for the schools. "The Negro colleges in the South will be a necessity for many years," he wrote. "These schools will be needed if the church does not want to deprive highly deserving students of educational opportunities. . . . The decision of the Supreme Court . . . did not preclude the necessity for these colleges." He quoted Benjamin Mays on black colleges: "'They have the capacity to meet the student on his own ground.'" Gross's repeated references to George Washington Carver (who had studied at Simpson College) may have seemed a little old-fashioned, but he also spoke of Martin Luther King, Jr., as exemplifying the famed Methodist union of knowledge and vital piety.

While traveling about the country, mostly by train, giving speeches, writing articles, and handling the myriad details of board administration, Gross also found time for certain special projects. One of them was the construction of a new building to house the Board of Education. When the board was created in 1939, its staff used an older building in downtown Nashville. Other executives wanted to buy and remodel an abandoned church building near the existing offices, but Gross had other ideas. He saw to it that a capable architect was chosen. He obtained the services of a Boston sculptor to create large bronze medallions for the outside of the building. Perhaps because the whole project exceeded the estimate, the medallions became known as "John Gross's pennies." Gross made decisions for the building in some detail, even though he was but one of the two division secretaries to use it. He arranged for the purchase of dining room furniture from Marshall Field in Chicago, and he decreed that no smoking would be tolerated in the building. Ashtrays were hard to come by, visitors found, and the interior of the board building breathed the pure air of Methodist doctrinaire piety, if not of Methodist doctrine. The Board of Education building was dedicated in 1952 and was named in honor of Bishop Paul B. Kern, the first chair of the board.

From his large office on the second floor of the Kern Building, Gross could survey the "empire" of more than 130 Methodist-related schools. But by the time he occupied his new office, Gross found a new problem on the agenda of the church, one that he was less experienced in dealing with. The denomination needed more clergy, and questions were being raised about the need for more schools of theology. A series of studies of theological education in the Methodist Church began in 1946, and in 1952 Gross created a new Section on Ministerial Education. In 1956 the General Conference approved the establishment of two new theological schools, one at Kansas City, Missouri, and the other at Delaware, Ohio. The University Senate approved the accreditation of these new seminaries and certain broad aspects of their structure. Gross's responsibility for these actions was not that of immediate involvement, but rather that of bringing in capable staff, coordinating plans with bishops and other church agencies, and seeing that his division retained responsibility for academic quality and Methodist relations.

The Gross years saw the ground laid for important changes that came later. The Section on Ministerial Education eventually became a department and had responsibility for a number of areas affecting ordained ministers, including courses of study (the route by which preachers could become ordained outside the seminaries), pastors' schools, in-service training, and oversight of the theological schools themselves. One of the most important accomplishments of the department was cultivation of a new plan for support of the seminaries, a plan that began under the Gross years but did not bear fruition until it was approved by the General Conference of 1968.

In his last report to the board on retirement, Gross noted that his twenty-four years "covered the greatest period of growth higher education in the United States has known." Properly feted and with a painting of him placed in the Kern Building, he left office but did not stop working. He continued to speak and write and served as a consultant to Florida Southern College. His wife died in 1966. From 1968–69 he acted as interim president of Pfeiffer College, a Methodist school in North Carolina. He died Feb. 1, 1971, in Nashville.

An assessment of Gross's contribution to Methodist higher education should take account of the fact that he was not an intellectual but a practical executive and an interpreter. His philosophy, while important, remained eclectic and unformed. His personality and his modus operandi as a superb bureaucrat are the qualities that enabled him to accomplish what he did. Education was "the church in action," to use one of his phrases, and results were what mattered most, not careful reflection or even clear policy.

Because Gross came from a family whose members had little formal education, and from a culture where education was not highly prized, he admired intellectuals and scholars but knew himself to be outside their circle. He read widely, however, and had a certain rough philosophy of the context in which church higher education fitted. That context included a strong bond between Christianity and Western civilization. In a statement whose theme appeared over and over again in his speeches and writings, Gross proclaimed:

> The Christian church must bear witness to the university of the intimate connection existing between our Christian faith and the civilization which we envision for our nation and world. Christian society must be rooted in Christian ideals. What we value most in America comes from the Christian heritage.

These ideals were sometimes translated into personal virtues, in Gross's thought. Liberal arts could be merged naturally into the curriculum of a church-related school because "they regard the person as central. Such virtues as justice, prudence, courage, faith, hope, and love are identified by these convictions with personality growth." Gross also liked to quote theologian Nels Ferre on "the heart of the Christian faith—truth and love—in ultimate personal terms."

This personalistic twist to the Western civilization-Christianity theme led Gross to consider the development of individual leaders to be the most important way for the church to influence the culture. Gross repeated many times that the education of leaders for both church and culture was one of the chief purposes of church colleges. In a fairly typical statement made in 1957, Gross stated that church colleges should focus "upon those persons who have the ability to transform their private Christian sentiments into public opinions."

The antithesis of this individualistic Christian culture lay in secularism. Gross constantly warned about the growing secularistic spirit in America and the world. He thought "a dominating technical civilization may destroy our cherished human values," and said that a secular outlook "makes for materialism and social conformity." These evils Gross saw as related to Communism. "The world today is divided between those that see man as a machine and those that proclaim his creative destiny as an individual," Gross stated in 1962. "Communism, secularism, and selfish concern take rootage quickly if Christian concern is missing from education."

Gross saw the development of church colleges within the context of the great Western universities, particularly Oxford, Cambridge, and Harvard. Within this context he placed Methodist colleges as indigenous to the Wesleyan appreciation for learning. He liked to repeat the phrase that Methodist schools should be "Christian without apology and Methodist with pride." He consistently listed the two most important purposes of a church college to be cognates of "knowledge and vital piety"— usually phrased as "academic quality" and "Christian spirit" by Gross.

Gross thus offered a sound rationale for higher education from the perspective of the church. "The church-related college ought not to be thought of as something distinct and apart from the church," he wrote in 1941. "It is a phase of the Church in action." "The Christian college is an integral part of the Church's educational program," he wrote in 1957 in "The Case for a Christian College." But from the perspective of the culture the need for Christian colleges was not so clear. Against a tide of rising secularism, Gross could only appeal to the need for "spiritual values" and a resistance to materialism and Communism. He could not satisfactorily explain why society needed church colleges.

Except for prudential reasons, that is. The church needed higher education because it provided leaders, he stressed. But the culture also needed these leaders. He pointed out that historically the church colleges had prepared leaders for both church and state. The church-related colleges, as part of the independent sector in higher education, could maintain academic freedom and the opportunity to experiment. He deplored McCarthyism for its threat to academic freedom and suggested the American effort in the space race had been hampered by this harassment.

This blend of prudence with an individualistic emphasis characterized not only Gross's philosophy but his style of leadership as well. Perhaps because he himself had been a college president, right from the start of his work on the Methodist Board of Education he established close working relations with Methodist college and university presidents. He met annually with the university presidents. The University Senate related to the institutions chiefly through the presidents. Similarly, Gross cultivated bishops. (Gross himself at times entertained hopes of being a bishop and did receive some votes in the jurisdictional conference.) This establishmentarian approach proved to be a two-edged sword. It gave the Division of Higher Education great status in the church, and it enabled Gross to accomplish his personal objectives, like fund-raising. But it also placed the division at a certain distance from the local church, from students, and 'from other constituencies whose support was vital for the division's work such as the annual conferences.

Gross's conception of himself as a president in another role led him to conceive of division staff as parallel to a college faculty. He sought capable individuals and then left them to their work. He had no patience with the notorious Methodist penchant for tinkering with organization. He told his staff, "I have tried to solve the problem of interstaff rivalry by making you all major generals." (There seemed to be no doubt who the general was.) He hired several men with Ph.D. degrees so they would be able to work with academics without fear of intimidation. The tenure of the staff in his administration tended to be lengthy. Gross also felt that staff members, like college faculty, should know their fields and keep up with developments. "What have you been reading lately?" was one of his favorite greetings. Gross established a policy of providing paid study leaves for the professional staff, although his demands on the staff often meant the leaves had to be delayed or neglected.

Gross worked himself and his staff hard, but he had the ability to assume a detached air once a project was completed. In the intensity of work he could become heated, but he did not bear grudges. He also had a sense of humor. When a staff member encountered him in the lobby of a hotel where a meeting was being held, he asked Gross about his hotel room. "Oh, it's fine," Gross replied, "but I had to move the Gideon Bible out of the way before I could get into it." He once told the story of the Tennessee mountain preacher who explained the certainty of the divine call: "You know it when God calls you. A call from him is like a kick in the jaw by a spotted mule." Then, after a pause, the preacher added, "Excuse me, Lord, for comparing you to a spotted mule."

Gross seemed to be the right man in the right place at the right time. When the newly united Methodist Church established its new structures, it needed strong leaders. It got one in Gross. It also needed leaders who knew how to accomplish the most within the system. This Gross did in a way that few others could. Despite the pressures and changes of economic depression, war, and technological developments, Gross not only kept the Methodist system of higher education together but strengthened it in important ways. His particular accomplishments lay in creating strong institutional ties and in undergirding financing. He was limited in his ability to understand the changing role of students, the positive aspects of the new technological age, and the need to identify with the local churches and annual conferences. Nevertheless, much of what United Methodist higher education is today can be attributed to the Gross personality, style, and confidence in Methodist faith.

SOURCES

Gross published several small books, some of them written with the aid of his staff. They include:

You and Your College, co-author with Boyd M. McKeown (Nashville: Abingdon, 1945).

A History of Cokesbury College (Nashville: Parthenon, 1947).

Education for Life (New York and Nashville: Abingdon-Cokesbury, 1948).

John Wesley: Christian Educator (Nashville: Methodist Board of Education, 1954).

Martin Ruter: Pioneer in Methodist Education (Nashville: Methodist Division of Higher Education, 1956).

Methodist Beginnings in Higher Education (Nashville: Methodist Division of Educational Institutions, 1959).

The Beginnings of American Methodism (Nashville: Abingdon, 1961).

Most of the quotations from Gross in this essay came from files of his addresses and articles in the United Methodist Board of Higher Education and Ministry archives, Kern Building, Nashville, Tennessee. Some of the more important of these materials are:

"The Church in Action," undated typescript with pencil note, "Methodist Messenger, Oct. 41, Arkansas Methodist 9/2/41, Kentucky Methodist 9/18/41, Zions Herald 9/17/41."

"The Church College Must Be Different," *Christian Advocate* (21 Jan. 1943): 9, 29–30.

"Educational Institutions in Time of Crisis," undated mimeographed typescript, apparently from World War II.

"Responsibility of the Church for Higher Education," typescript, March, February, 1950.

"Manpower and the Colleges," *Christian Century* (28 Mar. 1951): 399–401.

"Evangelism and Leadership," typescript, 27 Oct. 1955.

"Protestant Higher Education," *Christian Century* (11 Apr. 1956): 453–55.

"The Case for the Christian College," typescript, 7 Nov. 1957.

"The Trend Is toward the Church College," undated typescript, apparently from the 1950s.

"Leadership for Christian Society," typescript address to Methodist Board of Education, January, 1962.

Untitled typescript, apparently an address delivered at Emory-at-Oxford, Oxford, Ga., 12 Sept. 1962.

"The Bishops versus Vanderbilt University," *Tennessee Historical Quarterly* 22 (March 1963): 3–15.

"The Three-Dimensional Study of Campus Relationships," undated but apparently 1968 or later.

"God Needs Educated Men," untitled typescript, apparently 1969 or later.

"The University Idea in the Methodist Church," typescript, 1965.

Gross's reports to the Methodist Board of Education can be found in the board's annual reports, 1942–65.

Biographical sketches of Gross can be found in "John Owen Gross," *Who's Who in America with World Notables* (Chicago: A. N. Marquis, 1968–69), vol. 35, 900; "John Owen Gross," *Who's Who in the Methodist Church* (Nashville: Abingdon, 1966), 513; and Myron F. Wicke, *The Methodist Church and Higher Education, 1939–64* (Nashville: Methodist Division of Higher Education, 1965), 72–94.

9

Robert S. Maclay
(1824–1907)

by Charles E. Cole

A MERICAN METHODISTS IN the nineteenth century understood the mission of the church to be comprehensive and universal. Mission meant not only domestic and "foreign" missions, it
meant evangelism, education, health care, social work, and the whole
range of ministries that Christians traditionally associate with the nature
of the church. This universal aspect of mission meant that all persons
were potential members of the church and were assumed to be children
of God.

We do not have this unified vision of mission today. Mission may
mean medical institutions, and it may even mean colleges and schools—
but only those overseas. Mission may mean the notion of being "sent,"
as in the divine commission in Matthew 28, but professionals in church-
related higher education are rarely thought of as being under this divine
mandate. In the bureaucracy as in the local church, mission and higher
education have been sundered, and by a sort of historical amnesia, few
United Methodists seem to remember that they were once part of the
same reality.

It seems worthwhile, then, to ask how Christian leaders in the nineteenth century conceived of themselves and their mission. What did
they consider their task to be, and how did they in fact do their work?

To call attention to this problem may seem a diversion from what
many see as the real issue—that of the church's complicity in Western
aggrandizement through the linking of Western civilization and Christian missions. The interesting question in this context would be the role
of higher education. Was it through the identification of civilization with
Western conceptions of knowledge, for example, that Africa, Asia,

ROBERT S. MACLAY
Photo courtesy of United Methodist Commission on Archives and History.

South America, and other areas first became exploited by the colonialists? And did the missionaries channel into higher education the most compliant leaders of non-Western countries? These and other questions remain intriguing, but for two reasons they will not be pursued here.

The first reason is that the unsavory subjection of Christianity to Western political, commercial, and military overlords has been well established. We can readily concede that the church made a historic mistake in accommodating itself so completely to notions of Western superiority. The other reason, though, is that the present project seeks to tell the story of outstanding leaders in higher education. This biographical form will allow us some window into the complex and global aspects of Western Christian chauvinism, but the other dimension of the unity of mission seems more suitable for a single life story.

The story told here is that of Robert S. Maclay. Maclay's life sheds light on Christian higher education because of several remarkable achievements. By some measurements, he seemed the conventional missionary—pious, hard-working, anti-Catholic, superior if not arrogant in his assumption that Christianity offered the hope of salvation to heathens who were damned without the saving word. But unlike many other Westerners who labored among Asians, Maclay learned the languages of the people whom he served—no small accomplishment, as the small number of Americans who speak Chinese and Japanese today will attest. Unlike others, he did not become ill but remained in vigorous health while on the field, returning home on furlough only at ten-year intervals—an achievement of sorts because it reveals his toughness and endurance. And also unlike others, he did not serve for only a few years but maintained a continuity that enabled him to become a leading figure in missions in his denomination and one of the most influential in the entire Protestant missionary enterprise in the nineteenth century. Finally, Maclay completed the circle to his home church and native land, engendering a concern for intercultural and international theological education that today bears visible fruit.

Maclay was born February 7, 1824, in Concord, Pennsylvania, the fourth of five sons and one of nine children born to Scotch-Irish parents. The Maclays had emigrated to America from northern Ireland in the 1730s, although they were transplanted Scots. Two Maclays served as U.S. senators from Pennsylvania in the 1790s and early 1800s, and the American Maclays lived comfortably. Robert Maclay's parents became members of the Methodist Episcopal Church (MEC), and all five of their sons became Methodist preachers. Robert, or "Sam," as his siblings called him, entered Dickinson College, Carlisle, Pennsylvania, as a preparatory student and went on to receive the B.A. degree in 1845. Dickinson was founded shortly after the American Revolution and identified with Methodism in 1833. When Maclay was a student the school offered a classical curriculum and had a small but distinguished faculty, among them John M'Clintock, later an editor of *Quarterly Review* and president of Drew University, and J. P. Durbin, who served as secretary of the MEC Missionary Society from 1850 to 1872. On graduation, Maclay became a circuit preacher on trial in the Baltimore Conference, which at that time reached into several states.

Maclay's interest in China developed in the context of a growing national and ecclesiastical interest. Americans had begun trading with China in 1777, but commercial relations increased significantly only after Great Britain developed its own trade in Asia in the early nineteenth century. The churches, too, began to think of a worldwide mission, and a few Protestant missionaries had gone to China early on, beginning with the Anglican, Robert Morrison, in 1807. (Roman Catholics had been in China since the sixteenth century.) In 1835 Willbur Fisk, then president of Wesleyan University and a member of the MEC Missionary Society, proposed a China mission. Nothing happened immediately, however, and not until a commercial treaty was signed between China and the U.S. in 1844 were these plans realized. In 1846, the MEC sent two missionaries.[1] According to one anonymous source, Maclay was asked to consider going to the China mission by Robert Emory, the president of Dickinson. After staying on the circuit for a few months longer, he was appointed as a missionary to China in the fall of 1847.[2] Leaving New York on October 13, 1847, he sailed with another missionary, Henry Hickok, and Hickok's wife. As the ship made its way around the Cape of Good Hope and through the Indian Ocean, Maclay and Hickok studied Chinese, Greek, and Hebrew. Maclay learned to rise early and dress and even shave in the dark—a habit, he wrote in later years, that served him in good stead during his life. Finally, after passing through Hong Kong, the missionaries reached Fuzhou (then Fuh-chau or Foochow) on April 15, 1848. The Chinese authorities refused permission for the missionaries to live within the city walls, and for many years the missionary compound was located outside the city on an island in the Min River and on the bank opposite the city.

Maclay was still single but knew to whom he intended to be married. Henrietta Sperry, a 25-year-old Methodist teaching in a church school in Newark, had heard Maclay give his farewell address and had seen him ordained deacon. The two met, then began correspondence. She herself wanted to be a missionary, and when Maclay wrote asking for her hand in marriage, she consented and sailed to China in 1850. The wedding took place in Hong Kong with an Anglican bishop presiding.[3]

Maclay immersed himself in the study of the Chinese language immediately on his arrival in China in 1848. Like other missionaries, he worked at first through interpreters, then gradually learned to preach directly in Chinese. The main tasks the Methodist missionaries undertook were preaching, handing out literature, and doing limited medical work. Another major project was education. Three day schools for boys were opened, and in 1850 Henrietta Maclay opened the first school for girls. The curriculum in these schools mixed secular and religious disciplines, and the numbers participating were relatively small—in May, 1849, each of the boys' schools had about 20 enrolled, and Mrs. Maclay's school opened with 10 students and eventually reached an enrollment of about 25.

Maclay felt he was in "the *van-guard*, the *advanced corps* of western nations," and his reflections from this period show that he held conventional views of the Chinese and of his role as missionary. The Chinese, he wrote, "are ignorant of the Saviour. I think I am correct in saying that this vast nation is totally ignorant of the true character of Christ as the Saviour of sinners. . . . Missionaries . . . are sending out rays of light into the thick darkness of heathenism. . . . the millions of this benighted Empire are the slaves of sin, the bondsmen of the Devil." The Western missionary brings a superior word: "The missionary alone probably can see the true condition of the heathen among whom he labors. It is his business to understand their necessities. . . . I am far from home and Christian Society and surrounded by heathenism dark and polluting."[4] Although Maclay criticized the Chinese for their idolatry and immorality, he also defended them: "Some writers, misled by the free rough manners of our people, have given them a bad name. A little acquaintance removes this unfavorable impression."[5]

Like the other missionaries, Maclay loved to relay anecdotes of the Chinese to readers at home. Many of these stories are likely to strike today's readers as patronizing and reflective of stereotypes. But Maclay had enough self-transcendence to laugh at himself occasionally. While on a walk in the country where few foreigners went, he found himself the object of curiosity. "They were very anxious to see my head, and to gratify them I removed my cap," he wrote. Then, "the moment my head was bare they laughed most immoderately. I saw the tears running down the cheeks of several, while they seemed almost beside themselves with delight." (Maclay's short and blond hair apparently caused the humor.) He described a Chinese boy entering a service of worship while carrying ducks in his hands. "The poor ducks were evidently ill at ease," Maclay stated, "and in their own vernacular loudly expressed their dissatisfaction with present arrangements." Another time a family argument next to the church became so loud Maclay had to stop preaching, "listening to screams and the vilest language." One man left the assembly to break up the fight, but failing, he returned, "giving vent to his feelings in a deep guttural, the purpose of which I fortunately did not understand," Maclay wrote. Not all experiences were amusing, however; when the Chinese laughed at Christians kneeling to pray, Maclay felt it was a "cross" and "one of my sorest trials." He and other missionaries often encountered critics and hecklers, and Maclay's tactic was to listen and turn away wrath with soft answers.[6]

Maclay's own understanding of his task as a missionary was that of teaching "Gospel truths," of " planting seeds" that would one day ripen into a "harvest." This seed–harvest metaphor recurs again and again throughout his writings and provided a rationale for continuing to work even though converts were few in the early days.[7] Maclay also emphasized the work of the Holy Spirit in this process: "the work is *the Lord's*," he wrote, but exercising skill and talent made necessary "the *human machinery* in this great work of God" (italics in original).[8] This belief in the Holy Spirit was sometimes linked to what Maclay believed to be an approaching divine consummation. In 1854, he wrote: "The character of the people, the increasing faith of the Churches . . . and the recent wonderful developments of Christian knowledge and principles in the very heart of this vast empire . . . indicate to me that Christians are justified in expecting glorious results speedily to follow the preaching of the gospel in China." Over the decades Maclay emphasized this expectancy, a sense of seeing divine power at work in the changes occurring in China and Japan.[9]

Maclay exulted in his work, and unlike others he seemed to have no health problems. "I am amazed at my continued health in this climate," he wrote in early 1851. Others did not fare so well. The wife of Moses White died after only eight months, and White himself became ill. Hickok failed in health, and the superintendent of the mission, Judson D. Collins, suffered from typhoid. Both left for home in 1849, and Maclay was made superintendent of the mission. Reinforcements arrived in 1851—Issac Wiley, a physician, and his family; James Colder and wife; and Mary Seely, who shortly after her arrival married the widower White.

The powers of the superintendent were very broad, and both White and Wiley complained of Maclay's supervision. The reasons are not altogether clear, although the pressure from the Taiping rebellion exacerbated the problem. The Taipings were a crypto-Christian group who from 1851 to 1864 led an armed revolt against the Qing (Ching) dynasty. Young Maclay became concerned about the safety of the mission and debated whether to remove them to another location. Wiley, White, and probably Colder managed to pass a resolution at a meeting of the mission on September 30, 1852, aimed at abolishing the office of superintendent: "*Resolved*, that in view of the dissatisfaction felt by the Mission with the Office of Superintendent, Brother Maclay be, and hereby is respectfully requested to resign that office." Maclay responded: "I stated to the Brethren that I was ready to resign the Office as soon as released by the Board . . . in so far as I am personally concerned they need have no delicacy of feeling in reference to the abolition or suspension of the Office."[10] Wiley complained to the board executive, Durbin, that news of the rebellion "has produced already, unwarrantable alarm in the mind of our superintendent and his family, and that under the influence of his own fears, he has done no little toward exciting uneasiness in the minds of others."[11] But the dissenters had made a tactical mistake in moving that the office itself be abolished. Durbin at first replied that the missionaries had misunderstood the duties of the superintendent and that abolition of the office would contravene the policies of the church. Later, when he learned the conflicts were personal, he reproached the complaining members for not being honest with him.[12]

The issue resolved itself when all the missionaries except the Maclays left, mostly for health reasons, although in the case of Colder an additional factor was his dissatisfaction with MEC polity. He eventually withdrew from the MEC ministry. White had also had problems with Maclay's predecessor as superintendent, J. D. Collins. White published a translation of Matthew in vernacular Chinese, and Collins thought it better to use more scholarly language. Thus some of the conflicts could have had causes other than Maclay's "despotism," as Mrs. White put it. Nevertheless Maclay emerged as a stable and reliable leader. He had acted with the precise amount of humility and firmness that elders of the church preferred. This same conservatism also contributed to an image of Maclay as a cautious official—someone who "took no risks," and whose administration was characterized by "judicial fairness, wise caution," as later writers phrased it.[13] This image would remain with him throughout his career.

The Taiping revolt failed and never reached Fuzhou, although the MEC mission did in fact retreat to Hong Kong for a short time in 1853. After the departure of the other missionary families, the Maclays served for more than a year as the only MEC missionaries in Fuzhou. Of course, other Americans and English were serving there, so they were not totally isolated. Two MEC missionaries who arrived in 1855 were both Dickinson men—Erastus Wentworth had been a science professor there, and Otis Gibson was a graduate.

The restored mission expanded its activities. During the decade two churches were built besides the chapels already being used. Stations were established in the countryside outside Fuzhou. But not until July 14, 1857, was the first Chinese baptized. His name was Ting Ang and it had taken the mission nearly ten years to make him the first convert. The number of converts did not rise quickly, although some Chinese became preachers by the 1860s. The Fuzhou mission became the base for MEC expansion to Beijing (Peking) and into Jiangxi (then Kiangsi) Province in the 1860s.

Maclay continued to have "uninterrupted good health," although a daughter born in 1851 died in her second year. Finally, Maclay asked for a furlough in 1859. He had been in the field for more than a decade, a period in which the casualty rate of missionaries was more than two-thirds. Of 36 missionaries sent to Fuzhou by three missionary societies by 1858, 10 died and 13 were forced to return to the United States. Maclay already had such stature that on his departure Durbin had to reassure the remaining missionaries that the board had not lost confidence in the mission.[14] On the ship that carried the Maclays to the United States in 1860, their three-year-old daughter, Clara Isabel, died.

On his furlough Maclay received an honorary doctor's degree from Dickinson College and toured churches speaking about the China mission. One of his visits reinforced a decision by young Nathan Sites at Ohio Wesleyan University to become a missionary to China. He went to Fuzhou, served under Maclay, and spent his career in China. Maclay's furlough also gave him time to complete a book, *Life among the Chinese: With Characteristic Sketches and Incidents of Missionary Operations and Prospects in China*, published in 1861. In it Maclay maintained his ambivalent stance toward the Chinese. Chinese literature, like its religions and philosophies, had reached a point of "exhaustion." China's civilization is "hopelessly effete." And yet certain "conservative" elements had enabled China to remain stable. Among these elements were its classical education and respect for parents. Apparently, Maclay had begun to shift in his thinking about China. Instead of the light-darkness metaphor, he began to use a historical metaphor. After describing the difficulties of mission work in China, Maclay wrote that China's "day of preparation is long and toilsome." Maclay urged his readers not to "sit down in despondency" in the face of this struggle. "The cycle of wondrous events has already commenced in China. . . . There are indications that the Gospel is already arresting the attention of the Chinese in an extraordinary degree." And finally, Maclay struck an almost triumphant tone: "Progress is inevitable; and we believe that China is now thrown open fairly, fully, and, we hope, finally, to Christianity and foreign intercourse." China, he concluded, "is on the eve of great changes."[15]

The Maclays returned to China refreshed. When their ship reached Java after three months at sea, Maclay wrote, "To my surprise, I found myself indulging with my boys in a downright race, with hop, skip, and jump, over the beautiful sward in front of the governor's residence."

The next decade reflected slow but steady expansion for the mission. The entire Protestant missionary effort in China could report only 2,576 converts by 1865, but by 1871 Maclay reported 1,009 at Fuzhou alone. The first church was built within the city walls of Fuzhou in 1865. When Bishop Calvin Kingsley visited China in 1869, he ordained seven Chinese as deacons, elevating four immediately to elder. The educational effort was modest. From the original day schools, boarding schools had been established in the 1850s. Yet in 1870 Maclay could report only 27 students in the Baltimore Female Academy, and there was no boys' school. A press had been established in 1865, and it produced Bibles, hymnbooks, and other literature.[16] Even though no college was established during the Maclay superintendency, the Foochow Anglo-Chinese College began in 1881 with Maclay, by then in Japan, lobbying for its establishment.[17]

Maclay was nearing the end of his Chinese ministry. He and his wife had decided to send their children home to the United States for their advanced education, and one son, Charles Sperry, died at age 13 in 1868 while attending Pennington Seminary in New Jersey. After many years of effort, Maclay completed *An Alphabetical Dictionary of the Chinese Language in the Foochow Dialect* in 1871, with C. C. Baldwin as co-author. In a day when resources were scarce for those wanting to learn Chinese, the book promised to help not only missionaries but business people and diplomats as well. Maclay received another furlough in 1872, attended the General Conference in New York, and again went on the lecture circuit, using New Haven as a base. He himself had proposed that a mission to Japan be established, and in late 1872 he was commissioned as the superintendent of the MEC mission to Japan. He went with four assistants. Maclay maintained the headquarters at Yokohama along with I. H. Correll, while Julius Soper went to Tokyo, and others went to Hakodate and Nagasaki.

In contrast to China, Maclay found the Japanese relatively open to the missionaries. After Commodore Matthew Perry landed in Japan in 1853, the Japanese began to open their country to the West. The Japanese appeared to accept Christianity as part of Western civilization, even though governmental restrictions prevented the missionaries from working in all areas of the country. The people of Japan "have fully decided to accept modern civilization," Maclay wrote in his first report in 1873. Once again Maclay set out to learn a new language. He also joined an interdenominational committee already at work translating the New Testament into Japanese.[18] Only a year after arriving, Soper was preaching in

Japanese in Tokyo, and on October 4, 1874, Correll baptized the first two converts in the MEC mission.

The first educational effort came through the Women's Foreign Missionary Society of the MEC. The society sent Dora Schoonmaker to Tokyo in 1874, and she organized a day school for girls. Other day schools and Sunday schools were opened in rapid succession during the 1870s. In 1878, a secondary school for boys was opened in Tsukiji, Tokyo, by Soper and three Japanese converts, one of whom was Sen Tsuda. Tsuda represented the Japanese government on international missions and later was elected to the Diet. Then in 1879 Maclay opened a theological school in Yokohama.

These educational institutions marked one of the most significant differences with the China mission. The Japanese mission used the schools not only for evangelism but for training leaders. Bolstered by a $10,000 gift from John F. Goucher, a Baltimore minister who served on the MEC Missionary Society, the Yokohama school became "Methodist Missionary Seminary." Its curriculum included courses in theology, "the common English branches" of study (not further described), and Chinese. The seminary offered both preparatory and undergraduate studies, by today's definitions. All teachers were at first Americans, although in only a few years Japanese were added to the faculty. Some Japanese felt the Americans should have learned their language faster, but missionaries like James Blackledge disagreed. After listing his various duties, Blackledge asked rhetorically, "What time is there for the study of the language with our time so filled up?"[19]

The seminary moved to Tokyo in 1882 and merged with the boys' school. With another gift from Goucher the mission purchased twenty-five acres of land in Aoyama, part of Tokyo. In 1883 the institution was named Eiwa Gakko (Tokyo Anglo-Japanese College), and Maclay became its head. Its constitution stated: "It shall be the aim of the Tokyo Ei-Wa-Gakko to furnish a thorough Christian education and especially to train young men for the ministry of the church."[20] The combined school had 150 students, and by 1883 four were graduated from the seminary. Three became preachers immediately, and the fourth, Yujiro Motora, went to Boston University School of Theology for further study. He returned to Japan to teach after receiving a Ph.D. in psychology at Johns Hopkins University.

Besides Tokyo Eiwa Gakko, the MEC had other educational institutions: Cobleigh Seminary in Nagasaki, girls' schools in Nagasaki, Hakodate, Fukuoka, and Yokohama, and the girls' school in Tokyo begun by Schoonmaker. In addition, some missionaries taught courses in Japanese universities—W. C. Kitchen taught English and Christian ethics at Keio Gijiku in Tokyo, a prestigious private university, in 1886. These growing educational efforts were but one part of the expanding MEC work in Japan. An annual conference was organized in 1884. Maclay and eight other MEC missionaries were charter members, as well as five Japanese, including Sogo Matsumoto, who became the first Japanese presiding elder. In the absence of a bishop, Maclay was elected to preside over the conference, which he did for several years.

Although the Japanese mission developed well, Maclay suffered a loss in 1879 when his wife died. Henrietta Sperry Maclay had organized schools for girls in China and had supported the movements to abolish foot-binding and infanticide for Chinese women. She bore eight children but by the time of her death, only four survived. Like her husband, she learned Japanese when the Methodist mission was established in Japan. Less is known about her contribution to the Japanese mission, but she was playing the organ for worship when she died of apoplexy in Yokohama, July 28, 1879. Maclay stoically reported in his annual report, "Mrs. Maclay, after twenty-nine years of faithful missionary toil, passed, by a sudden and glorious transformation, from the courts of the Lord's temple on earth to the sanctuary on high." In 1881 Maclay traveled to London to speak at the Ecumenical Council of Methodism and returned by way of San Francisco, where he married Sarah A. Barr.[21]

Maclay's view of Christianity in Japan combined optimism with a conservative religious approach. He wrote in the 1880s that "Japan presents today the unparalleled example of a great non-Christian nation awaiting, in a voluntarily assumed attitude of expectant receptivity."[22] He saw many advantages for Protestants in emphasizing education. It "tended powerfully to counteract and remove the terror and hatred of every thing connected with Christianity, which . . . had continued with unabated force through nearly two hundred and fifty years." It also placed young Japanese who would become leaders "at the formative period of their lives, under the training of Protestant missionaires." But the most important reason was: "It enabled the trained thought of Japan to estimate at their true value, and give a triumphant answer to, the utterances of flippant skepticism, so attractive to imperfectly educated minds, which would classify Christianity with the exploded and effete religions of the world, and claim that not the prudent Christian statesman, but the brilliant free-thinking scientist, is the true apostle of the career of progress upon which the Japanese have now entered."[23]

Within the immediate context in which he was writing, Maclay meant by "prudent Christian statesman" a missionary who affirmed the increasing emphasis on education in Japan. In contrast to his earlier days of condemning the "heathen," here he had only words of praise for the Japanese as they laid the foundation for the Westernization of their country. He praised embassies sent to foreign countries, youth studying in

European and American universities, the system of schools established in Japan, the Western scholars and scientists the nation employed to begin its educational system, and its compulsory laws in education. Because of these steps, "the authorities of every mission operating in Japan have felt constrained to shape their policy so as, in some way, to identify themselves with and help forward this educational movement."

Maclay must have intended the "statesman" image to have a more literal meaning as well. In Korea he worked at high governmental levels to open the country to Christian mission. Although both China and Japan had dominated Korea at various periods, in Maclay's day China dominated. The United States, wanting to open relations with Korea, went through the Qing dynasty to do it. When the United States made a treaty with Korea in 1882, the Korean government sent a legation to Washington. One of the Americans who traveled across the United States with the Korean special mission was Goucher. He instigated a move that led to Maclay's being sent to Korea to prepare the way for Methodist missions there.[24]

Maclay's goal was to assure government toleration of the mission. He landed at Chemulpo and then went to Seoul, arriving on June 24, 1884. The treaty between Korea and the United States made no provision for religion. Maclay did not meet official government representatives but simply talked informally with Koreans and discussed the prospects for missions with Western representatives. On July 3 Maclay received a message from the king "to authorize our society to commence hospital and school work in Korea." This decision Maclay attributed "to the Lord." Despite some difficulties ensuing from an abortive coup d'état later in 1884, three MEC missionaries established the work in Korea in early 1885.[25]

Here then was the statesman at work. Maclay continued as superintendent of both the Korean and Japanese missions until 1888. He was sixty-four years old and wrote Secretary Reid of the MEC Missionary Society that he would like "a period of needed rest" before attending General Conference, to which he had been elected. At the conference he was appointed dean of the Maclay College of Theology, which his brother Charles had just endowed and which was opening its doors in San Fernando, California.

Charles had also begun a career as a Methodist preacher in Pennsylvania, and like his brother he aspired to be a missionary. He went to Santa Clara in 1851 and served as a pastor until 1856, when he retired for health reasons. He stayed in California and managed a farm and other business interests. He was elected to the California Legislature as a representative and then a senator in the 1860s and was closely associated with Leland Stanford when Stanford was both a railroad entrepreneur and governor. Charles participated in the founding of the University of the Pacific in 1851, a school that began in Santa Clara before moving to its present location in Stockton.[26] He founded the town of San Fernando in 1873–74.

In the 1880s Charles donated ten acres for a school of theology. He built a building and endowed the school with utility stock and real estate. The school opened in the fall of 1887 with three faculty members, including the dean. Ten students enrolled. The dean died within a year, and Robert Maclay was then appointed dean. The school became one of several schools in the University of Southern California, begun in 1880 as a Methodist institution. The college of theology curriculum included not only theology but home and foreign missions. But land values deflated, and when Charles Maclay died in 1890, provisions of his will prevented officials from selling the land he had bequeathed for endowment. By 1891 financial cutbacks left Robert Maclay as the sole faculty member. He continued until 1894, when he retired. The school continued to struggle and was actually closed from 1899–1907. Eventually it re-opened and as the School of Theology at Claremont now exists independently of the University of Southern California and as one of thirteen United Methodist schools of theology in the United States.

Maclay lived in retirement in San Fernando, tending an orchard and occasionally writing for publication. In his last years Maclay seems to have moved from ambivalence toward Asia to clear admiration. In 1895 he wrote of China: "May I not say it is entitled to the credit of being the first nation known to history that gave unchallenged credentials of honor to literature that ennobled the scholar, that made education the key to political preferment, that exalted reason above force, that esteemed the pen mightier than the sword, the statesman higher than the warrior; and that, in the interest of society, inscribed 'Knowledge' over its gateway to all official positions in government service?"[27] He was not affluent and had a difficult time maintaining himself in his last years. In 1900 two of the missionaries who had served with him, S. L. Baldwin in China, and M. C. Harris in Japan, arranged for a $500 grant to Maclay from the MEC Missionary Society. In 1904 Mrs. Maclay died, and on August 18, 1907, Maclay died of "old age," according to the death certificate.

What were the contributions of this man whom colleagues referred to in death as "a gentleman of the old school," "a clear thinker," a "saint" who possessed an "urbane manner" and who "made no mistakes"? Maclay broke no new ground in religion or theology, although he knew as much as any Westerner about Asian religions. His theology reflected the orthodoxy learned in his youth, and it was a practical theology after the Wesleyan mode—a combination of the sense of God's active power at

work in history with the need to labor and to get things done. His religious orthodoxy led him to posit education as merely instrumental. In
China he considered day schools and boarding schools chiefly as ways to
make converts. By the time he got to Japan he could see the importance
of leadership training, but again leadership he defined as having a limited content—chiefly male clergy.

Despite these limitations, Maclay held a vision that was not only remarkable in his day but remains so even today. He believed that education grew out of theology, thus stating affirmatively for the church what
many United Methodists and other Christians still have trouble grasp-
ing. In working from such a premise, Maclay placed himself in the great
tradition of Christian educators from the founders of the medieval universities of Europe to those of Harvard College. Maclay had no difficulty
accepting a broad liberal arts education for students because he believed
that faith preceded understanding. And as a Methodist, he also believed
reasoning grew out of faith and was consonant with it. This breadth of
vision may explain his impatience with "skeptical scientists," since he
himself apparently had no difficulty reconciling science and religious
faith.

Maclay also conceived of education as an essential part of the church's
mission. He lived historically much nearer the time when the churches
had been the original sponsors of educational institutions. Although today it is worth remembering that higher education constitutes a critical
part of the church's mission, Maclay and other Christian leaders of his
time could hardly conceive of mission without education, which they
placed on a par with preaching and evangelism. This sense of the unity
of the church's mission would do much to help the church regain its
place in the culture if it could be recovered and redefined for our own
day and time. To this unitary vision of mission Maclay brought also a
commitment to accessibility. Despite his proscription on theological
education for women, he placed no such limits on the importance of
education for non-Western people. This emphasis on accessibility of
church-related schools and colleges to Asians and other non-Westerners
remains one of the enduring legacies of Maclay and his generation of
leaders.

Did Maclay acquiesce in Western imperialism? Yea and nay. Clearly
Maclay conceived of missions and Western civilization as nearly one and
the same thing. Perhaps he did this unconsciously, and perhaps we are
being unfair to impose our standards on him and his day, but to keep the
record straight we need to note this unfortunate and destructive integration of profane power with sacred ministry. This continuum between
Western civilization and Christianity can be seen in the assumptions that
Maclay and other missionaries made about the "heathen," particularly in

China, and also in their willingness to place Christian missions under the guns of Western militarism.

At the same time, we can also see in Maclay's case a gradual change in his conception of Asians. Like many others, the longer he stayed in Asia, the more he began to appreciate Asian history and culture. Maclay did not become an Asian—he kept on shaving early in the morning to preserve his appearance, and he confidently acted as if Western institutions were superior to Asian—but he saw to it that Asians were given the opportunity to advance and were given leadership positions. Only some Asians? In the case of Japan, some of these leaders emerged as creative and powerful figures in their own right, and they are still revered by Japanese today. Therefore it would be a perverse sort of judgment that criticized the Japanese for affirming these leaders. Maclay also tried to interpret Asian culture positively to American Methodists.

Finally, Maclay sensed that God was actively at work in the changes being brought about in Asia. He continually stressed the need for the churches to live in a state of expectancy. Was this a reflection of Maclay's romantic American vision of progress? Or was it a part of a millennialist interpretation of the Bible, where historical changes hid themselves in symbol and cipher? The exact nature of Maclay's optimistic outlook remains outside this limited study, but surely we can affirm the value of remaining open to the future as we contemplate church-related higher education. When many of Maclay's contemporaries could see only disaster arising from historical change, he saw the power of God at work. Because Maclay learned to exercise this power both in the church and the world, he laid foundations that still support the mission of church-related higher education today.

NOTES

1. The first two missionaries were Moses C. White and Judson D. Collins, who arrived in Fuzhou Sept. 30, 1847. *Widening Horizons,* vol. 3 of *History of Methodist Missions,* Wade Crawford Barclay (New York: Board of Missions of the Methodist Church, 1957), 367.

2. "Robert Samuel Maclay, Missionary in Japan," *Gospel in All Lands,* 1886, 21.

3. "Mrs. R. S. Maclay," *Proceedings of the General Conference of Protestant Missionaries in Japan* (Tokyo: Methodist Publishing House, 1901), 720–21. Having a bride sent from the home country was a common practice. When Maclay's brother, Charles, was preparing to leave the East Coast to go to California as a missionary, he wrote: "Bro. Kidder wishes me to go to California single & will make arrangements to send me a wife, but I don't believe in the principle exactly." (*Charles Maclay Journal,* vol. 6, 25 Feb. 1851, Huntington Library, MC 143. Re-

produced by permission of *The Huntington Library, San Marino, California*.)
Charles managed to get married before sailing.

4. Typescript of letter, 26 Sept. 1848, Fuh-Chau, Maclay correspondence. The
correspondence is a part of the holdings of the Archives Department, General
Commission on Archives and History, The United Methodist Church. Permission to quote from this and other missionary correspondence has been granted
by the General Board of Global Ministries of The United Methodist Church.

5. *Missionary Advocate* 6 (July 1850), dated Fuh-Chau 9 Jan., 7 Feb. 1850.

6. These quotations and incidents are taken from the *Missionary Advocate* from
1850 through 1852. Similar incidents appear in the *Christian Advocate* for the same
period.

7. References to this theme appear throughout published works, but some examples are: *Missionary Advocate* 9 (May 1853): 10; 11 (May 1855): 10; 14 (April
1858): 6; and 15 (July 1859): 27. See also "Opening Fields," an address Maclay
gave to the MEC Missionary Society in 1872 and published in its *Fifty-fourth
Annual Report*.

8. The belief in the Holy Spirit as the initiating and empowering divine agency
can be found in many places in Maclay's early writing. Some examples are: *Missionary Advocate* 5 (January 1850): 77; 7 (November 1851): 58; 9 (May 1853): 10; 10
(October 1854): 50; 10 (November 1854): 57; and 25 (19 Oct. 1869): 27. See also the
Christian Advocate 22 Sept. 1852.

9. *Missionary Advocate* 10 (November 1854): 57.

10. Maclay to Durbin, 7 Oct. 1852, Maclay correspondence. Maclay added in a
note marked "Private!" that he wished the board had communicated more regularly with him during his superintendency. "Still it is all right," he wrote loyally.
He also wrote about Colder's unhappiness in this letter. Quoted with permission. Maclay never displayed any ill will toward those opposing him in this conflict. The Maclays named their fifth child, Clara Isabel (born in 1856, died in 1860)
after Isabel White, the wife of Moses C. White, according to John W. Krummel,
Tokyo, in a letter to Charles Cole, April 19, 1985. Maclay spoke in complimentary
terms of White, as when he wrote of two missionaries accompanying him on a
ship in 1861, "in studying the dialect they have been very much aided by Brother
M.C. White's excellent little Manual on the Fuhchau Colloquial, and I would
recommend this work to all who may hereafter come out to join our mission in
Fuhchau." *Missionary Adocate* 17 (January 1862): 74.

11. I.W. Wiley to J.P. Durbin, Fuh-Chau, May 4, 1853, United Methodist Archives, Wiley correspondence. Used with permission. Afterward in the letter
Wiley conceded the threat might be real: "If the rebel has gone to the north we

are not now, and most probably will not for some considerable time, if ever, be in danger here. Should this report, however, prove incorrect, we will most probably be driven from Fuh-Chau."

12. The two letters from Durbin to the "Wiley and White Committee" are dated Dec. 4, 1852, and Jan. 20, 1853. United Methodist Archives, *China Letterbook*. Used with permission. Durbin wrote that "you have constantly declared [your steps were taken] not from personal dislike to the Officer, but from conscientious dissent from the Office. Oh, my Dear Brethren, I cannot resist the apprehension that there is trouble among you personally. . . . This issue will break up the China Mission."

13. The first phrase comes from J. O. Spencer, who served under Maclay in Japan, in "Robert S. Maclay, D.D.," *The Japan Evangelist* 4 (October 1896): 10. The second comes from an anonymous article, "Robert Samuel Maclay, Missionary in Japan," *Gospel in All Lands* 40 (1886): 213, and is actually part of a resolution honoring Maclay from the Japan Annual Conference. The organizer of the 1885 conference at which the resolution was passed was then-Bishop Isaac Wiley, one of Maclay's former antagonists in China.

14. The statistics here come from Barclay, *Widening Horizons*, 379. The reassurance was expressed in a letter from Durbin to O. Gibson, May 24, 1861, United Methodist Archives, *China Letterbook*. Used with permission. "You are evidently under an impression that the Board and Cor. Secty. have lost confidence in the Mission. . . . you say, you have 'heard on good authority, that the Cor. Secty. has said, that now Maclay has left the Mission, there is no one left capable of conducting it, or in whom the Board can put confidence.' . . . There is not a word of truth in the statement."

15. *Life among the Chinese* (New York: Carlton and Porter, 1861), 6. Other quotes are from pp. 155–57, 342, and 347.

16. Many of these statistics come from Barclay, *Widening Horizons*, 382–83, although the figures on the overall Protestant work appeared in *Missionary Advocate* 20 (January 1865): 1. See also *Fifty-Second Annual Report of the Missionary Society of the MEC for the Year 1871* (New York: MEC Missionary Society, 1872), 48–51.

17. Maclay had proposed a seminary for China in 1849, but such an institution would have been only a preparatory school. Of education he wrote: "We have employed this instrumentality, because we thought it would be efficient in spreading among the people a knowledge of that Saviour who has died to save them. This is our ultimate object, and we believe the schools are eminently qualified to accomplish this." *Missionary Advocate* 5 (January 1850): 77. At first the Foochow College was also only a preparatory school and possibly the equivalent of a junior college.

18. Missionaries had arrived in Japan in 1859 from the Protestant Episcopal Church, Presbyterian, U.S.A., and Dutch Reformed Church. By 1860 American Baptists had arrived, and by 1869, Anglicans. Roman Catholics had been in Japan since the sixteenth century but had been virtually exterminated. New missions revived Roman Catholic work in Japan in the 1860s. See Barclay, *Widening Horizons*, 664n. The biblical translation was completed in 1880. See Otis Carey, *A History of Christianity in Japan: Protestant Missions* (New York: Fleming H. Revell, 1909), 148. The translation committee's schedule was perfectly suited to Maclay's style, since it met daily from 5 A.M. to noon. *Sixty-first Annual Report of the Missionary Society of the Methodist Episcopal Church for the Year 1879* (New York: MEC Missionary Society, 1880), 159.

19. Blackledge in Yokohama to John M. Reid in New York, June 28, 1886, United Methodist Archives, Blackledge correspondence. Used with permission.

20. Quoted by Milton S. Vail, Aoyama, to Bishop S.M. Merrill, United Methodist Archives, Vail correspondence. Used with permission.

21. The details of Mrs. Maclay's death are couched in terms appropriate for her time: "The stroke came while she was presiding at the organ, during the Japanese Sunday services in the Yokohama Church. The Japanese preacher announced as the closing hymn, 'Rest for the weary'; during the singing of the last stanza the hands of the organist dropped, and she fell unconscious into her husband's arms. She was buried in the foreign cemetery in Yokohama." Anonymous, "Mrs. R. S. Maclay," *Proceedings of the General Conference of Protestant Missionaries in Japan*, 1901, 721.

Of the Maclay children who lived to maturity, Robert Hall (1852–1929) received degrees from Syracuse University and returned to China, where he worked as a businessman, interpreter, and judge; Arthur Collins (1853–1930) was graduated from Pennington Seminary and Wesleyan University and taught in Japanese universities before returning to the U.S. to earn a law degree from Columbia and practice law in New York City; Alice Minette (1859–96) married a clergyman from Mississippi, W. B. Cooper; George Hugh Erwin (1858–78) studied in Pennington Seminary and was a student at Syracuse when he died of typhoid in his sophomore year; and Edgar Stanton (1863–1919) was graduated from Syracuse University, worked as a newspaper reporter in New York, and was the official historian of the U.S. Navy. He also edited the *Journal of William Maclay: United States Senator from Pennsylvania, 1789–1791* (New York: Frederick Ungar, 1965 reprint of 1927 ed.).

Maclay married Sarah Ann Barr on June 6, 1882. They had no children.

22. "New Japan," 11-page typescript, undated but apparently from the 1880s, in the Aoyama Gakuin archives.

23. "Education in Japan," *Manual of the Methodist Episcopal Church: A Quarterly Magazine* 2 (January 1882): 44. Maclay also gave in this article a summary of the MEC education work in Japan, referring to the seminary in Yokohama as "a

training-school" (p. 45). Quotes in the next paragraph come from this same source.

24. Barclay, *Widening Horizons*, 741–42. Maclay described his visit in detail in "A Fortnight in Seoul, Korea, in 1884," *Gospel in All Lands* (January 1896): 354–60. His comment on the origin of the initiative was: "The opportune proposal of Rev. John F. Goucher, D.D., of Baltimore, to give liberal aid in founding the Korea Mission, was cordially accepted by the missionary authorities of our Church. My visit to Seoul was the result of this proposal."

Maclay described the consent of the Korean king in another article written a decade after the event. He wrote that he had already met in Japan a member of the Korean department of foreign affairs, Kim ok Kuin. When he arrived in Korea he presented a letter to Kim with "an expression of our desire to come to Korea, together with a brief statement of the lines of work upon which it was our purpose first to enter." The letter was submitted June 30 and Maclay received a reply from the king through Kim. Kim was involved in the attempted coup later in 1884 and after fleeing the country and living in exile, was assassinated in Shanghai in 1894, according to Maclay. "Korea's Permit to Christianity," *Missionary Review of the World*, vol. 9 (new series) (April 1896): 289–90.

25. The first two MEC missionaries were Dr. William B. Scranton, a Yale graduate and a physician from Cleveland, Ohio, and his mother, Mrs. Mary F. Scranton, a Women's Foreign Missionary Society missionary. Barclay, *Widening Horizons*, 742–44. Mrs. William B. Scranton later joined the two in Korea.

26. Charles Maclay was on the first board of trust for California Wesleyan College, as the school was first named, and served until 1873. He also served as secretary of the board from 1858 and as treasurer from 1862. Letter from Ronald H. Limbaugh, director, Holt-Atherton Pacific Center for Western Studies, University of the Pacific, Sept. 26, 1984.

Another Maclay brother, William J., taught Latin and Greek at the school beginning in 1854 and served as president for a few months in 1857. Rockwell D. Hunt, *History of the College of the Pacific, 1851–1951* (Stockton: College of the Pacific, 1951), 23, 26.

27. *Christian Advocate* (16 May 1895): 307. Showing his belief in biblical literalism, Maclay went on to sketch how the Chinese might have originated in the Middle East and journeyed to their present habitat.

10

John M'Clintock
(1814–1870)

by Michael D. Ryan

J OHN M'CLINTOCK'S LIFE was a magnificent blend of scholarship, churchmanship, and citizenship. His was a mind alive, a true embodiment of the principle of lifelong learning so much touted in these days of continuing higher education. His contribution to the Methodist Episcopal Church (MEC) and the high quality of his citizenship, tested in the full bloom of his maturity, which coincided with the Civil War, derived directly from his intellectual cultivation. From the time of his conversion to Jesus Christ as a seventeen-year-old chief clerk of the Methodist Book Concern in New York City in the year 1831 to his premature death in Madison, New Jersey, on March 3, 1870, as the true founder and first president of Drew Theological Seminary, John M'Clintock placed his erudition in the service of his Lord. This meant for him first and foremost serving his church as a preacher and a teacher, and then using all his influence as a churchman in the struggle for justice in his nation, which for most of his life legally allowed what he considered to be the moral abomination of slavery.

Daniel Drew, who believed it was better to be handy with a rake than a pitchfork, used the money he took in bear-market skulduggery in the New York Stock Exchange to buy the seminary as a memorial plaque for his own name. It opened its doors to a new class in November of 1867. M'Clintock spent the last two years of his life organizing the seminary, recruiting both faculty and student body, gathering books for the library around his own personal holdings and (in addition to doing the work of the president and registrar) functioned on occasion as a janitor and carpenter. He brought the crucial ingredient for the founding of a seminary—a knowledge of the history and the current status of the several

JOHN M'CLINTOCK

Photo courtesy of Drew University.

theological disciplines, including biblical studies; church history; historical, systematic, and practical theology; and church polity. All of these he had combined with a first-rate knowledge of classical languages, mathematics, history, and philosophy, besides the belles lettres of current culture in English, French, and German. So he came with the first curriculum in his head and a vision of how that might be communicated and utilized to produce a truly educated ministry for the MEC. To take proper measure of this man and his learning one must know his story.

By the standards of the typical twentieth-century educational pattern in America, M'Clintock's higher education began in 1822, when at the age of eight he entered the grammar school of the University of Pennsylvania. The second son of an Irish immigrant couple from Tyrone County, who met and married in this country and who operated a dry goods store in Philadelphia, M'Clintock was given a classic grammar school education based on the British model. Latin and Greek constituted the basic curriculum along with the fundamentals of arithmetic, English grammar, and composition. His teacher, Dr. S. B. Wylie, who would later publish his *Greek Grammar* (1838), drilled the students in all the forms of grammar and as exercises had them write out analyses of passages of Latin and Greek poetry and prose. Students were expected to provide an accurate translation, make notes on the etymology of the chief words, state the rules of grammar that applied, comment on the syntax and the poetic meter of the text, and clarify the references to facts of history or to ancient mythology, as the case would be. Young M'Clintock flourished under the discipline, taking genuine delight in the knowledge gained in this way from every passage of an ancient text. He learned his lessons so well that later when he was a college student and audited Wylie's classes on Homer, he could follow Wylie without a text, for he had virtually memorized Homer as a grammar student.

M'Clintock cherished the memories of the Philadelphia of his childhood. Born on October 27, 1814, he was given his father's first name, and he grew up in a large household with four brothers and three sisters. They lived in an apartment in back of the dry goods store, where famous Methodist itinerant preachers often came for a meal or to stay overnight. His parents, John and Martha, were faithful members of Saint George's, Philadelphia's oldest Methodist Society, and they maintained a home where discipline and frivolity were tempered by piety. The "City of Brotherly Love" was small in comparison to large cities today. Nestled between the Delaware and the Schuylkill rivers, it afforded many delights for growing children. Swimming and boating in summer, ice-skating in winter, ball playing on Bush Hill to the northwest, and hiking along the rivers and into the marshlands on the south were typical activities. All were within walking distance of the stately town houses and

churches around city hall. When he was eleven years old, he was enrolled in a weekly catechetical class that was just being formed by two
ministers of Saint George's. M'Clintock enjoyed the classes and the singing, prayer, and exhortation so much that he went out to enlist other
members. He clearly reflected the religious commitment of his parents.

M'Clintock's childhood came to a rather abrupt close when at the age
of fourteen he was made a full-time clerk in the family store. From the
standpoint of his parents it was part of his education to learn the mercan-
tile business, but he was plagued by a wandering mind filled with the
scenes he had learned to envision from the Songs of Anacreon or the
Aeneid of Virgil. Often scolded for not paying attention to details, he
was not very happy in the store, although it made it possible for him to
accept his first full-time job away from home. He was hired in 1830 at age
sixteen as a clerk in the Methodist Book Concern in New York City,
where he went to live in the home of a Methodist preacher, the Rev.
Samuel Merwin.

New York was in the full bloom of summer when young John arrived
to assume his duties in the book concern. He explored the city in eve-
nings and on weekends took longer walks or went swimming in the East
River, which then was so clear that one could see the bottom in the deep-
est part. With many business errands to run he was able to write to his
parents after a short time that he knew the town pretty well. The book
concern was managed by the Rev. John Emory, who was elected bishop
at the next General Conference, and the Rev. Beverly Waugh, who was
M'Clintock's immediate supervisor. It was thought that he might have to
take a crash course in bookkeeping, but M'Clintock, who kept all the
books when Waugh was ill, learned the procedures rapidly and after a
year was made chief clerk. He was given the task of balancing the books
of the business which annually grossed more than a quarter of a million
dollars.

During the summer and fall of 1830 M'Clintock occasionally went to
hear different preachers in the city, but for the most part he attended the
services of his host, Merwin. His correspondence with his father shows
that he appropriately was concerned with a choice of what career path to
follow. His father, writing to him on December 27, 1830, made three
suggestions: one, to go to college and finish his education; two, to stay
there and learn the business so that he might one day open his own book
store; and three, to come home and give himself to the dry goods store.[1]

M'Clintock, who received the letter from Philadelphia the next day,
immediately replied, making it clear that his own preference was to go to
college, and he already had in mind entering the new Wesleyan University in Middletown, Connecticut, that was going to open in October,
1831. He was confident that his knowledge of business was sufficient so

that he could always be sure of finding work as a clerk, if he did not succeed in a profession. Finally, he negated outright the dry goods business on the grounds that it was injurious to his health.[2] Whatever M'Clintock was to do, it would be by way of higher education.

For the first eleven days of February, 1831, a revival was held in the congregation led by Merwin. M'Clintock attended every session and was soon under conviction for his sins. He answered not one but three altar calls, and late one evening while in prayer after the meeting, Merwin came and knelt beside him and prayed for M'Clintock and his family. He came away assured that his sins had been forgiven by the Lord whom he had resolved to serve always. Mrs. Merwin, who mothered him, was especially happy. M'Clintock continued to attend all the meetings, which were held three times a day, with prayer sessions in between. During the rest of that winter and spring, the young convert attended class meetings every Friday night, prayer meetings on Saturday nights, and regular services every Sunday. He saved $250 towards the $300 costs for attending college, and he sent home for books to use with a tutor in preparation for college. These included his texts of Julius Caesar, Sallust, grammar, and his Greek Testament. The classics, combined with the basic text of his faith, came to represent the character and the content of his lifelong quest for learning. From the outset of his vocational pursuit, higher learning was joined with his commitment to Christ. Like Saint Augustine and Saint Thomas, M'Clintock took to heart the commandment to love God with all your heart and with all your soul and with all your mind.

It was another year—in the fall of 1832—before M'Clintock finally started college. He was persuaded to remain with the Methodist Book Concern until after the General Conference of the MEC in May, 1832. Emory was elected a bishop and Waugh was made head of the book concern. M'Clintock returned home in June and continued his preparation for college. He made some fine resolutions for a daily discipline of prayer, Bible study, and religious readings around his other studies but found he could not maintain it. Once again his lively mind carried his attention to fields afar from his present life, and he finally reduced his resolutions to two general aims: to have "a clean heart" and "a clear head."[3]

He went to Wesleyan University in early September, but shortly after his arrival he was prostrated with a severe illness. This was but the first of many periods of illness throughout his life which would take him out of his normal course of activities. He went home to recuperate, and then late in October he enrolled in the freshman class of the University of Pennsylvania. He had to work hard to catch up with the rest of his class, and by the spring of 1833 he was well along in his college program. In

March, 1834, he took a set of examinations which allowed him to skip most of the sophomore year and to be enrolled in the junior class with the rank of number fourteen. By July he was number six in distinction in his class.

M'Clintock's commitment to Christ and to higher education were not as easy to reconcile as one might expect from the standpoint of a twentieth-century observer. The polity of the church allowed young men to be called to the ministry and to be placed under the discipline and care of a conference without regard for their progress in a college education. It was not yet normal for ministers to have a college education, much less a seminary education beyond college. Privately he had resolved to "bend all his studies toward the ministry"[4] and to wait for the workings of God's providence to open the way into ministry. The ministers of his conference did not blush at making themselves the instruments of God's providence, for they decided together and simply informed him on March 24, 1833, that he was "on trial as an exhorter in the Methodist Episcopal Church."[5] M'Clintock said that it was done without his knowledge or seeking, but he accepted it as God's will. In November of that year he preached his first sermon and was frankly embarrassed by his effort. He was made a local preacher in December, 1833, and after a month's probation received his license in January, 1834. All the while he was studying hard for his college courses and the examinations for admission to the junior class in March.

During the summer of 1834 the nineteen-year-old local preacher helped out in the circuit of Flemington, New Jersey, with regular preaching assignments and other pastoral responsibilities. In September he suffered with his whole family the pain and embarrassment of the failure of his father's dry goods business, a result of causes which he did not enumerate. He returned in September to his studies at the University of Pennsylvania, fending off a number of calls to the pastorate. When a friend of his was forced to leave the charge of Elizabethtown, New Jersey, M'Clintock was persuaded to accept the appointment to that charge. Like many a Methodist student minister from that day to this, M'Clintock found himself with a full load of college studies plus full pastoral responsibilities. When the provost of the university got wind of M'Clintock's situation, he objected to his prolonged absence from the campus, and so John spent most of the winter of 1835 in Philadelphia pursuing his studies. He was tutored in advanced mathematics by a member of the faculty, achieving a very high level of competence in that discipline. During this same period he was advanced in the ministry of his church, having become a traveling preacher in April, 1835. When he was graduated from the university with honors on July 26, 1835, at the age of twenty, he had laid well his foundations for a dual career in the preaching ministry and in higher education.

His move to higher education was rather sudden and could therefore be interpreted as providential. He wore himself out after eighteen months in his first pastoral charge after graduation in Jersey City, New Jersey. His throat was raw from preaching three times every Sunday, and for some weeks he spit blood and suffered chest pains. On the advice of a physician he gave up the pulpit ministry. When it became known that he was available for a teaching position in a university, he was offered a professorship in mathematics and natural philosophy at La Grange College in northern Alabama (not to be confused with another school of the same name in Georgia). The faculty at Dickinson College in Carlisle, Pennsylvania, also offered him a position in mathematics, but at the lower rank of assistant professor. On the advice of his teachers he accepted the Dickinson appointment and moved to Carlisle with his new bride Caroline Augusta (née Wakeman) in the summer of 1836.

Like young Jonathan Edwards who a little more than a century before had become senior tutor at Yale College when he was twenty-one years old,[6] John M'Clintock became a teacher of mathematics when he was twenty-one. He found the faculty most congenial, especially young Robert Emory, the professor of classical languages and the son of his erstwhile employer, Bishop Emory. Teaching deepened his knowledge of math, which he augmented by covering the history of math as well as teaching an advanced course on mathematics beyond the textbooks. At the same time he took advantage of the library and pursued a program of studies that he set for himself, which included further readings in the classics, Latin and Greek, logic, metaphysics, history, law, poetry, and belles lettres. Resolving not to be a narrow mathematician, he geared himself for leadership in what his biographer, George R. Crooks, called "the second, or educational, era of the development of American Methodism."[7]

John Wesley's maxim "Getting knowledge is good, but saving souls is better,"[8] had been perversely used by many Methodist preachers to oppose education itself. In their view all one needed for ministry was a conversion experience, a Bible, a fluent tongue, stout lungs, and a horse and saddle. M'Clintock with his future friend and colleague James Strong would challenge this anti-intellectual stream in Methodism in the mid-1850s and successfully make the case for seminary education beyond college as a desideratum for ministry. That is, for theological education as a graduate enterprise. Strong, the Christian layman and Greek scholar who later would produce *The Comprehensive Concordance of the Bible*, incited a heated controversy that began in *The Christian Advocate and Journal,* December 22, 1853, with his plea for "A Central Theological Seminary" for the MEC. Thomas E. Bond, the editor, in a reply on January 12, 1854, officiously opposed the idea, arguing that the church could stand on the successful record of Methodist preaching. George Hughes wrote a long lampooning reply, entitled "A Central Salvation Seminary," for the January 19, 1854, issue, which ridiculed it by suggesting that it would have a professor of prayer meetings, another of class meetings, a pastoral professor and one of manual labor. The degree offered would be a P.P.R.: "a Professor of Plenty of Religion."

But Strong also found his defenders. R. S. Moran argued in the January 26 issue that it would amount to disobedience to the gospel imperative not to use the appropriate means to reach "a large class of persons to whom we have not now access." D. T. Leech of the seminary at Concord, New Hampshire, was drawn by Hughes's satire into the fray and in the February 16 issue presented an outline of the very impressive curriculum of that school which surely must have been intimidating to those who opposed a seminary. E. E. Griswold supported Strong's contention of the ineffectiveness of Methodist preachers in the cultural climes of New York and Baltimore by citing statistics, showing that while the population of New York City had increased in the previous decade from 347,874 to 602,075, the number of members of Methodist Episcopal churches actually declined by four hundred, and Baltimore, which had enjoyed a similar increase in total population, showed a decline of one thousand members.[9]

M'Clintock spent eleven years at Dickinson College. After his first year he was made a full professor of mathematics and in the middle of his fourth year after another debilitating throat infection he became the professor of classical languages, filling the vacancy created by the departure of his friend Robert Emory. In the spring of 1839 when he was himself recuperating, his infant daughter Sarah died after a short illness. For solace John turned once more to his studies, reading the Book of Job and other books of the Bible, but also indulging himself with such fare as Byron's *Journals,* essays by S. T. Coleridge from his journal *The Friend,* and Coleridge's *Aids to Reflection in the Formation of a Manly Character,* which made a profound impression on him.

His private studies continued apace during the next seven years. In April, 1840, he was ordained an elder of his church, and he plunged more deeply into theological studies. In that year he also began to learn Hebrew (he was then twenty-six), which he pursued intensively for two years. In the fall of 1842 he turned to the German language and before the year was over he was reading Goethe's *Wilhelm Meister* as a way into the language and culture of modern Germany. By the year 1846–47 he was able to do a translation of the *Life of Christ* by the German church historian and Berlin professor, A. Neander, and to see it through to publication.

M'Clintock continued to expose himself to a broad range of scholarly and theological opinion, which made him acutely aware of the narrow-mindedness that he found in Methodism. During his illness of 1839, he wrote in his diary in the entry for January 17:

> There is too much *prescription* in the Methodist Church, and there is too much *proscription* for individual opinions. A man can hardly be independent with any hope of rising in the Church. This state of things causes a mean, truckling spirit to grow up among the young men, which in a great degree, renders them intellectual slaves to a few not very intellectual masters.[10]
>
> (Italics in Crook's text.)

Two great issues animated M'Clintock throughout his mature years. The first was the freedom of Christians to cultivate their minds and to use reason to understand truth and reality. This placed him squarely in the tradition of Augustine, who taught that "every good and true Christian should understand that wherever he may find truth, it is his Lord's."[11] He loved to cite to his students interested in theology the concluding passage of Coleridge's *Biographia Literaria:*

> that the scheme of Christianity, though not discoverable by human reason, is yet in accordance with it; that link follows link by necessary consequence; that religion passes out of the ken of reason, only where the eye of reason has reached its own horizon, and that faith is then but its continuation.[12]

The other great issue of the day that challenged his resources and consumed much of his time and energy was slavery. The General Conference of 1844 had placed it squarely on the agenda of the church as the presidential election of that year did for the nation. M'Clintock closely followed developments in his nation and church. Early in the year 1847, Bond agreed to publish a series of articles in *The Christian Advocate* in which M'Clintock called for the extirpation of slavery from the land. These articles elaborated a position that he took in a letter written the previous year to a friend in England who had proposed an American branch of the Evangelical Alliance to include churches from both North and South because it would be "practicable" to do so. M'Clintock's reply included the following remarks:

> Is a general alliance of Christians practicable if the American branch admits slave-holders indiscriminately? . . .
>
> Perhaps in all this I am influenced by my feelings. To tell the truth my abhorrence of slavery grows apace. Year after year I feel more and more that

something should be done by every good man in this land to deliver it. . . .

But Oh! what a sad subject it is. Even writing to you in quietness, I find my heart beating violently with agitation. Tonight at least, I can dwell on it no more. God have mercy upon us, and upon our favored but guilty country. I trust him still, but I could not trust him if I did not follow my honest convictions.[13]

The year 1847 marked the beginning of what was perhaps the climactic passage of M'Clintock's life, which exhibited several rather sudden turns both before and after this one. It was the year in which he became embroiled in a dispute over three runaway slaves from Maryland. He was subsequently charged with inciting a riot outside the Carlisle courthouse, along with twenty-eight black codefendants. When he was acquitted himself, he and his lawyers appealed the verdict, which found thirteen of the blacks guilty and sent ten to prison. They won the appeal before the Pennsylvania Supreme Court and all the blacks were released from prison.

It all began for M'Clintock on June 2, 1847, when he went to the post office to fetch his mail. He was told that two Maryland slaveowners were in the process of receiving a certificate from a local magistrate returning three slaves to them. M'Clintock rushed over to the courtroom and went to the bar where the lawyers for the defense of the blacks were seated and asked them if they were aware of the recent Pennsylvania law that made the whole proceeding illegal. They were not, nor was the judge aware of it, and no copy of the law could be found in the courthouse, so M'Clintock rushed back to his study and brought his newspaper copy of it, which the lawyers then used as the basis for their petition.

The new Pennsylvania law was an answer to the U.S. Supreme Court and to federal law which struck down previous Pennsylvania laws aimed at protecting fugitive slaves. The new law acknowledged federal jurisdiction over such cases, but made it an offense (with severe penalties) for any Pennsylvania officials, sheriffs, or magistrates to perform any function in the return of runaways. It also made it illegal for slaveowners to employ violence or physical force in recapturing their alleged slaves. When M'Clintock returned to the courthouse with his copy of the law, the fugitives were being rushed into a waiting carriage. At that moment the crowd of blacks seized them away, and while M'Clintock and the lawyers watched in amazement, one of the slaveowners gave chase and was severely beaten when he tripped and fell. The man, a Mr. Kennedy, died some weeks later, which added gravity to the case.

With two lawyers as eyewitnesses as to his conduct during both of his visits to the courthouse, he was acquitted, but a number of false witnesses were brought forward, and the jury had to determine who was giving truthful testimony. When the jury read its verdict, the trial judge surprisingly protested it, expressing his opinion of M'Clintock's guilt. But the jury had spoken and M'Clintock was free.

The case was covered by several newspapers in New York and Phila-delphia, so M'Clintock, who was already known in Carlisle and in church circles as "that damned abolitionist," gained a national reputa-tion and some notoriety for his involvement. When the trial was behind him, feelings were still running strong against him among the southern sympathizers in Carlisle. Then in the spring of 1848 his good friend Robert Emory died. All this worked together in his decision to leave Dickinson. Once again offers came his way, but this time it was for the presidency of such colleges as Lima, Newark, and Allegheny. He turned them all down and accepted instead his election by the General Con-ference of 1848 to the editorship of *The Methodist Quarterly Review*.

M'Clintock took up residence with his wife, his daughter Augusta, and his son Emory in Jersey City, so that they could be near his wife's family. From there he commuted to New York City, where the office of the *Review* was located at 200 Mulberry Street. It was a new setting and in a significant way it was a whole new career which happily required the combined gifts that he brought as a scholar and churchman. As the edi-tor of the foremost journal of Methodism, M'Clintock became a mentor for the ministers and intelligent laity of the church, a role which he took very seriously.

Anticipating the high scholarly tone that M'Clintock would give to the *Review,* the General Conference gave an official directive with his election, namely, that he should make the quarterly "more practical." In the very first issue he brought the matter before the readership. What could the directive to be more practical have meant? He was sure that it could not have been intended to lower the tone of the journal in literary style and scholarship. He understood it to mean that there should be more *scholarly* articles to deal with such *practical* matters for ministers as biblical exegesis, questions of faith, discipline, and church polity, as well as the social and political issues of the day. He went on to say in that first editorial:

Nothing is gained to religion or the Church by attempts to cut off investigation or to stifle honest opinions. Time was when this was thought to be a Christian duty. There are, doubtless, some who think it such still, who would shut up men's minds forever in their own narrow enclosure, putting a barrier to in-quiry at the precise point which they have reached, as if wisdom must die with them. To these men every new view of the wants or the duties of the Church is heresy, and all scrutiny of an old one presumption. With such men we have no sympathy.[14]

Throughout the eight years of his tenure as editor of the *Review*, M'Clintock maintained its quality and the critical stance vis à vis both his church and society at large. He ordered articles reviewing the latest trends in theology and philosophy. An example was one critically appraising Auguste Comte's positivist philosophy. Comte himself wrote a response to the editor expressing his appreciation for the "conscientious review," calling it a "generous proceeding, to which I have been but little accustomed from the French press."[15]

The new form of expression, written rather than oral, favored M'Clintock's health. Then in March, 1850, his wife died. It dealt him a severe blow, for he believed almost to the end that she would rally and survive. To recover from his melancholy he went with a party of friends to Europe in the summer of 1850, and a whole new world of associations opened up for him. The party went on to Germany after a two-day stop in Britain, and then visited Bremen, Berlin, where they were entertained by professors from the university, and Munich, which simply charmed them. After a tour through Switzerland and the Rhineland of Germany they went to Paris, which M'Clintock called "the capital of Europe," an impression which never left him. He went back to Europe twice in the 1850s, again for the summer in 1854 with his second wife, Catharine (the widow of his friend Robert Emory and the woman he had married in October, 1851), and again in the summer of 1857, when he went with Bishop Matthew Simpson as a delegate from the General Conference to the Wesleyan Conference of Britain. M'Clintock cemented relations with British Methodists and German scholars and churchmen. A cosmopolitan by culture, M'Clintock moved easily into the international set of Christians associated with the Evangelical Alliance.

In 1853 he and Strong started *The Cyclopaedia of Biblical, Theological, and Ecclesiastical Literature*, a work involving many hands which he worked on for the rest of his life, and which was completed in ten volumes in 1881, eleven years after his death. This monumental work of scholarship was reprinted in 1970 because, as the publisher's announcement put it, "the *Cyclopaedia* is unique for its comprehensive scope, the detailed character of its work and its accuracy."[16] No greater compliment could be paid to a scholar and editor than to have his work reprinted a century later. M'Clintock was the type of scholar who enjoyed collaborative enterprises, such as the publication of a series of Latin and Greek elementary grammars, entailing a new approach to language instruction, which he and Crooks published in 1845.

In 1852 M'Clintock moved to New Brunswick and the next year back again to Carlisle, where the family settled in a large comfortable home on the edge of town with a splendid view of South Mountain. The house had a spacious library where he continued to edit the *Review*. Under continuing pressure to make the *Review* "more popular," that is more "suited to the practical and utilitarian tastes of the people," he relinquished the editorship at the General Conference of 1856, and in 1857 he returned to the pulpit ministry. He was appointed pastor of Saint Paul's MEC in New York City, but did not take up his duties until after another summer in Europe, when he went with Bishop Simpson. In September he represented his church at a Berlin Conference of Christians from All Lands. To the pulpit of Saint Paul's he brought the full powers of a mature scholar who matched learning with eloquence, and he literally attracted crowds to services in the new edifice, where the poor and the wealthy, among the latter Daniel Drew, came to listen and to admire, if not fully to comprehend.

In 1860 M'Clintock's career took another sudden turn, one that catapulted him into the international limelight. In that year he accepted the invitation to become the senior minister of the American Chapel in Paris, France. The chapel had been founded by the American and Foreign Christian Union of the United States and was to become under M'Clintock a nineteenth-century model of a Protestant interdenominational ministry, tailoring prayer and worship services to meet the needs of more liturgical Episcopalians, as well as those evangelicals who preferred extemporary prayers and preaching. M'Clintock never preached from a manuscript, but he did read the morning prayers from the Episcopal Prayer Book at 11:15 A.M. on Sundays. Then at noon he would introduce the sermon with extempore prayer.

During his stay in Paris from 1860–64, which coincided with the first three terrible years of the Civil War, the American Chapel became a rallying point for Americans in Paris. Many famous persons, some from the South, were exposed to the preaching of a man who did not hesitate to apply the gospel to the chief issue between the warring parties—slavery. After the war broke out in 1861, many Americans and interested Europeans came to the chapel for news and also to convey European views of the war and political developments around it. Out of the pulpit M'Clintock became a propagandist for the Union cause. Agénor Étienne De Gaparin, a reformer and writer, pled for the Union cause in *The Uprising of a Great People.* M'Clintock translated it into English and circulated it in England. He entered many a hall in London, Paris, and in several cities in Germany as an advocate and spokesman for the North. In April, 1861, he spoke to the Wesleyan Missionary Anniversary in Exeter Hall in London and seized the opportunity to refute an editorial of the *London Times* of the previous day which declared, "The Great Republic is no more." Turning history to his purpose, M'Clintock asked his audience of patriotic Methodist Britons if it would have been appropriate for a prophet to have said at the outset of the colonial rebellion in America

that "Great Britain was no more?" He was sure of the antislavery sentiments of the British Methodists and so soon turned the meeting into a
rally for the Union cause. But M'Clintock did not make an altogether
favorable impression on his hosts. At one point he was obviously irri-
tated by the proceedings and was so undiplomatic as to tell his hosts—
after receiving a resolution only minutes before it was time to speak to
it—that meetings were better prepared in American conferences. No
wonder that some of the British speakers had some barbs for him in their
speeches.[17]

The M'Clintocks returned to New York in 1864. John was so weak
that his son Emory had to carry him aboard the steamer. Back home in
New York he declined a public dinner that would have honored him for
his public service. He was persuaded to return to the pulpit of Saint
Paul's, but after a year which saw the assassination of Lincoln, whom he
dearly loved, he retired to "Brown Farm" at Germantown outside Philadelphia. His discourse delivered on Lincoln's death was reconstructed
from carefully taken notes and published together with Lincoln's first
and second inaugural addresses and his Gettysburg Address. It may
have been his finest hour in the pulpit, ending with a plea to quench all
desire for vengeance:

> I have been sorry to hear from the lips of generous young men, under the
> pangs of the President's assassination, sentiments of bitterness and indigna-
> tion, amounting almost to fierceness. It is natural, no doubt, but what is natu-
> ral is not always right. Indulge this spirit, and you may hear next that this
> man's house or that man's should be mobbed. Mobs are alien to our northern
> soil; they belong to another atmosphere than that of free schools and free men.
> The region of slavery was their natural home; let us have none of them. And
> soon, when the last shackles shall have fallen, and throughout our land, from
> sea to sea, there shall be no master and no slave, the blessed Peace shall come,
> for which we have looked, and prayed, and fought so long, when the Republic
> shall be established upon the eternal foundations of Freedom and Justice, to
> stand, we trust, by the blessing of God, down to the last syllable of recorded
> Time.[18]

M'Clintock was never to enjoy a real retirement. The General Conference of 1864 had created a large committee for the centenary of American
Methodism in 1866. In 1865 a central committee of six people was
formed to organize the benevolence work. M'Clintock became the chairman, working on it for two years, and was gratified to learn that total
contributions for all purposes came to seven million dollars. While serving in this capacity, he learned that Daniel Drew wanted to establish an
educational institution and that he wanted M'Clintock to be the organizer and first president. After a period of negotiations the agreement

was consummated and M'Clintock moved his household and his library one more time in the early summer of 1867 to the mansion of the Gibbon estate in Madison, New Jersey, the home of the new Drew Theological Seminary. During the academic year 1867–68 he taught Theological Encyclopaedia, his own version of the way that the various disciplines of a theological curriculum combine to form a coherent enterprise for understanding and communicating the Christian faith in the present age.

In 1868 he attended his last General Conference, held in Chicago, and lifted his voice for yet another cause: membership of the laity in the General Conference. Although that goal was not attained in his lifetime, his speech for it before the conference helped to move things in that direction. The conference appointed him trustee on the first board of education formed by the General Conference. The trustees met in New York in December, 1869, to lay the groundwork. C. C. North, who reported for the board to the next General Conference, wrote a reminiscence of M'Clintock's participation at that meeting:

> In a day spent in discussions which were to consolidate the whole movement and send it forth organized for its work, M'Clintock shone conspicuously in amplitude of suggestion, in scope of comprehension, in vigorous application and broad sympathy for the chief object of the movement—the education of young men for the ministry.[19]

Perhaps nothing sums up the spirit and the total import of the life of M'Clintock as well as his own words in a letter of June 18, 1864, to James M'Cabe, congratulating him for his strong stand against slavery in the independent paper called *The Methodist:*

> My residence in Europe has confirmed all my fears of the dangers of ecclesiastical corporations. Nothing but free criticism can save them from rotting. We Methodists are but men. . . . There must always be men, in every ecclesiastical and political body, who shall work for the best good of the body, without holding the form of power in it. I am content to be one of these men in our Church.[20]

NOTES

1. Letter of his father, John M'Clintock, to his son John, 27 Dec. 1830, included in George R. Crooks, *Life and Letters of the Rev. John M'Clintock, D.D., LL.D.* (New York: Nelson & Phillips, 1876), 24 ff. This brief biography of M'Clintock was written in almost total reliance on this larger work for the factual data of M'Clintock's life. The author is responsible for the selection, organization, and interpretation of the data.

2. Letter of John M'Clintock to his father, 28 Dec. 1830, 25 ff.

3. Crooks, *Life and Letters*, 34.

4. Crooks, *Life and Letters*, 36.

5. Crooks, *Life and Letters*, 36.

6. Perry Miller, *Jonathan Edwards* (Cleveland and New York: Meridian Books, 1949, 1964), 39.

7. Crooks, *Life and Letters*, 77.

8. Wesley's maxim was repeated by Crooks, *Life and Letters*, 41.

9. E. E. Griswold, letter to *The Christian Advocate and Journal*, published on 23 Feb. 1854.

10. Crooks, *Life and Letters*, 83 ff.

11. Augustine, *On Christian Doctrine* (Indianapolis, New York: Bobbs-Merrill, 1958), 54.

12. S. T. Coleridge, *Biographia Literaria* (New York: Dutton, Everyman's Library, 1906, 1971), 289. Crooks quoted an earlier edition without a page reference on p. 122 of his work.

13. Crooks, *Life and Letters*, 138 ff.

14. Crooks, *Life and Letters*, 211.

15. Crooks, *Life and Letters*, 230 ff.

16. Brochure by Arno Press advertising the reprint of J. M'Clintock and J. Strong, *The Cyclopaedia of Biblical, Theological, and Ecclesiastical Literature*, in 1970.

17. The meeting of the Wesleyan Missionary Anniversary was covered by *The Methodist Recorder, The General Christian Chronicle* in the May 2, 1861, edition. M'Clintock's remarks were printed along with other speeches. The Rev. W. M. Punshon responded to M'Clintock with a view sympathetic to the Confederacy, saying, "I am sure there is no Christian Church, there is no Christian heart in England, that wishes ill to the great country of America. The only thing that we wish is, that, as the old veil of the Temple was rent in twain from the top to the bottom, the old banner of the States may be in like manner rent in twain, with all the stars on one side, and all the stripes on the other. (Loud applause.)"

18. John M'Clintock, *Discourse Delivered on the Day of the Funeral of President Lincoln*, reported by J. T. Butts (New York: J. M. Bradstreet & Son, 1865), 28 ff.

19. Letter of C. C. North to G. R. Crooks, included in Crooks, *The Life and Letters*, 394 ff.

20. Letter of M'Clintock to James M'Cabe, June 1864, cited in Crooks, *Life and Letters*, 363.

11

Daniel L. Marsh
(1880–1968)

by Joanne Carlson Brown

It has been said that all men in their outlook on life develop either into Platonists or Aristotelians. President Marsh is one of those rare individuals who have learned to combine the idealism of Plato with the realism of Aristotle. He thinks like an idealist and carries out his ideals with the practicality of a realist.[1]

DANIEL L. MARSH was many things: a minister of God, a poet, a husband and father, a gardener, an eloquent public speaker, an idealist, a realist, an optimist, an author, an educator, and a man of great physical and moral strength who possessed a wonderful sense of humor. But Marsh favored one characterization given him—"the friendly President of a friendly University"[2]—and, indeed, this is how he is best remembered, as the man who "took a moldering collection of brownstones . . . in 1926 and built a multiversity,"[3] his beloved Boston University. Marsh's vision and his superb administrative skills propelled Boston University into the ranks of the country's top-rated universities. He demanded no less of the faculty, trustees, and students than he did from himself—dedication to the ideal of a united university and commitment to work for the reality of that ideal. Included in the ideal were not only freedom of thought but also the Methodist heritage of learning, virtue, and piety.

Marsh was born on a farm in West Newton, Pennsylvania, April 12, 1880. He attended the country school near his home and taught in the one-room school house when he was sixteen. He received his A.B., Phi Beta Kappa, from Northwestern University in 1906 and his A.M. from

DANIEL L. MARSH

Photo courtesy of Mugar Memorial Library, Boston University.

Garrett Biblical Institute in 1907. His mother had dedicated him to the ministry as a young boy and he fulfilled her desires, earning his S.T.B. in 1908 from Boston University School of Theology and entering the ministry in the Western Pennsylvania Conference of the Methodist Episcopal Church (MEC). Marsh served a suburban Pittsburgh church for five years before being chosen general superintendent of the MEC Union of Pittsburgh, a post he held for thirteen years with time out to serve as an army chaplain during World War I. During this time he was also editor of the conference newspaper, *The Pittsburgh Methodist*. It was his skilled management of these varied ministerial tasks which prompted Bishop Francis J. McConnell to nominate and urge Marsh to accept the presidency of Boston University. Marsh was elected to the presidency in December, 1925, and assumed his duties February 1, 1926, at the age of 46, one of the youngest college presidents at the time. Marsh retired in 1951 but remained active in the university community until he died in 1968.

The image which emerges from a study of Daniel Marsh is complex. He is often praised for his discipline and willingness to work. He is described as an optimist, a good friend, and a fair opponent who was always clear about where he stood on issues.[4] On the other hand, Marsh was also somewhat of an autocrat who demanded things be done his way. He stood firm in his opinions, even if they were unpopular. Whether one agreed with him or not there was no denying that Marsh was a superb administrator and a shrewd business person. These qualities helped him work the near-miracle of turning Boston University into a leading university. But it was Marsh as a person—his sense of humor, his physical and mental and spiritual strength, his love for "his" university, his uncompromising principles, and his optimism—which gave the institution its life.

Marsh's main accomplishment was the creation of a true university. He did this under less than favorable conditions. During Marsh's presidency the country and the world experienced four years of prosperity, eleven years of depression, five years of war, and five years of international tension. During this time, Marsh unified the university, coordinated its program, and fostered tremendous growth. Boston University went from a scattered conglomeration of four undergraduate colleges and five professional schools in 1926 to seven undergraduate colleges and eight graduate schools in 1951. The faculty grew during that time from 412 to 1,503, the student body from 9,687 to 34,202. In addition, Marsh was justifiably proud of the financial state of the university. When he assumed office, Boston University was $425,000 in debt, small by today's standards but a significant amount in 1926. The university was operating in the black when he retired.

These were not easy times for fiscal management, but Marsh showed

resourcefulness as a leader. For the university to survive during the depression, it had to find ways of conserving resources. Marsh made cuts
in the administrative expenses of the university and then turned to the
"family" of the university for help. He asked all employees of the university, administrators, faculty, and staff, to take a 5 percent wage reduction. He offered three reasons for his request. First, since all shared in
the university's affluence, all should take part in the university's economy in depression. Second, employment with reduced salaries was better than unemployment if the school were forced to close for lack of
funds. Third, no one class of persons should be an exception to the nationwide program of economy—"an economy that is good for the soul of
the nation."[5] No one was compelled to take the reduction; however,
Marsh was pleased to announce 100 percent participation in the plan.[6]

Marsh was probably proudest of the new university campus. He had
resisted pressure from a number of trustees to sell real estate the university held on the Charles River to maintain short-term solvency. He had a
vision of physical as well as spiritual unity, and by the time he retired the
campus on the Charles was nearly complete, providing the growing university with modern, adequate buildings and a physical reminder of
how far it had come.

And it had come far. Marsh, the architect of the university, saw as his
main task the transforming of the campus from diversity to a university.
When he assumed office, students were enrolled in nine well-separated
departments with no university consciousness. There was not even a
telephone listing for the university which included all the departments.
They were all listed separately.[7] His goal was to create a feeling of loyalty
to the university, not to the separate colleges. To do this he stressed
coordination and cooperation rather than competition. In the first article
he wrote for *Bostonian*, the Boston University alumni magazine, he
raised this theme.

> Since the whole is always greater than any of its parts, Boston University is
> greater than any single college or school connected with it. Not only greater
> than any of its parts, but greater even than the sum of them; for there is an
> unexplored reminder, a glorious plus, in the synthesizing unifying whole that
> is greater than the sum of the separate units. In algebraic terms, it may be
> expressed thus:
>
> BU = CLA + PAL + ST + LAW + MED + S.ED + SRE + GRAD + X[8]

He created general university bureaus and offices to institutionalize
this coordination, instituted general admissions, replaced departmental
placement services with an all-university placement service, instituted
The Hub as the yearbook for the entire university, created a General

Alumni Association, appointed the first full-time alumni secretary, and appointed roving professors. But institutional unity was not enough. There had to be spiritual unity as well. To that end Marsh designed an official flag for the university and wrote a university hymn designed to rally all the ideals and vision he cherished for his alma mater.

Marsh was a firm believer in coordination in education—not just among departments, although that was crucial, but among all aspects of education. In a speech delivered at the Emory University centennial, he outlined his program of coordination. He advocated coordination between universities and colleges through exchange programs. He felt it was essential to coordinate the high school program with the college one so there would be a logical sequential progression in one's education. There should be a coordination of the curriculum which would reflect the value of the liberal arts. Such coordination, under faculty control, would include the extracurricular activities as well, since quality education involved the whole person, not just the mind. Educational trends must be integrated with social trends—the university had to be coordinated with contemporary life if it were to remain a relevant member of the community. And the university must be coordinated with the church—not in a narrow sectarian way, but in sharing the values upon which each rested.[9]

Boston University grew because Marsh instilled these values in those around him. But the university also grew because Marsh was president. Being a college president was a calling for Marsh. In his reply to the induction address at his inauguration, he voiced this sentiment. "When I heard your voice calling me to this post, I heard it as the call to duty, as the voice of God; and so, hearing it, there was nothing for me to do but to accept."[10] He expected others to join in that sense of calling. In his inaugural address he issued his call to his community to join together to give reality to the ideals.

My task . . . is to preserve in a materialistic age the ideals which have made Boston University great. Comradeship in the common task is to be the keynote of my administration. . . . I shall expect from the trustees an unalloyed loyalty and unfailing support, and I know that I shall have it. . . . I regard my associates in the staff of administration and in the faculty as coworkers, to be loved, trusted, and leaned upon . . . I expect from the community—Boston and all New England—financial assistance.[11]

College presidents have to have many qualities which would enable them to live up to their calling and draw others into loyalty to that calling. He had a slight prejudice toward clergy. From history and contemporary examples he held that ministers made better presidents than any

other profession, all other things being equal.[12] This idea is also reflected
in the importance he placed on faith in God.

> A college president must have a great faith in God. A faith that will enable him
> to remain serene in the midst of calamity, and to maintain poise in the pres-
> ence of petty and pugnacious emotionalism, that will enable him to lift his
> eyes to the far horizon; to see the long course of history to which the single life
> and this vast work belong; to trust Him who encompasses all centuries and all
> places in His mind and purposes.[13]

But a president must also be practical. A college president had to
have life experiences, to be educated, to be an authority on college administration, and to be well-acquainted with social sciences. The president must also be versed in the theory *and* practice of business and have
a firm grasp of human behavior. In order to have power and influence, a
president had to possess certain characteristics: unimpeachable character, health, patience, fairness, common sense, a sense of humor, intellectual flexibility, loyalty, courage, tact, and an ability to speak
persuasively in public.[14] This was Marsh's ideal, and he gave reality to
that ideal in many ways.

Marsh was a very effective speaker, a consummate fund-raiser and
public relations person. These tasks were inseparable for him. Marsh
became one of the most widely quoted men in Boston while president of
Boston University, thus fulfilling a promise he had made to himself
when assuming office—that if he accomplished nothing else during his
term of office, the public would be made aware of Boston University.
Through his statements about education and society, his poetry and his
work for the church and community, the world heard of Boston University and understood what its president was aiming to achieve. Support
came to the university by way of financial gifts, students, and prayers.

Marsh was asked at the beginning of his term if he were going to be
an administrator or an educator:

> I told him [the reporter] I expected to be both; that I regarded a University
> president as an administrative-educator, and an educational-administrator;
> that I conceived of an administrator as one who could get all parts of a complex
> machine to work together harmoniously for the accomplishment of the ma-
> chine's purpose, and the purpose of the University was education.[15]

Marsh's theories and practices of education also contributed to his
success at Boston. He often used his linguistic skills to bring home a
point about the nature of education.

What is education? I believe we can still find the best answer in the etymology of the term. Our word comes, as you know, from two Latin words, *e*, meaning "out," plus *ducere*, "to lead"—to lead out. Into this old definition it is my purpose to put new meaning. It used to be thought that education consisted in leading out the different mental faculties, such as memory, imagination, reason. But if mental psychology has taught us anything, it is that we are unitary beings—we are one self. Therefore, I am thinking of it as the leading out of the whole individual into a personality. Except a man be born again he cannot see the kingdom of education. Vivifying education does not come by knowledge alone, nor by experience alone, but by knowledge, observation, reflection *and* experience.[16]

This "leading out" theme is a prominent one in all his writings. Education leads one out into a full personality where one is at home with self and the world—the physical world, the world of people and the world of thought. One is a full participant in this world—an actor, not a passive recipient. And this is because of the transforming nature of education. It not only gives one certain skills and knowledge and facts; its true value is that it trains the mind to think.[17] Marsh did not believe in the ivory tower idea of college. Higher education was not time away from the real world, but a time for passionate engagement in the world with its myriad problems and possibilities. One refrains from the "work" of the world in order to pick up clues which will guide one in the quest of Marsh's "full-orbed" education, a process which lasts a lifetime. Education must never be aloof from life, it becomes routine, bookish, anemic. But life must never be aloof from education—from "vital intelligence"— for then it becomes mechanical, inhuman, and dull. For Marsh, education was the very essence of creative living.[18] To that end Marsh asserted that Boston University stood for a liberal and useful education.

We sponsor a scholarship whose results are not valued for their own sake nor for the sake of their utility to the individual, but for the sake of their service to the community,—a scholarship whose devotees regard themselves as custodians of a sacred trust for the benefit of the nation and the whole wide world. . . . We aim at an education that makes a living and that makes life worth living.[19]

The university must never be allowed to forget its purpose and becomes an entity for its own sake, cranking out uniform "products," and concerned for its own preservation rather than true education.

In education, the danger always is to mistake the shell for the kernel, to make the school a place of formal discipline through chosen materials instead of a guide and inspiration to creative living; to become so absorbed with curriculum, and research, and honors, and institutional prestige as to forget that if we are to save and heal and fortify the social order we must give every individual the opportunity to think, the stimulation to think, the materials with which to think constructively. The educational institution was made for the youth and maiden, not the youth and maiden for the institution. Not the institution, but life itself is the hope of the world. Schools and books and labs and all other products of the intellectual life must minister life.[20]

As much as Marsh promoted Boston University the institution, he did not forget why the university existed—to provide an education to people who would use it to improve the world in which they lived.

Marsh was frustrated by those who misused the idea of education or dismissed its value to society. Marsh believed that education shaped the very core of society and thus was society's best weapon for defending its values. To Marsh democracy as a form of government was impossible without free (in all sense of the word) education.

Many people get wrought up over what they call "subversive influences" and "subversive activities." The thing that the fascist or the communist is most afraid of is unregimented education. I wish our victims of communist-phobia could understand that you cannot kill an idea by damning, or imprisoning, or shooting somebody who holds it. The way to get rid of an idea is to supplant it with a better one. The surest way to disseminate the right idea is by education.[21]

Marsh believed all people should be able to obtain an education no matter what class they belonged to or what the economic times. It was society's duty to ensure that all worthy students are able to secure an education. To that end he fought hard for federal government aid to colleges during the depression. Marsh was chosen by the Association of American Colleges to be its legislative representative. He took its proposal for federal aid to private colleges and universities to Washington and lobbied for its passage. The association was making four requests: (1) work-study; (2) low-interest refinancing loans to institutions; (3) student loans; and (4) low-interest building loans.[22] While not all goals were achieved in 1935, they have become part of the fabric of government-school relationships since.

Education had to be free not only in the financial sense but also in the academic sense. Marsh firmly believed in and fought for academic freedom, which meant that each professor or student is free

to seek the truth in his own way, to form his own opinions, to arrive at his own conclusions, and to announce his own convictions. He is not to be limited by patented dogma, fainthearted consideration, inherited tradition, or acquired prejudices. He does not need to bend the knees to error, not to fawn before flattery nor to cringe before denunciation.[23]

For Marsh, academic freedom was not an end in itself; rather it was a means to an end. The end was the aim of all education—the discovery of truth. But this freedom was not only a right, but a responsibility to be exercised in a manner which contributes to society. And it was religion which most guided this responsible use of education.

Religion pioneered education in all centuries. It has established the schools and fostered the atmosphere where learning could take place. But more importantly to Marsh religion has given education a sense of responsibility. "It [religion] requires us to make our quest of truth in a spirit of affirmation rather than of negation, of reverence rather than irreverence."[24] It does this through enabling synthesis. It shows that all truth is one. Religion insists that education is not enough in itself without a religious sense of the "incommensurate value of human personality."[25]

To illustrate his understanding that religion occupied the central place in higher education, Marsh had the chapel placed in the center of the Charles River campus to serve as its focal point. He allowed the trustees to name the chapel after him because it symbolized the ideals for which he had worked so hard—the unity of the university and the centrality of religion in education. Inscribed in the narthex of the chapel are his words: "Let this Chapel at the center of the University campus signify forever the centrality both of intellectual and experimental religion in education and also of devotion to God's righteous rule in human lives."

Despite his emphasis on religion in education, Marsh never advocated one religion over another and made it very clear that proselytizing went against the spirit of Boston University.

> We hope that nobody at Boston University will be ambitious to proselytize believers from one faith to another; but at the same time we earnestly hope that the quest for truth in every classroom will be conducted in such a spirit of reverence rather than of irreverence, of affirmation rather than negation, that the Jew will be a better Jew, the Catholic a better Catholic, the Unitarian a better Unitarian, the Methodist a better Methodist, and all of them better citizens because they have been students at Boston University.[26]

Marsh based his assertions on the clause on religious freedom in the Boston University charter.[27]

This is not to say that Marsh downplayed the Methodist connection of Boston University. In fact, he held it as a major benefit of the university. He was proud that Methodist evangelistic passion revived interest in education. The growing church needed trained leadership, both clergy and lay, and established educational institutions which would combine the two values most important for the growth of church and society—religion and education.[28] Marsh encouraged Methodists to attend Methodist colleges *and* graduate schools. He advocated an educated ministry and argued against the 1939 decision to allow lay and supply pastors to administer communion.

Education, as Marsh well knew, depended heavily upon teachers for its quality. Marsh saw his job as an administrator as that of attracting the best teachers and then fostering an atmosphere where they would be encouraged to do their best work.

> The successful president keeps his faculties working in their proper places, while at the same time he works for the unity of his organization. He has such singleness of purpose, so believes in his institution, and is so consecrated to its service, that he creates an *esprit de corps* that causes the college to operate smoothly and effectively. The faculty members are so encouraged and inspired that only seldom does a professor lose his sense of calling and cease to be an evangelist for the subject he teaches.[29]

This is his view of the teacher—an evangelist for the subject—one who loves the subject so much that that love and enthusiasm spreads to the students. This teacher is not a tyrant, but one who sees the student as a traveling companion on the path to truth who looks for guidance and support. For Marsh the ideal teacher was

> one who secures the student's cooperation in the great business of self-education. He will free the student from arbitrary requirements that handicap him in forming a programme appropriate to his needs. He will decentralize responsibility for learning, skillfully shifting it from teacher to learner.[30]

Marsh recognized the power teachers have over students and encouraged its proper use. It is a gentle, subtle power which encourages but never directs. Marsh insisted his professors have strong academic credentials and excellence in classroom teaching. But he also insisted on a moral quality in his professors. He wanted each of his teachers to have an experiential knowledge of religion as well as an intellectual knowledge of the subjects to be taught. Marsh asserted, "We have no place in our organization for one who is off-color in a moral way, or who can sneer at and ridicule that which is right."[31] Marsh would never require a specific creed of his teachers, but he did demand religious values and expected them to lead a moral life. He himself provided an example for the university. In keeping with the conventional piety of the time he did not smoke or drink and could not believe anyone connected with Boston University would either.

But Marsh's example of the moral life went beyond personal habits. He was a Boston personalist by training with Borden Parker Bowne and by predilection. He was a strong proponent of the Social Gospel and believed in the idea of the dignity of all work. To Marsh persons needed to be conscious that no matter what their area of work, they were co-workers with God. This knowledge would give workers a sense of dignity and enable them to make a life as well as a living.[32] People had to be willing to work to alleviate not only the symptoms of society's wrongs of hunger, poverty, drunkenness—but also to work to eliminate the causes of injustices of every sort. "In attacking the cause of poverty, the builders of the Kingdom of God will have to interest themselves in wages, sickness, unemployment, desertion or non-support, domestic difficulties, delinquency, and many other causes."[33] The church had to concern itself with justice. It should be directing the great social movements of the day. The church must reach up toward God in worship, but should not fail to reach out toward humanity in service.[34] Evangelism is not only to proclaim certain principles to certain groups,

> but to organize all of life around the principles enunciated by Jesus—the sacredness of personality, the superiority of human rights over property rights, the brotherhood of man, the Golden Rule, fair play, justice, faith in God and man, love as the strongest bond between men and nations.[35]

To this end the church had to be involved in the labor movement. If the church abandoned labor, it would be taken over by "materialistic philosophy." He supported the Interchurch World Movement's investigation of the steel strike in 1919 as a way of gaining the confidence of the workers that the church was committed to bettering their conditions. The church must work to transform individuals who will in turn transform their society. "Before we can have a Utopia we must have Utopians. The Church must produce men and women who represent the attitude and the consequent behavior of Jesus Christ."[36] Marsh worked and wrote against all forms of prejudice—against women, blacks, Jews, Roman Catholics, and immigrants. He pushed for assimilation of immigrants. He wanted a homogeneous society which was Americanized. He strongly asserted freedom of speech, of press, and assembly for all—even those with whom he disagreed. He asserted that one could be a Christian and a radical. But he condemned bolshevism as being false to the ideals for which it purported to stand—it was the arch-crime against democracy.[37]

Marsh felt that America was "the Messiah of nations." It had a special mission to be the preserver of freedom. He compared it to Israel of old. It must protect itself from the enemies of democracy, which is the best form of government since religion is at its foundation. The enemies of democracy for Marsh were: luxury of wealth, industrial and group selfishness, intolerance, and the notion that physical science has given its verdict in favor of violence and against social justice.[38]

True to his convictions, Marsh was a pacifist. He promoted the League of Nations and attempted to revive the idea in 1939 as the world drifted toward yet another World War. He was against drafting eighteen- and nineteen-year-olds in the 1940s and coauthored a resolution from the National Association of Schools and Colleges of the Methodist Church opposing a compulsory draft for peace time.[39] Marsh worked for reconciliation after World War II, strongly supporting the creation of a United Nations with real powers. As early as the 1930s he was advocating disarmament. Marsh also argued for the creation of a Jewish state in Palestine in 1944.

Marsh had views on many other social issues as well. He was against the teacher's oath law proposed in 1934. He felt that evolution was not incompatible with the Bible of Christianity. He felt, in fact, that it was part of God's plan because the laws of nature are God's mind. But he rejected Social Darwinism. Marsh advocated the historical criticism of the Bible, supporting Shailer Matthew's emphasis on the search for the historical Jesus and his assertion that the Resurrection was demonstrated by science—not chemistry or biology, but the only science that has anything to do with it—the science of history.[40] Marsh supported Prohibition, abhorred jazz, and believed that because of television, "we are destined to have a nation of morons."[41]

Marsh was an active and devoted Methodist. He was a Wesleyan who upheld the importance of faith and holy living. "The genius of Methodism is found in its insistence that religion does not consist in any mere intellectual assent to creedal dogma, but in experience and life."[42] He firmly believed that Methodism was one of the great forces of the world—all due to Wesley's lead.[43] Marsh wrote into the *Discipline* of the MEC certain provisions concerning city society organizations, provisions that gave the work of church unions a new standing.[44] He was a powerful figure and at times even a "king maker" in the General Conferences from 1916 to 1948, including the Uniting Conference in 1939. Marsh was a strong supporter of the Epworth League, which he saw as a self-help organization. In it young people would learn by doing while being imbued with an intelligent and vital piety.[45] And he was a member of the Methodist Board of Education from 1929 to 1952.

Marsh's social and church opinions were part and parcel of the ideals which shaped a great educational institution. For Marsh, who as a personalist could not compartmentalize his life, all thoughts and experiences are directed to the same goal—quality of life. Marsh saw this personalism as his guiding force and that of Boston University.

> The driving power that is to take the good ship Boston University across educational seas and land it safely at the port of Unselfish Service, is Personalism, or Personalistic Idealism. . . . Personalism views the whole universe as a society of persons. It takes into consideration the sum total of experience. Its sovereign test of every experience is, What kind of person will this make? It estimates all things in terms of their efforts upon persons. By this standard must be judged educational processes, industrial relations, social contracts, political movements, and all the rest. Its dominant principle is the dependence of individual culture upon the moral and spiritual values.[46]

Marsh lived and ran "his" university according to these principles. He guided Boston University for twenty-five years through troubled times and succeeded in creating a true university where freedom and responsibility were ideals held up for all to strive toward. When he retired in 1951 many thought he had worked a near-miracle. He was named chancellor for life of the university by the trustees. Marsh was the right man for the job at the time he was called, but it was also the right time for him to retire. A new type of leadership was needed. Marsh, somewhat autocratic in his administration, made the decisions and then sought approval based on the loyalty he demanded. He made sure he was never opposed by using politics and persuasion. He saw what was needed and he did it. For that Boston University, and indeed society, should be grateful. He guided the university with skill and with love. He sought to instill ideals into a world that seemed to have forgotten to look beyond itself. He used all of his varied gifts to give reality to those ideals. Perhaps this is best expressed in the last stanza of Boston University hymn he wrote as one way to unite the university:

> *O Vision Splendid! Thine the art*
> *To make all visions real:*
> *The call to serve with all the heart*
> *Is blazoned on thy seal.*
> *O Boston University,*
> *O Alma Mater true,*
> *We live to give reality*
> *To Ideals of B.U.*[47]

NOTES

1. Resolution presented to President Marsh by faculty senate, Boston University, 7 Dec. 1950, written by Prof. Samuel M. Waxman. Marsh Archives, Boston University.

2. Silver Anniversary Press Book, Marsh Archives, Boston University, 5.

3. *Time* (31 May 1968): 62.

4. *The Pittsburgh Methodist* 16 (April–June 1926): 2.

5. *Bostonia* (January 1933): 3–4.

6. *Bostonia* (October 1932): 4.

7. *Bostonia* (1966): 7.

8. *Bostonia* (October 1926): 4 n.8. The initials stand for the various schools and departments at the time: CLA—College of Liberal Arts, X—Christ, etc.

9. Daniel L. Marsh, "Co-ordination: A Proper Watchword for the University of Tomorrow," *School and Society* 45 (13 Feb. 1937).

10. *Bostonia* (July 1926): 67.

11. *Bostonia* (July 1926): 68.

12. Marsh, "College Administration—A Science and an Art," delivered at Cornell College, 25 Apr. 1944, Marsh Archives, Boston University, 3–4.

13. Marsh, presidential address to the Association of American Colleges, reprinted in *Boston University News*, 30 Jan. 1951, 2.

14. Marsh, presidential address, 2.

15. Marsh, *Annual Report*, 1950. Marsh Archives, Boston University.

16. *Bostonia* (1934): 7.

17. Marsh, *The Youth of America* (Cincinnati: Methodist Book Concern, 1923), 37.

18. *Bostonia* (1938): 7.

19. *Bostonia* (July 1926): 75.

20. *Bostonia* (1938): 6.

21. Marsh, *The American Canon* (New York: Abingdon Press, 1939), 79.

22. Marsh, "Federal Government Aid to Colleges Report," Report 5, *Educational Association of the Methodist Episcopal Church*, 1935, 52.

23. Marsh, "Religion in Education in a Time of Change," Methodist Division of Higher Education (5 Jan. 1962), pamphlet no. 1017-H.E., 7.

24. Marsh, *Charm of the Chapel* (Boston: Boston University Press, 1950), 37.

25. Marsh, *Chapel*, 15.

26. Marsh, *Traditions of Boston University* (Boston: Boston University Press, 1945), 9.

27. "No instructor of said university shall ever be required by the trustees to profess any particular religious opinions as a test of office, and no student shall be refused admission to, or denied any of the privileges, honors or degrees of said university on account of the religious opinions which he may entertain; but this section shall not apply to the Theological Department of said university." Cited in Richard Morgan Cameron, *Boston University School of Theology*, 1839–1968 (Boston: BUST, 1968), 19.

28. Marsh, "Methodist Education in Retrospect," *Forward Together*, National Methodist Educational Conference, 1936.

29. Marsh, "College Administration—A Science and an Art," 7–8.

30. *President's Report*, 1933, Marsh Archives, Boston University, 29.

31. Marsh, "Higher Education Plus the Highest Education," 15, Baccalaureate Sermon, Boston University, June 1927, Marsh Archives, Boston University.

32. Marsh, *The Youth of America*, 97.

33. Marsh, *Youth*, 183.

34. Marsh, *The Faith of the People's Poet* (Indianapolis: Bobbs-Merrill, 1920), 209.

35. Marsh, *The Rights of Young Methodists* (Cincinnati: Methodist Book Concern, 1924), 75.

36. Marsh, *Youth*, 109.

37. Marsh, *Youth*, 146, 150.

38. Marsh, *The American Canon*, 30, 155.

39. Minutes of the National Association of Schools and Colleges of the Methodist Church (January 1945): 7.

40. Marsh, *The Faith of the People's Poet*, 195.

41. *Time* (31 May 1968): 62.

42. Marsh, "We Learn to Do By Doing," *The Epworth Herald* (14 May 1932): 467.

43. Marsh, *Rights of Young Methodists*, 83.

44. Francis J. McConnell, *Pittsburgh Methodist* (April–June 1926): 7.

45. Marsh, *The Rights of Young Methodists, passim*.

46. *Bostonia* (July 1926): 80–81.

47. Marsh, *Traditions of Boston University*, 50–51.

12

W. W. Orwig
(1810–1889)

by Charles Yrigoyen, Jr.

I T IS IMPOSSIBLE to write a history of the Evangelical Association without reference to William W. Orwig. He was one of its foremost leaders in the nineteenth century. There was hardly a major area of his church's life in which he was not active. His influence and labors were particularly evident in the denomination's publishing operations, missions, and higher education.

Orwig was born on September 25, 1810, near the town of Orwigsburg, Schuylkill County, Pennsylvania. His family was of German descent. Orwig's great-grandfather migrated from Germany in the eighteenth century. Although it is difficult to trace the religious background of his family, there is little doubt that his parents were pious and godly people. Jacob Albright, the founder of the Evangelical Association, enjoyed the hospitality of their home on more than one occasion.[1]

In 1815 Orwig's parents moved the family to Buffalo Valley, Union County, in central Pennsylvania. On June 4, 1826, while attending a camp meeting with his friend, Daniel Brickley, Orwig experienced conversion and afterward became convinced that he should become a preacher.[2] Two years later, on June 2, 1828, at nearby New Berlin, Pennsylvania, he was received into the ministry of the Eastern Conference of the Evangelical Association by Bishop John Seybert. He was appointed to the Center Circuit and in the years following served the Lebanon, York, and Schuylkill circuits, all in Pennsylvania.[3]

In 1833, at the age of 23, Orwig was elected presiding elder (superintendent) of the Zion District of the Eastern Conference. Three years later he was placed in charge of the New York District. After only three months in New York, Orwig was elected by the General Conference to

W. W. ORWIG

Photo courtesy of United Methodist Commission on Archives and History.

be the church's book agent and editor of *Der Christliche Botschafter*, the denomination's newspaper founded in 1836.[4] He took up his duties at the publishing headquarters in New Berlin, Pennsylvania, in 1837.

Orwig returned to the pastorate in 1843 and served churches in York and Baltimore in the West Pennsylvania Conference. In 1849 he again assumed the editorship of *Der Christliche Botschafter*, a position he held until 1854 when the publishing house was relocated to Cleveland, Ohio.[5] Orwig did not move with the publishing operations. Instead, he settled in Carlisle, Pennsylvania, where he spent two years writing a history of the Evangelical Association. He published a number of other volumes during his lifetime, including a catechism, a work on pastoral theology, and an extensive treatment of sanctification and Christian perfection.[6]

In 1856 Orwig became principal of Union Seminary, one of the earliest educational institutions related to the Evangelical Association. In the nineteenth century "seminary" was the name given to many different types of educational institutions, including those presently called secondary schools and colleges. After three years as principal of Union Seminary, Orwig felt it best to demote himself to assistant principal so that his popular and competent colleague, Francis Hendricks, could become the chief executive of the school.[7]

The General Conference of the Evangelical Association meeting in Naperville, Illinois, in October, 1859, elected Orwig to the episcopacy. At the end of his four-year term he was not re-elected bishop. He was chosen again, however, to edit *Der Christliche Botschafter* from 1863 to 1869. Thereafter, Orwig was treasurer of the denomination's missionary society for four years and ended his active ministry as a pastor and presiding elder in the Erie Conference of the Evangelical Association.[8]

Following his death on May 29, 1889, Orwig was eulogized by many in his church. In a memorial address Bishop Rudolph Dubs praised Orwig's accomplishments and importance. He said that Orwig "was, in his day, the most progressive leader in our church. . . . The Evangelical Association never had a greater or a better man. He was one of the 'founders' of our church. No one else did more for the establishment and building up of our church."[9]

Orwig was especially appreciated for his efforts on behalf of higher education. Shortly after Orwig's death one writer noted his contribution in that area:

He was one of the chief champions of the cause of education in our church, and probably did as much, if not more than any other, to initiate and develop it among us. He advocated it strongly, in the days when the cause was anything but popular among our people, and when many saw little good and much evil in higher institutions of learning. But he had strong convictions upon this subject, and had the courage to promulgate and advocate them. He was ahead of his generation upon this point. Comparatively few were at first in sympathy with his ideas, but he won a great victory with his mighty pen, and the institutions of learning in our church to-day owe a great debt to him.[10]

Like other Protestant churches in America in the earlier nineteenth century, the Evangelical Association experienced considerable controversy regarding higher education for its members and its preachers, especially the latter.

Many believed that education would generate serious problems for the church. Formal learning would destroy piety, weaken an individual's spiritual life, and hinder experiential religion. In the case of preachers, their education would create a chasm between the pulpit and the pew. Preaching by educated young men might be too sophisticated and complicated for the vast majority in a congregation to understand. Furthermore, the strongest opposition to Evangelical Association founder Jacob Albright and his colleagues came from persons who were generally well-educated. Academic training was, therefore, regarded at least with great suspicion.[11]

On the other hand, there were those who held that the church was under obligation to give consideration to the intellectual and cultural needs of its members. They were concerned that other denominations might surpass them in providing for the cultural and educational requirements of their people, thereby attracting Evangelical Association members and preachers to other churches. To some, the very existence of the Sunday school, the Evangelical Association catechism, and its publishing house and periodicals were indications that the church was prepared for the next logical step, namely, the establishment of its own educational institutions. They believed that educated preachers would not weaken the church but strengthen it. Finally, they were afraid that their most promising preachers, who on their own initiative attended the schools of other denominations, might be enticed to leave their church if it treated as suspect the person who had received college training.[12]

In the two decades beginning with 1840 the dispute over the role of higher education and the church reached a critical point in the Evangelical Association. Orwig assessed the situation in 1841 as follows:

As to a liberal education and higher institutions of learning, we can only say that they were still too much underrated and neglected by us as a denomination; although some of our members learned to see and feel their importance. The time evidently had not yet arrived for the Association to establish higher institutions of learning; nevertheless, more might certainly have been done for the promotion of science and general culture, than really was done. The great abuse of learning, and of higher literary institutions, both in Europe and America, with its consequent injurious results, had filled many of our members, not only with indifference, but even with prejudices against every thing of the kind; and that the abuse of a good cause never proves anything against the cause itself, these friends did not take into consideration. . . . as the Association was frequently charged with being, as a body, hostile to learning and literary institutions, we were, at length, compelled to express ourselves in public on this subject.[13]

The 1843 General Conference of the Evangelical Association declared that the church was unjustly charged with despising education and institutions of learning, especially for its preachers. A spiritually qualified preacher who also possessed a good education could accomplish much more for God than the "unlearned man, though he possess the same measure of divine unction and grace."[14] Although it was not yet advocating college training for its clergy, the General Conference recommended to all candidates for its ministry that they "take proper measures to store their minds with as large an amount of useful information, as they possibly can, or to endeavor to become *learned* and *literary men,* who have also the unction of the Holy Ghost."[15]

The Evangelical Association in 1843 was plotting a course which not only recognized the importance of higher education for its laity and preachers, but which would also result in the organization of its own institutions of learning. While acknowledging that his church was not yet prepared to establish such schools in 1843, Orwig commended a proper plan of study for preachers and expressed his hope that

> although we think highly of private study and self-made men, yet we do not wish to be understood, as if we regarded higher institutions as superfluous and useless—far from it, such institutions, provided they are conducted by pious men, are unquestionably a great blessing to the Church and to the world; for, if there were no learned, pious men, who were educated in such institutions, our holy religion would not have been defended so triumphantly and spread so victoriously. . . .[16]

In the years following the 1843 General Conference the number of those advocating an academically trained ministry and higher education increased. Among the most influential was John Dreisbach (1789–1871), one of the church's most effective and revered leaders. Dreisbach argued that while a classical education was not a necessity for a preacher, it certainly was not a disadvantage. In fact, he said, "human learning, sanctified by the Spirit of God . . . [was] highly advantageous to a minister for greater usefulness in his calling."[17]

When the General Conference of 1847 met in New Berlin, Pennsylvania, Dreisbach presented the following motion:

> Resolved, that with the consent of the majority of our church members there should be established a nursery of general knowledge, and that this institution be connected with manual labor, in order to afford the scholars an opportunity for defraying the expense of their instruction, boarding, etc.[18]

The vagueness of Dreisbach's proposal and lingering apprehension about the worth of education led to its defeat by the membership. This ended the first effort of the Evangelical Association to found an educational institution for its constituency.[19] Those who favored higher education, however, including Orwig, perhaps its foremost proponent, were not dissuaded. Their determination was voiced in one of the denomination's newspapers:

> All that we have to do is to make a second effort. And it is altogether likely that the first one did more for the cause of education than a great many are aware of. We believe that there are many in the Evangelical Association that voted against the "Mental Nursery" who since have seen the folly of their conduct, and would now pursue a different course. . . . We may look in any direction we please, and see better times ahead . . . let us unite in a solid phalanx, and make use of all the legal and sanctified [means] within our reach, and the cause must advance.[20]

There were two efforts to establish schools by annual conferences in the Evangelical Association. The Pittsburgh Conference, which was organized in 1852, established Albright Seminary in Berlin, Somerset County, Pennsylvania, in 1853. Financial problems and other difficulties, however, raised questions about its continued existence. The Ohio Conference decided to found a school in 1855 at Greensburg, Ohio. Officials of the Pittsburgh Conference welcomed the opportunity to close the financially plagued Albright Seminary and to merge it with the newly begun Greensburg Seminary. In 1865 this school, too, was forced to close because it lacked suitable financial support.[21]

In the meantime, the West Pennsylvania Conference under Orwig's leadership instituted an Education Society and laid plans for an institution of higher learning at New Berlin. The optimism of the society was communicated in the following statement published in 1851:

> The cause of education is one of so much importance, and is so extensively appreciated in the present age, that no intelligent Christian can, with safety to his religious character, take a stand against it.

The "Education Society of the West Pa. Conference," is still as much convinced as ever, of the propriety and the advantages of education. And in view
of the Society's usefulness in the past, and its prospects for the future, the
members feel encouraged to continue their efforts with renewed energy for
the promotion of education.[22]

When it was decided to move the Evangelical Association publishing
headquarters from New Berlin to Cleveland in 1854, Orwig urged the
West Pennsylvania and East Pennsylvania annual conferences to purchase the vacated property, which, he stated, "might easily be arranged
for an academy or seminary of learning."[23] Orwig's proposal was favorably received and the raising of funds was begun for a new school. Orwig was elected a trustee of the proposed institution and appointed one
of two agents to collect funds for it. Speaking as one of the solicitors,
Orwig reported to the church's constituency:

Now we do hope that our friends, generally, will wake up to this matter
and at once resolve to make a mighty effort for the consummation of the project. We do not know that they could leave a better legacy or heritage to their
children and posterity than a good and permanent Institution of Learning; for
certainly knowledge is better and of vastly more value than riches. . . . The
benefits of having a good Institution of Learning within our reach; to educate
our sons and daughters, are, in our estimation of much more moment, than
the ability to distribute farms and houses, or any kind of perishable property,
among them.[24]

In 1855, the trustees elected Orwig the president of their board and
principal of the institution, to be called Union Seminary (so named because it was to be in Union County, Pennsylvania). Fund-raising for the
new school was moving ahead. Orwig was reluctant to accept the position of chief administrative officer but finally consented after five months
of deliberation. Perhaps Orwig's hesitation may be accounted for by the
modest estimate of his intellectual abilities by himself and others. One
contemporary wrote of him: "His intellect does not seem to be of that
brilliant order which startles and amazes the world, although he is far
removed from being dull or slow."[25]

This assessment of Orwig's intellect may be somewhat misleading.
Although he may not have been much of an original thinker, he certainly
was a bright and thoughtful person. His writings attest to his sound
scholarly competence, insight, and ability to communicate. Furthermore, he felt sufficiently capable not only to serve as an administrator,
but also to occupy the chair of "moral science and the German language"
when the school opened.[26]

The formal opening of Union Seminary at New Berlin took place on

January 3, 1856. The first-year enrollment pleased Orwig and the school seemed to him to have a very useful and promising future. He continued to seek financial support from the people and churches of the Evangelical Association to ensure its permanent life.[27]

From its earliest days, Union Seminary enrolled both male and female students. Orwig is given credit for insisting on the importance of education for women as well as men. One historian of the Evangelical Association stated:

> It is tardy justice to say that *co-education* in the Evangelical Church owes its introduction to Bishop *W. W. Orwig,* one of the founders, and first President of Union Seminary, at New Berlin, Pennsylvania. . . . When this institution was projected, in 1854, the co-education of the sexes was still in its experimental stage, and strenuously opposed by many of the leading men of the Evangelical Church.
>
> Bishop Orwig was a man of broad and advanced views on this subject, and it is chiefly owing to his wise counsels that both sexes started on an equal educational footing in the scholastic history of the church.[28]

The second catalogue of the school, published in 1857, described its course of study: "the course of instruction in this institution embraces all the branches usually taught in seminaries and academies of the higher grade, adapted to prepare students for active business life, teaching, the study of a profession or for any class in college."[29] The curriculum included courses in English, mathematics, the natural sciences, the "mental sciences" (psychology, ethics, theology), Latin, Greek, German, and French. In 1857 Union Seminary opened a "normal department" for the training of teachers for public schools.[30]

Orwig led the infant school through its earliest years, doing his utmost to enlist qualified students, supervise proper instruction and orderly campus life, and guarantee its financial stability through endowment. The size of the student enrollment (264 by 1858), progress in the solicitation of funds, a religious revival at the school, and the founding of seminary literary societies in 1858 were signs of advancement to Orwig.[31]

On July 15, 1859, apparently feeling that it was to the advantage of the school for him to step aside as its principal, Orwig submitted his resignation to the trustees. The board accepted his desire to relinquish his position but realizing his value to the institution, and by his consent, elected him assistant principal. At the same meeting Orwig urged the board to explore making Union Seminary a college. He also accepted re-election as president of the board, a position he held for a few years thereafter.[32]

Orwig was elected a bishop of the Evangelical Association on October 17, 1859, at its General Conference in Naperville, Illinois. During the term of his episcopacy (1859–63) and after he remained an advocate for education in his church. Union Seminary, the school he had given so much of his energy to found, was rechartered in 1887 as Central Pennsylvania College. Today, after mergers with other institutions, the school continues as Albright College in Reading, Pennsylvania, one of the fine church-related liberal arts colleges of the United Methodist Church. It owes its life to many, not least of whom is William W. Orwig, a man with virtually no formal education himself. Yet he stands as one of the most prominent pioneers for higher education in the Evangelical Association.

NOTES

1. Rudolph Dubs, "Memorial Discourse," *Evangelical Messenger* (4 June 1889): 356.

2. A. Stapleton, *Annals of the Evangelical Association of North America* (Harrisburg, Penn.: Publishing House of the United Evangelical Church, 1900), 535.

3. Dubs, "Memorial Discourse," 356.

4. F. Wilbur Gingrich and Eugene H. Barth, *A History of Albright College* (Reading, Penn.: Albright College, 1956), 46.

5. "Our New Bishop," *Evangelical Messenger* (9 Dec. 1859): 196.

6. W. W. Orwig, *History of the Evangelical Association*, vol. 1 (Cleveland, Ohio: Charles Hammer, 1858). This volume was also published in German. This is a substantial volume and has been used by many historians as a basis for their work. Although apparently planned, Orwig never published a second volume of this work. W. W. Orwig, *Katechismus über die Hauptlehren der christlichen Religion, für die Jugend in der Evangelischen Gemeinschaft* (New Berlin, Penn.: J. C. Reissner, 1847). Several editions of this work were published. W. W. Orwig, *Pastoral-Theologie* (Cleveland, Ohio: Verlag der Evangelischen Gemeinschaft, 1877). W. W. Orwig, *Die Heilsfülle, Heiligung und Vollkommenheit nach Massgabe der Heiligen Schrift* (Cleveland, Ohio: Verlagshaus der Evangelischen Gemeinschaft, 1872).

7. Gingrich and Barth, *History*, 81.

8. Dubs, "Memorial Discourse," 356.

9. Dubs, "Memorial Discourse," 356.

10. Dubs, "Memorial Discourse," 360.

11. Gingrich and Barth, *History,* 15.

12. See Raymond W. Albright, *A History of the Evangelical Church* (Harrisburg, Penn.: The Evangelical Press, 1942), 211–18.

13. Orwig, *History of the Evangelical Association,* 1:336–37.

14. Orwig, *History of the Evangelical Association,* 1:368.

15. Orwig, *History of the Evangelical Association,* 1:368.

16. Orwig, *History of the Evangelical Association,* 1:369.

17. Orwig, *History of the Evangelical Association,* 1:395–96.

18. *Evangelical Messenger* (22 July 1848): 55.

19. Gingrich and Barth, *History,* 19–20.

20. *Evangelical Messenger* (8 Mar. 1850): 17.

21. Gingrich and Barth, *History,* 22–28.

22. *Evangelical Messenger* (22 May 1851): 38.

23. *Evangelical Messenger* (4 Jan. 1854): 4–5.

24. *Evangelical Messenger* (29 Mar. 1854): 52.

25. *Evangelical Messenger* (9 Dec. 1859): 196.

26. Gingrich and Barth, *History,* 48.

27. Gingrich and Barth, *History,* 53–56.

28. A. Stapleton, *Flashlights on Evangelical History* (York, Penn.: n.p., 1908), 144.

29. Gingrich and Barth, *History,* 58.

30. Gingrich and Barth, *History,* 59–60.

31. Gingrich and Barth, *History,* 64–67.

32. Gingrich and Barth, *History,* 81.

13

John Wesley Powell
(1834–1902)

by Charles E. Cole

M OST OF THOSE who contributed to church-related higher education in America were leaders in institutions. They were bishops, preachers, presidents, patrons, and teachers who founded schools, developed them, and maintained them. But some came out of church schools and colleges whose contributions were of a different kind, contributions by way of adding to the cultural base of knowledge and demonstrating that church-related college education had humanitarian values. Such a person was John Wesley Powell.

The Utes called him *Ka-pur-rats*—"arm off," and the fact that he lost most of his right arm while fighting as a warrior no doubt increased his esteem among many, whites no less than native Americans. He spoke Ute "passably well," according to one observer, and he spent much of his adult life trying to understand native Americans and to interpret their life and culture to a dominant white society. In his role as scientist he could be high-minded, "one of Plutarch's men," as a Smithsonian official called him, and at his home in Washington in 1878 the Cosmos Club was created by Powell and his peers Henry Adams, Clarence King, and John Hay.

But the scientist wanted something more than knowledge. A "born fighter" and a "gallant leader," as others called him, he knew how to implement knowledge in government policy and structures. Always his political designs were intended to carry out reforms for the sake of the human and the natural worlds alike. In these tasks he could be merrily engaged, humming his way down the corridors of his Washington domain, standing off congressional committees with reams of statistics, using his personal charm to calm the fears of both enemies and suppor-

185

A PHOTOGRAPH TAKEN BY JOHN K. HILLERS IN THE 1870s:
JOHN WESLEY POWELL POSES WITH TAU-GU, A PAIUTE LEADER.

Photo courtesy of National Anthropological Archives, Smithsonian Institution.

ters. His enduring legacy consists not only of the anthropological and geological enterprises that he began and that continue today, but of a vision of the land and of human society that still challenges us.[1]

Powell was born March 24, 1834, in Mount Morris, New York. His parents were English immigrants, and his father, Joseph Powell, had been a lay Methodist preacher in England. On arriving in the United States in 1830 he continued to preach while also working as a tailor and farmer. The mother taught her children the Bible, and at age five young "Wes," it was said, could recite the Gospels from memory. The family moved several times, and Powell spent part of his childhood in Jackson, Ohio, in the southern part of the state. There he first discovered the stimulation in observing nature by being tutored by a self-educated man who collected artifacts and read widely. When the family moved to southern Wisconsin in the 1840s, Powell met native Americans for the first time, Winnebagos who camped on the Powell farm. They had just returned from a meeting in Chicago where they had traded their territory to federal officials in exchange for goods.

The Powell family later moved to northern Illinois while Powell *pater* combined farming with preaching. As a young adult John Wesley spurned his father's entreaties to enter the ministry. The son displayed his interest in nature by hunting for fossils, collecting shells, and traveling the rivers of the upper Mississippi Valley by boat to explore the natural world. And although father and son disagreed on John Wesley's future profession, they agreed on another burning issue of the day: abolitionism. Joseph felt so strongly about the matter that he left the Methodist Episcopal Church in the 1840s while the denomination dithered over the slavery issue. He became a preacher in the newly formed "Wesleyan Methodist Connection," later the Wesleyan Methodist Church. His involvement was deep enough to lead him to become a trustee of Illinois Institute, forerunner of Wheaton College, a school founded by the Wesleyan Methodists.[2]

While John Wesley Powell waited to express his own hatred of slavery by fighting in the Civil War, he attended school on and off, spending some time at Illinois Institute and also at Illinois College in Jacksonville and at Oberlin. He never earned a degree. During periods when he was not in school himself, he taught school in the Midwest and lectured on the lyceum circuit. By the outbreak of the Civil War he had completed most of the tasks of young adulthood, except for marriage, a rite he carried out in 1861 after entering military service as a volunteer. Teaching himself engineering, he learned something about bridge-building and defense construction and eventually became the captain of the artillery unit that was engaged at Shiloh. Here he lost his right forearm during battle. He actually rose to the rank of lieutenant colonel, but "major" became his enduring sobriquet as a result of his military experience. His amputation did not end his participation in the war, and he returned to fight at Nashville and Vicksburg, cementing a relationship with U. S. Grant that would pay large dividends after the war.

Returning home after the war, he had to choose between a political post that offered monetary rewards and a position as a teacher of geology at Illinois Wesleyan University, Bloomington. For whatever reasons, he accepted the latter and taught at Illinois Wesleyan for two years. He accepted a post at Illinois State Normal University, also in Bloomington, in 1867, although he taught there while still on the faculty at Illinois Wesleyan.[3] More importantly, he immediately launched a proposal to obtain state financing for the Illinois Natural History Society. After he had lobbied for the measure and it passed, he was offered the position of curator, in addition to his teaching duties. Accepting this offer, he then used part of the museum's funds to underwrite his first field trip, officially called the "Rocky Mountain Exploring Expedition."

Powell developed what we now call "multiple funding" to a fine art. On this first trip he assembled the following resources: $500 from the Illinois History Museum, a requirement that each member of the party pay personal expenses, permission to draw supplies from the U.S. Army commissary, railroad passes from four lines, parcel transportation from American Express and Wells Fargo, a loan of scientific equipment from the Smithsonian Institution in return for topographic measurements, and in return for specimens, $500 from Illinois Industrial University and $100 from the Chicago Academy of Sciences. In order to obtain help from the U.S. Army, he traveled to Washington and made a personal request to U. S. Grant. There he also met Joseph Henry, secretary of the Smithsonian.

The party was assembled out of people Powell knew personally. Besides Powell, the twelve members of the party included Powell's wife, Emma; Powell's brother-in-law, A. H. Thompson, Bloomington school superintendent; and others who were amateur naturalists, including three college seniors. All were from Illinois. Each member of the party was styled with a scientific name, designating his or her duties. Mrs. Powell was called an "assistant ornithologist," for example, though her scientific credentials were nonexistent.[4] The purpose of the party was twofold: to make scientific measurements and collect specimens, and to investigate mineral deposits. The latter purpose belonged especially to Powell, in light of his geological expertise.

The party traveled to northern and central Colorado, climbed Pike's Peak, and explored the headwaters and first eighty miles of the Platte River. Powell collected minerals around Central City. Powell and his wife remained in Colorado for two months after the rest of the party returned to "the States." He wrote in the official report: "I spent the months of September and October in that region, making an exploration of the head-waters of the Colorado River (or the Grand, as the upper part of the river is called). As I hope to complete the exploration of that river next year, I defer this part of my report."[5]

Here then was the prototype for all the expeditions that Powell was to lead later: funds from several sources, including in-kind contributions and loans; contacts with government and other officials in Washington; a party made up of nonprofessionals whom Powell knew by personal contact; the statement of dual purposes, one scientific and the other practical; and the exploitation of one project for the next.

In 1868 Powell led a second expedition to Colorado. The party made the first ascent of Long's Peak, then explored the area from the head-waters of the Grand to the Green River.[6] Powell also encountered the Ute Indians on this trip. The trip lasted into the winter, giving Powell just enough time to return home and launch the expedition that made him famous: the first boat trip down the Colorado River through the Grand Canyon.

The country from the western boundary of Colorado down through the plateaus of southern Utah and northern Arizona remained virtually unknown in the 1860s. Only bits and pieces had been identified: Father Silvestre Velez de Escalante had crossed the Colorado near Glen Canyon in 1776. Lt. J. C. Ives of the U.S. Army had traveled up the Colorado as far as Diamond Creek, which is in the lower Grand Canyon, in 1857. There were Mormon settlements in the region, including Callville, on the lower river, and one participant in the famous Mountain Meadows massacre, J. D. Lee, had settled just below the Crossing of the Fathers.[7] Thus numerous parties had penetrated to the Colorado and had crossed it, but no known survivors had ridden the length of the river. A prospector named James White was dragged from the river at Callville in 1867, incoherent and vaguely claiming to have ridden a log raft through the Grand Canyon; but Powell interviewed White and was convinced he had not been the first through the Grand Canyon. Most historians have agreed with Powell.[8]

A more important context is that of the surveys then under way in the West. Clarence King launched his Fortieth Parallel Survey in 1867, mapping on either side of the Central Pacific and Union Pacific railroads from northern California to the Missouri River. Lt. George Wheeler began mapping large parts of the West in 1871. And F. V. Hayden led the United States Geological Survey of the Territories beginning in 1869. Thus Powell's trip down the Colorado was critically timed in that it staked out an area for more detailed exploration even though it fell within the scope of the other surveys, particularly the Wheeler survey.[9]

Powell had four boats made especially for the 1869 expedition. As before, he assembled a party out of those he knew, although this was to be an all-male party, made up of ten men (one dropped out before the run through the Grand Canyon). The party pushed off at Green River Station in Wyoming Territory on May 24, with enough supplies to last ten months. Although the upper part of the Green posed no serious navigational problems, one boat disintegrated against a rock in Lodore Canyon, providing the name Disaster Falls for the site. From then on the trip consisted of easy stretches, followed by rapids. The Major had from the start placed one boat in front to reconnoiter, and when rapids or falls appeared too dangerous to navigate, the boats would be pulled to the side and "lined" down, or a portage would be made. Sometimes the party stopped to rest for a day or two, and the men climbed out to take measurements at various points. On July 8, Powell and George Bradley, an army sergeant, climbed up "six or eight hundred feet," according to the Major. The one-armed explorer got stuck, unable to go up or down. Hanging on to the rock with his one hand, the Major found it barely possible to let go in order to take hold of the drawers that Bradley extended to him from above.

Marble Canyon proved to be one of the most difficult parts of the journey. Its sixty-five miles provided a mixture of great beauty and terrifying rapids, with the shiny sparkling surfaces of rock in the three-thousand-foot canyon exhilirating the men but the numerous cataracts forcing them to portage, line, and run hair-raising rapids. Afterward the Major realized they were just then on the threshold of the "great unknown," that part of the Colorado that was least known to whites. Their supplies dwindling, they passed the Little Colorado River and entered the Grand Canyon proper about August 10. First a chilling rain, then heat that rose to 125 degrees, afflicted them as they passed one rapid after another. Finally on August 27 they came to what Bradley called "the worst rapid yet seen," and the prospect caused three of the party to leave the next morning, climbing out to walk overland only to meet death at the hands of the Shivwits, a plateau tribe, a few days later. Powell and the rest of his party passed the rapids successfully and reached the Mormon settlements on August 29.[10]

Powell became a national hero as a result of his feat, and he capitalized on his momentum to launch another expedition down the Colorado two years later. This one was more amply financed and included a congressional grant of $10,000 for a "Geographical and Topographical Survey of the Colorado River of the West."[11] The Smithsonian supported the second trip, which really began a mapping of the Plateau region of southern Utah. Powell sent photographers into the field, and he initiated his language studies of the Utes and other native Americans of the region. Powell's work with the natives of the Great Basin and Colorado Plateau has been hailed as a "pioneering effort," partly because many of the people had never had contact with whites before 1870.[12] For a short time he served as a special commissioner to investigate policies toward native Americans, and it was in this connection that in 1874 he testified to Congress on his attitudes toward native Americans in the West.

> When white men are near them they pilfer a little from them and then the white men shoot them and the Indians retaliate. Troops are then sent in to subdue the Indians for troubles which might have sprung from slight causes and on affairs which might have been trivial we spend thousands of dollars. . . . I think that we ought to withdraw every soldier from that territory.

Powell testified that with inducements the native Americans would willingly move onto reservations, but he drew back from supporting the idea of citizen rights for them: "The Indian knows nothing about courts nor how to protect himself. He must be protected through his agent by some means or other until he learns more about his own rights."[13]

Supporting the conventional program for Indians to become farmers, Powell argued for building mills, roads, and houses, but he nevertheless argued for the development of initiative:

> We think nothing should be *given* to an Indian, to eat, or to wear, as a gratuity. We wish to establish on these agencies a system by which those who work shall be rewarded; that they shall work for their clothing and food. . . . When an Indian finds that he can get his dinner easier to work for you than to dig for roots *(sic)* he will work for you.[14]

This short stint as an Indian commissioner did not lead Powell into policy-making for native Americans, but he continued to write and speak on what he regarded as enlightened policies toward the Indians for the rest of his life. Powell's knowledge of Indian life was such that Spencer Baird, director of the Smithsonian, could tell a reporter that Powell knew "more about the live Indian than any other live man."[15] And in his 1878 report to Congress Powell offered a rationale for a serious effort to carry out research on Indians:

> The field of research is speedily narrowing because of the rapid change in the Indian population now in progress; all habits, customs, and opinions are fading away; even languages are disappearing; and in a very few years it will be impossible to study our North American Indians in their primitive condition except from recorded history.[16]

In Powell's mind, the practical problems of Indian administration merged with the scientific problem of understanding the historical relationships between the tribes. Merely to propose a reservation and training policy was not enough. Which tribes should be placed on reservations together? Powell knew that tribal names and geographical proximity were no clue to the historic relationships between the tribes. Language was the key, Powell thought, but to understand the linguistic affinities of tribes required more scientific research. And it was this congruence—or tension—of scientific and practical interests that led Powell to formulate the proposal for the formation of the Bureau of American Ethnology in 1878. The BAE came into being through a rider that Powell caused to be introduced to the bill creating the United States Geological Survey, a consolidation of the previous King, Wheeler, Hayden, and Powell surveys. Powell was named director of the BAE in 1879 and remained in that position until his death.

The purpose of the BAE combined the practical and scientific impulses that brought it into being. The wording of the authorizing legislation stated merely that an appropriation of $20,000 was granted to the BAE "for completing and preparing for publication the *Contributions to North American Ethnology*, under the Smithsonian Institution." Actually the bureau as Powell conceived it was to carry out ethnographic research "to produce results that would be of practical value in the administration of Indian affairs." But on a larger scale the bureau would carry out a "new ethnology," nothing less than a science of man. Thus the BAE combined politics and science.[17]

Linguistic research was the foundation of the bureau activities under Powell, but no aspect of primitive life escaped the army of scientists that Powell unleashed on the field. Ancient artifacts, observations of contemporary religion and culture, photographs—all were compiled on native Americans from the Arctic to the Isthmus of Panama. The research of these anthropologists was published in the annual reports of the BAE and in larger projects that took decades to complete.[18]

It is remarkable that Powell could generate such a program in ethnology while at the same time presiding over the work of the United States Geological Survey, which if anything commanded an even greater scope. The conditions that led to the formation of the USGS were, like the BAE, both natural and historical. By the middle of the nineteenth century the American plains had been called the "Great American Desert," a designation that appeared on maps and that appeared to be confirmed by the reports of Forty-niners and those on the Oregon Trail. But against this notion had been posited the opposite claim that "rain follows the plow." This popular idea emerged from the experience of settlers who crossed the Mississippi while applying the techniques of agriculture familiar in the East—techniques that depended very much on sufficient rainfall to produce crops and sustain livestock. And as these settlers moved past the 100th meridian, their notion that "rain follows the plow" seemed confirmed, because in the early 1870s climatic conditions allowed planting and grazing on the Great Plains just like that carried out by farmers in Ohio and Illinois.

Powell saw clearly that there was a difference in the lands beyond the 100th meridian. These received enough rainfall to grow crops, but not enough to sustain intense cultivation over long periods. He dubbed this the "subhumid" region to distinguish it from the true desert areas to the West and the wetter areas to the east. Powell argued that these subhumid areas required special measures, measures that might also be applied to the desert and mountainous areas on both sides of the Rockies. For one thing, he thought the basic land unit should be larger than the 160-acre quarter-section familiar to homesteaders: it should be 2,560 acres, or four sections, to allow settlers with only small amounts of capital to compete with large cattle companies. Each unit should have at least 20 acres of irrigable land within its boundaries. On better irrigated lands the homesteads could be 80 acres. Grazing lands should be divided by watersheds and not rectangular grids.

Powell also wanted administrative reforms to end inefficient and corrupt practices. Whereas land speculators regularly used dummy homestead entries to seize valuable timber and mineral lands, Powell urged classification of lands by the government with restrictions on their use. Against the practice of the General Land Office in handing over land-parceling surveys to private companies, Powell argued the government should do its own surveying. Powell even had the vision to suggest the cooperative unions could control pasture lands, an idea he had seen in practice by Mormons in Utah and Hispanics in New Mexico. These cooperatives would solve the problem of landowners controlling an entire stream by buying land at its head.[19]

Efforts at reform were aided by the return of dry conditions to the subhumid belt in the 1870s and 1880s. Grasshoppers stripped Kansas farmlands and cattle died in Wyoming.

Powell lobbied for adoption of his proposals through the National Academy of Sciences, which recommended several of them. Only the proposal to consolidate the surveys passed, however, a seemingly inauspicious start. The survey began with the appointment of a prestigious director—Clarence King, whom Henry Adams was to tout in his *Education* as having enough talent to be "the richest and most many-sided genius of his day." But the genius sought wealth, and after a year, King had resigned and Powell was named to succeed him. He began by expanding on King's conservative interpretation of policy. When the USGS

was established in 1879, it was charged with survey of the "national domain." Did this mean only public lands, or did it include private lands,
as well, since these carried many of the mineral resources that legislators
were interested in? King had interpreted the phrase to mean public
lands only, but Powell took the opposite view. To strengthen his hand,
he asked for and got an additional phrase in the enabling legislation:
"and to continue the preparation of a geological map of the United
States." By a sort of regressive logic, Powell and his office argued that a
geological map could only be prepared after topographical surveying.
Thus the addition of a seemingly innocuous phrase gave the USGS the
authority it needed to pursue aggressively a program that encompassed
the entire United States.

For the next decade Powell received ever greater appropriations for
the survey. He began to map the United States, a task that he originally
estimated would require 24 years and $18 million. (Today the USGS is
still engaged in producing the maps at the scale that Powell specified.)[20]
And when the severe winter of 1886 and drouths in following years dev-
astated the cattle industry and much of the farmland of the subhumid
belt, Powell again took up the cause of land classification and water al-
location that had been raised in the 1878 *Arid Lands* report. At first he
received the support of western congressmen, and an Irrigation Survey
was passed in 1888. But Powell made the mistake of taking the careful
scientific approach to the problem instead of the fast pragmatic one. He
wanted to complete the topographical mapping of the western region,
then make a survey of reservoir sites, canals, and the like. But when his
office began designating reservoir sites, speculators clamored for the
land adjacent to the areas. The commissioner of the General Land Office
then closed all public lands until all the sites could be designated. A
natural uproar followed, since land speculation and western development were virtually synonymous. The congressmen who had hitherto
supported Powell then saw that his leisurely methods of surveying
would take years, and they began to slash the Major's budget and demand line-item appropriations.

Powell, increasingly in pain from his amputated arm and realizing his
projects could not succeed politically, resigned from the USGS in 1894.
He continued to decline in health throughout the 1890s, even though he
held the directorship of the BAE until his death in 1902.

Any assessment of Powell's contribution to church-related higher education must take into account the fact that Powell was not an orthodox
Methodist in his adult life. He apparently did not worship regularly, and
during his river voyages he did not observe Sunday rest, an omission
that offended some of his party. He smoked a pipe and cigars, he played
billiards, and though he could quote the Scripture while making philo-

sophical arguments and even sing revival hymns on occasion, these seemed to be vestiges of the past for him, not signs of personal piety.

Intellectually, he understood religion as part of the mythologic phase of human development. He could accept religion in primitives, but it seems safe to say that science was Powell's religion, and intellect was the key to understanding ultimate reality. Late in his life he wrote that science acted on religion, not to destroy it, but to purify it. And, he added, science is not in conflict with religion, but with metaphysics, which as an idealistic empiricist he hated with a passion.

If, however, we consider the effect of religion in phenomenological terms, Powell seems to have expressed his Methodism in his talent for organizational efficiency. As the name connotes, Methodists believe in and practice a systematic approach to religion and the lived expression of that religion in daily life. This faith in organization and discipline began with the spiritual practices of the Wesleys, carried over into the discipline of the class meetings and conferences of ordained clergy, and today abundantly expresses itself in the way Methodists organize their church and try to organize the world. Powell was exposed to this Methodist faith as a child and like many others in his day, particularly in the Midwest, he coalesced science and religion into a single vision, one that had a particularly clear demonstration in reform efforts to clean up politics, the environment, and morality.

During the 1860s and 1870s, Powell demonstrated his comprehension of systems by leading exploratory expeditions and by carrying out projects that required the support of the federal bureaucracy. Later as director of the BAE and USGS, he became the civil servant par excellence, a living example of the honest and efficient government employee that Carl Schurz and other reformers extolled. When Powell's agencies were investigated by Congress in 1886, the majority report said the USGS was "well conducted, and with economy and care, and discloses excellent administrative and business ability on the part of its chief."[21] Powell referred to division of labor as "the fundamental law of political economy,"[22] and argued that government must surpass the private sector in its scrupulous attention to honesty: "The private employer assumes the integrity of his agent until the contrary is proved. The Government requires its agents to establish the integrity of all their transactions."[23] Whether it is true that the USGS under Powell became "the largest scientific organization of any kind in the world," it certainly reached gargantuan proportions by nineteenth-century standards, and more importantly, it established a tradition of efficiency and integrity in government scientific work that was widely admired.[24] Thus Powell proved himself to be a master of systematic exercise of power in a way that integrated the twin principles of efficiency and moral integrity. In this sense

Powell can be called "methodistical," even if his personal commitment to the denomination had become attentuated during his adult years.

Another indication that his religious formation affected his outlook as an adult lies in Powell's humanitarianism. He seems to have approached native Americans more out of innate curiosity, at first, than out of sympathy, but even his scientific detachment served to increase white understanding of native Americans. Powell did not depreciate primitives and tried to report on them with fairness. In his attempts to interpret the values of Indian culture to the white culture, however, he sometimes employed language that confirmed racist stereotypes: "In the dead stillness of the night the band of warriors with noiseless tramp, or in the canoes propelled by silent paddles, stole upon their victims and killed them without mercy, or skulked in ambush with the same result."[25]

In the same vein he could reproach students under his tutelage for identifying too closely with primitives they studied: "There is a curious tendency observable in students to overlook aboriginal vices and to exaggerate aboriginal virtues. It seems to be forgotten that after all the Indian is a savage. . . ." He went on to note, however, that the opposite was true about those who looked at native Americans from a distance—they tended to emphasize vices.[26]

On the whole, however, he seems to have had a moderate stance, both personally and professionally. He pointed out some of the errors whites had made with native Americans, such as failure to understand the democracy of the tribal system, ignorance of communal attitudes of property, and overestimation of the numbers of native Americans. And although he supported a policy of removal, he did so as a way of protecting Indians and trying to bring them into the inevitable process of acculturation. At some points he was ahead of his time, too, particularly in recognizing the integrity of tribal life and in understanding that even primitives had an intelligence and a basic humanity that made them closer to civilized humans than to animals. There seems little reason to doubt Powell's sincerity in writing, "When I stand before the sacred fire in an Indian village and listen to the red man's philosophy, no anger stirs my blood. I love him as one of my kind."[27] This broad-minded sympathy with native Americans seems consonant with his religious background, especially his father's concern with abolitionism. And though science and the humanities were other influences on him, his integration of these disciplines in a single vision enabled him to advocate native American interests in a humane way.

The second question about Powell is: how did he contribute significantly to higher education? In one sense his contribution was highly specialized. He helped to establish field work as an appropriate academic pursuit in the sciences, and he served as a "university examiner" for undergraduate courses at Illinois Wesleyan in 1874 and 1875.[28] But he served no institutional posts, gave no large bequests, and was a college faculty member for only a few years.

What though can be said of the impact of Powell on higher education as a whole through his leadership in geological and anthropological sciences, especially since the two agencies under his control established a sort of "official science" for his day? Academics did not always agree with the policies of the USGS and BAE—not surprisingly, since academics rarely reach a consensus on anything. But all across America, indeed, across the world, scientists benefitted from the research of the USGS and BAE. In the late part of the nineteenth century scientists were busy finding empirical data to confirm or refute the Darwinian hypothesis. The paleontological discoveries so well known today were just beginning to appear—Neanderthal man in 1856, the ruins of Troy in 1871, and the cave paintings at Altimira in 1879. Thus the research produced in such large quantities added greatly to the knowledge of early humanity, and the observations that Powell and his associates made of Numic and other native Americans were particularly useful because the tribes were virtually untouched by Western civilization.

Much of Powell's achievement lay in its consolidation of previous knowledge rather than innovation, however. Some debunkers of Powell have pointed out that the triangulation technique of surveying, the concepts of antecedent and consequent river erosion, the view that settlement patterns should be based on topography and hydrographics rather than the grid, and the land classification proposals espoused by Powell—all these had been promulgated in some form before Powell.[29] And yet the rebuttal only confirms the fact that it was Powell who made these concepts and proposals valid by embedding them in policy proposals of official government bodies or by implementing them on a broad scale.

Powell's contribution then, consisted of his intellectual leadership and his administrative genius in fields of study that coalesced with broad academic and research interests, rather than particular institutional accomplishments. Powell belongs to science and to humanity in their common effort to understand chthonic and human origins and development. Insofar as higher education has benefitted from the work of the BAE and the USGS, it has benefitted from the work of Powell.

We are left, then, with a question. How many cultural leaders were educated by church-related colleges? Powell was no exception, and a cursory survey of a few Methodist schools and colleges shows suggestively there were other such leaders: scientists, entrepreneurs, artists, doctors, lawyers, and many others.[30] Unfortunately, most institutional and religious histories pay maximum attention to clergy and academic leaders, and minimum attention to graduates who enter so-called secular pursuits. Yet what college, state- or church-related, would not be proud to claim a John Wesley Powell as one of its former students? Although Powell himself seems to have drifted away from the church, what about the church's disregarding of its own children? Why did not church-related higher education take as much interest in the scientists, artists, and business people it educated as it did in the preachers and bishops? As Powell himself like to remark, "Research begins with the known and proceeds to the unknown." If more research were done on the persons educated by church-related higher education, it might reveal that church-related schools and colleges have had an impact on the culture much larger than we realize.

NOTES

1. The evaluation that Powell spoke Ute "passably well" comes from Don D. and Catherine S. Fowler, *Anthropology of the Numa: John Wesley Powell's Manuscript on the Numic Peoples of Western North America, 1868–1880* (Washington, D.C.: Smithsonian Institution Press, 1971), 19. The Fowlers note that when taking down Numic tales, Powell omitted all scatalogical and sexual references, "thus rendering some of the story-plots unintelligible" (p. 19).

The quote about "Plutarch's man" is attributed to S. P. Langley, secretary of the Smithsonian 1887–1905, and is found in W. M. Davis, "Biographical Memoirs of John Wesley Powell, 1834–1902," *National Academy of Sciences Biographical Memoirs*, vol. 8, 1915. Davis was not altogether complimentary, however, and wrote Powell was guilty of "provincialism" in not giving enough credit to Europeans for his geological writings in the 1870s.

"Born fighter" comes from Bailey Willis, *A Yanqui in Patagonia* (Stanford University, Calif.: Stanford University Press, 1947), who as a young man worked in the field doing geological work under Powell.

"Gallant leader" was the romantic phrase of Samuel Bowles, who encountered Powell's party on the second trip to Colorado just after the climb on Long's Peak. Bowles, *The Switzerland of America: A Summer Vacation in the Parks and Mountains of Colorado* (Springfield, Mass.: Samuel Bowles and Co. 1869), 86.

2. William Culp Darrah, *Powell of the Colorado* (Princeton: Princeton University Press, 1951), is the best source for the details of Powell's early life. Powell recalled the incident of meeting Winnebagoes in "Proper Training and the Future of the Indians," *Forum* 18 (January 1895): 623. For the story about memorizing the Gospels see Mrs. M. D. Lincoln, "John Wesley Powell," *The Open Court* 16 (December 1902): 705.

For the Wesleyan Methodist Church see Ira F. McLeister and Roy S. Nicholson, *Conscience and Commitment: History of the Wesleyan Methodist Church of America* (Marion, Ind.: Wesley Press, 1976), 26–38. The church was based on certain organizational principles, such as inclusion of the laity in General Conference and the exclusion of bishops, as well as abolitionism, but indications are that Joseph Powell was concerned mostly about abolitionism.

3. Elmo Scott Watson, *The Illinois Wesleyan Story 1850–1950* (Bloomington, Ill.: Illinois Wesleyan University Press, 1950), 72–73, 84–85. See also Darrah, *Powell,* 73–79.

4. Three Illinois Wesleyan students and one faculty member went on the expedition. One of the students, Joseph C. Hartzell, later became a bishop in the Methodist Episcopal Church. See Watson, *Illinois Wesleyan Story,* 84–85. The titles that Powell bestowed on members of the party are listed in the official report he made to the Illinois State Board of Education, "Scientific Expedition to the Rocky Mountains. Preliminary Report of Prof. J. W. Powell to the Illinois State Board of Education," 3. The report from Powell is dated Dec. 18, 1867. Marcus Benjamin Papers, Smithsonian Institution Archives, Record Unit 7085, Box 4.

5. "Scientific Expedition to the Rocky Mountains, Preliminary Report," Marcus Benjamin Papers, 4.

6. The party on this trip included five students from Illinois Wesleyan, one from Illinois State Normal, and a former teacher from Illinois Wesleyan. See Watson, *Illinois Wesleyan Story,* 90–91.

7. Details about Lee's settlement are given in Frederick S. Dellenbaugh, *A Canyon Voyage: The Narrative of the Second Powell Expedition down the Green-Colorado River from Wyoming, and the Explorations on Land, in the Years 1871 and 1872* (New Haven: Yale University Press, 1926), 195, 211. Lee was finally executed for his role in the massacre.

8. The best account of the White adventure is given in William H. Goetzmann, *Exploration and Empire: The Explorer and the Scientist in the Winning of the American West* (New York: Alfred A. Knopf, 1966), 394–97.

9. See Goetzmann, *Exploration and Empire,* and also Richard A. Bartlett, *Great Surveys of the American West* (Norman, Okla.: University of Oklahoma Press, 1962).

10. The account of the first expedition down the Colorado was written by Powell and published in W. A. Bell, *New Tracks in North America* (London, no publisher, 1870). The best-known account by Powell is *Exploration of the Colorado River of the West and Its Tributaries,* first published in 1875 and later reprinted several times. But because Powell's notes of the first expedition were lost and he combined, apparently inadvertently, facts of both expeditions, historians have considered this source unreliable. Instead they have used other journals, the only complete one of the first expedition being that of George Young Bradley. This journal is in the New York Public Library and has been printed in the *Utah Historical Quarterly* 15 (January-October 1947), edited by Darrah and containing as well Powell's re-

port that appeared in Bell, *New Tracks*, and other letters, diaries, and newspaper articles stemming from the first trip.

11. Darrah, *Powell*, 152–53; and Goetzmann, *Exploration and Empire*, 553. This episode as well as the most thorough study of Powell's professional career is given in Wallace Stegner, *Beyond the Hundredth Meridian: John Wesley Powell and the Second Opening of the West* (Boston: Houghton Mifflin, 1954).

Before launching the second trip, Powell made a reconnaissance trip in 1870 to identify sites on the Colorado River where supplies could be delivered to the boating party. He met with the Shivwits on this trip, the same tribe that had killed three members of the 1869 party. He found them pacific and even smoked the peace pipe with them, with some unforeseen results: ". . . when the Indian pipe comes around, I am nonplussed. It has a large stem, which has, at some time, been broken, and now there is a buckskin rag wound around it, and tied with sinew, so that the end of the stem is a huge mouthful, and looks like the burying ground of old dead spittle, venerable for a century. To gain time, I refill it, then engage in very earnest conversation, and, all unawares, I pass it to my neighbor unlighted." Powell, *Exploration of the Colorado River of the West* (Washington: GPO, 1875), 129.

12. Don D. and Catherine S. Fowler, *Anthropology of the Numa*, 7.

13. Whether or not native Americans should be citizens was debated extensively during the 1880s. Powell's views were in keeping with those of other reformers who feared premature citizenship would make the tribes victims of speculators and other dishonest exploiters. See Loring B. Priest, *Uncle Sam's Stepchildren: The Reformation of United States Indian Policy, 1865–1887* (New Brunswick, N.J.: Rutgers University Press, 1942), 204–206, 208–13.

14. Handwritten MS no. 4024g, National Anthropological Archives, dated 13 Jan., apparently 1874, pp. 42–43, 46–47, 54–55. This testimony was printed in House Misc. Doc. 86, 22 Jan. 1874, 43rd Cong., 1st sess, vol. 2, pp. 8–12, where the wording differs somewhat from the handwritten version.

15. William C. Wyckoff of the *New York Tribune* in a letter to Powell, 10 Feb. 1874. BAE letters received, Record Group 57, National Archives, FM 156, no. 256.

16. House Misc. Doc. 5, "Report of the National Academy of Sciences on the survey of the territories," 45th Cong., 3rd sess., 3 Dec. 1878, p. 26.

17. According to Curtis M. Hinsley, Jr., Powell "blended the historical and classificatory orientations that had existed for decades within American anthropology. He thereby built into the Bureau a dichotomy of purpose that would both enrich and plague its operations for the rest of the century." And yet, "The founding of the BAE profoundly altered the context, force, and direction of nineteenth-century American anthropology." *Savages and Scientists: The Smithsonian Institu-*

tion and the Development of American Anthropology 1846–1910 (Washington, D.C.: Smithsonian Institution Press, 1981), 150–51.

18. Among these was "Linguistic Stocks of American Indians North of Mexico," which later appeared in the *Handbook of American Indians,* Frederick Webb Hodge, ed., BAE Bulletin 30, Part 1, A—M (Washington: GPO, 1907), backpiece. A photograph of the map appears in Seymour I. Schwartz and Ralph E. Ehrenberg, *The Mapping of North America* (New York: H. N. Abrams, 1980).

19. Henry Nash Smith, "Clarence King, John Wesley Powell, and the Establishment of the United States Geological Survey," *Mississippi Valley Historical Review* 34 (June 1947—March 1948): 40. Stegner also discusses these reforms. See especially 228, 315–16. The official agency interpretation was given in Brookings Institution, Institution for Government Research, *The U.S. Geological Survey: Its History, Activities and Organization* (New York: D. Appleton, 1919), 14.

20. *The USGS Yearbook Fiscal Year 1982* (Washington: GPO, 1982) states: "Currently, 15 states have complete published topographic map coverage at 1:24,000 scale, and, overall, 79 percent of the conterminous United States is available in published form at this scale." The scale 1:24,000 is used on a 7′ 30″ quadrangle, equivalent to an inch per half-mile.

21. Senate Report No. 1285, 49th Cong., 1st sess., 8 June, 1886, p. 52.

22. House Misc. Document 5, Report of the National Academy of Sciences on the survey of the territories, 3 Dec. 1878, 45th Cong., 3rd sess., p. 16.

23. Senate Report 507, Part 2, Dept. of the Interior, "Organization, Business Methods, and Work of the USGS," Cockrell Committee Report, 50th Cong., 1 sess., p. 395.

24. The quote comes from W. M. Davis, "Biographical Memoirs," 56.

25. Powell, "The North American Indians," N. S. Shaler, ed., *The United States of America: A Study of the American Commonwealth,* vol. 1 (New York: Appleton, 1894), 262.

26. *BAE Annual Report,* 1885–86, 35–36.

27. Powell, "Darwin's Contributions to Philosophy," *Proceedings, Biological Society of Washington* 1 (1882): 69. Smithsonian Miscellaneous Collections, vol. 25.

28. Letter, 18 May 1874, Prof. J. R. Jaques, Illinois Wesleyan University, to Powell, requesting him to be a university examiner and assuring him, "The office will not be burdensome. It will be mostly advisory." BAE Letters Received, Group 57, FM 156, no. 169. The Illinois Wesleyan catalogues for 1874 and 1875 list Powell as an examiner.

29. Goetzmann, *Exploration and Empire*, 423, 482. Goetzmann debunks any claims for Powell's originality, and rather sees Powell as a reformer: "A central theme runs through all of his thought: institutions and techniques devised in what he called the humid Eastern sections of the United States could not be successfully transplanted to the new and challenging Western environment. . . . It was a pedagogical mission, appropriately enough, and as civilization and its spokesmen gradually invested the West, it ultimately became a reforming mission" (pp. 562–63).

30. For example, Powell's own Illinois Wesleyan helped to educate Adlai E. Stevenson, vice-president under Grover Cleveland. Stanley F. Reed, a 1902 graduate of Kentucky Wesleyan College, distinguished himself as a justice on the U.S. Supreme Court. Wofford College in South Carolina educated three governors and two U.S. senators from South Carolina as well as eleven U.S. Army generals and two U.S. Navy admirals. Iowa Wesleyan College educated Belle Babb Manfield, the first woman to be admitted to the bar in the United States, as well as James A. Van Allen, discoverer of the radiation belts that bear his name. For this information I am indebted to Robert W. Frizzell, librarian and archivist at Illinois Wesleyan; Richard A. Weiss, bibliographer and archivist at Kentucky Wesleyan; Herbert Hucks, Jr., archivist at Wofford College; and the library at Iowa Wesleyan.

14

Martin Ruter
(1785–1838)

by Norman W. Spellmann

MARTIN RUTER PLAYED a crucial role in the founding of four Methodist schools, edited or wrote more than a dozen books, and helped develop the course of study for Methodist ministers before giving his life as a missionary in the Republic of Texas.

Born on April 3, 1785, in Charleston, Massachusetts, Ruter was the son of a poor blacksmith, who could not afford to provide any academic advantages. Nevertheless, as Ruter explained in his autobiography, "I had a taste for learning and a thirst for knowledge from my earliest recollections. This taste I cherished by improving diligently such opportunities as I had of private studies at home and in attending the schools in the neighborhood where I lived."[1] In 1793 the family moved to Bradford, Vermont, where Job Ruter and his wife (who had been Baptists) joined the first Methodist class formed in their neighborhood. Their home became a preaching place for Methodist itinerants. While in Bradford, young Martin came under the influence of Mrs. Margaret Appleton Peckett, an Englishwoman who had been John Wesley's housekeeper. Mrs. Peckett offered Ruter her firsthand Methodist witness and encouraged him to read her volumes of Wesley's works.

Soon after his family moved to Corinth, Vermont, in 1799, Ruter "experienced the pardon of sin and enjoyed peace of mind. The following winter I joined the Methodist Episcopal Church. . . . It sometimes occurred forcibly to my mind that I should be called to preach the gospel. After experiencing religion these impressions increased, and I turned my attention closely to the study of divinity." John Broadhead, presiding elder of the New London District, was so impressed with Ruter that he took the young man along on his travels for three months

MARTIN RUTER

Photo of a painting of Martin Ruter courtesy of Walter N. Vernon, Jr.

of instruction. At the end of this period, in the fall of 1800, Ruter was licensed to preach. When the New York Annual Conference met in historic John Street Church in New York City in June, 1801, the sixteen-year-old Ruter was received into the conference on trial by Bishop Francis Asbury and appointed to the Chesterfield Circuit.[2] To make up for his lack of formal education, Martin Ruter made a practice of private study which he continued for many years. He read widely in English literature and the classics, both ancient and modern. Through his own efforts, he gained a working knowledge of Greek and Latin. While serving a "mission" appointment in Montreal, Canada (1804), he became fluent in French and learned Hebrew from a rabbi. In these busy years, the young scholar also managed to achieve considerable skill in mathematics.

Ordained deacon in 1803 and elder in 1805 by Bishop Asbury, Ruter quickly rose to positions of trust and responsibility in the enlarged New England Conference. After serving pastorates in Northfield and Portsmouth, he was appointed to Boston in 1808. In that same year—as part of a move to change the General Conference into a delegated body—Ruter's colleagues chose him to be one of their seven representatives to the General Conference meeting in Baltimore. In 1809 the twenty-five-year-old minister was appointed presiding elder of the New Hampshire District.[3]

During this same period, Martin Ruter lost his wife of three years (1805–08), Sybil Robertson, and two children. In 1809 he married Ruth Young of Concord, New Hampshire. Eight children were born to this second union. From 1812 to 1813, Ruter located—that is, took an appointment at a fixed position rather than itinerating. He located, undoubtedly, for family reasons. "Well do I remember the interest he manifested for my welfare," his daughter later wrote, "from the first dawn of recollection till he was called to his reward from the plains of Texas. However multiplied were his public duties, he yet found time to devote hours, oft-repeated, through a series of years, to conversations with [us] on the subjects of religion, morality, science, etc." Ruter's letters to his wife from Texas movingly portray his care for each member of the family.[4]

After returning to the active itineracy in 1814, Ruter became involved in a project with Joshua Soule and John Broadhead to establish a Methodist academy in New England. Although there were only about 8,000 Methodists in New England at that time, they feared sending their children to the schools controlled by the "Calvinistic standing order." Under the influence of Broadhead, Ruter, and Soule, the New England Conference accepted a site in South Newmarket, New Hampshire, and authorized a subscription for a building. Ruter himself made the largest single contribution. The New Market Wesleyan Academy opened on September 1, 1817, with Moses White as instructor and a student body of ten boys and girls—"an early experiment in coeducation." Encouraged when the enrollment reached twenty-seven, the conference decided to incorporate the school. It elected a board of trustees and chose Martin Ruter to be the first principal.

In the meantime Ruter had been transferred to the Philadelphia Conference in 1816 and appointed to Saint George's, the largest Methodist church in America. "At thirty-two, Ruter was recognized as one of the most eloquent and forceful preachers of the Methodist Episcopal Church." His fellow ministers in the New England Conference gave him fifty-seven of the sixty-three votes cast on the first ballot for delegates to the 1816 General Conference—ahead of both Elijah Hedding and Joshua Soule. In recognition of Ruter's standing as the foremost scholar in the church, Asbury College (in Baltimore) conferred upon him an honorary master of arts degree in 1818.[5]

When Martin Ruter returned to New Hampshire to begin his duties as principal of New Market Wesleyan Academy in 1818, enrollment immediately rose to eighty students. His presence also inspired an increase in the number of courses. In addition to Latin, Greek, French, mathematics, and rhetoric, the academy advertised classes in logic, philosophy, ecclesiastical history, divinity, Hebrew, Chaldee, and Syriac.

Ruter's enthusiasm was contagious. On hearing so much talk of profound scholarship and high ideals, one observer declared that "every man began to look as though he knew twice as much as he did know." To establish a library, Ruter sought contributions from personal friends and former parishioners in Boston, New York, Philadelphia, and Baltimore. According to one report, he soon had eight thousand "impecunious Methodists of New England" doing their best to support the school.[6]

But Ruter was not permitted to work out his plans for the New Market academy. In 1820 the General Conference chose him to establish a new branch of the Methodist Book Concern in Cincinnati. Deprived of Ruter's dynamic leadership, the school—which had been poorly located—closed in 1823.[7]

By becoming a book agent at Cincinnati, Ruter did not cease to be an educator. Rather, as John O. Gross has explained, he was devoting his educational and administrative leadership "to further a form of adult education peculiar to Methodists. Self-education through reading was a definite part of their plan. The long list of books, Bibles, hymnbooks, *Disciplines* and church periodicals which were sold to the people by the circuit riders shows the vast amount of religious instruction given to the people of the frontier."[8] During his eight years as book agent, Ruter edited a number of works with instructional and cultural value: *The New*

American Spelling Book, The New American Primer, An Arithmetic, and *Juvenile Preceptor.* His specifically religious writings included *A Hebrew Grammar, Explanatory Notes on the Ninth Chapter of Romans, A Sketch of Calvin's Life and Doctrine,* and revisions of John Foxe's *Book of Martyrs* and George Gregory's *A Concise History of the Christian Church.* Ruter's most influential writing was the *Concise History,* which was included in the conference course of study for Methodist preachers for nearly fifty years.[9]

Following the example of John Wesley, Ruter labored to make edifying books accessible to Christian readers who had neither the money to buy most publications nor the time to read them. Of his work at Cincinnati, Ruter wrote: "Believing that I was promoting the interests of the Church, and my solicitude for the prosperity of the Concern in the West being very great, I used the greatest exertions in my power, and made as many sacrifices as my situation would permit."[10] In recognition of Ruter's scholarship and achievements, Transylvania University in Lexington, Kentucky, gave him an honorary doctor of divinity degree in 1822—apparently the first such award for an American-born Methodist preacher.

When the General Conference of 1820 recommended that all annual conferences establish academies, the newly formed Ohio and Kentucky conferences appointed a joint committee to look for a site. Ruter, living in Cincinnati, was named one of the Ohio commissioners. The best location seemed to be Augusta, Kentucky, where the state legislature had chartered Bracken Academy in 1798, giving it six thousand acres of land. The school was struggling, and its trustees happily negotiated with the representatives of the two Methodist conferences. Kentucky chartered Augusta College in December, 1822, under the auspices of the Ohio and Kentucky conferences. Despite its name, for several years the school operated as an academy while financial and educational foundations were established. In 1827 the trustees decided to complete the development of the school into a bona fide college and elected Martin Ruter to be its first president. Ruter, who was completing his second term as book agent, wanted to return to the itineracy. At the urging of Bishops Hedding and Enoch George, however, he finally accepted the presidency of Augusta. "I had long ago seen that the Church needed seminaries of learning and could not conduct its important interests without them," Ruter noted in his autobiography. "I therefore accepted the appointment, determined to see what might be accomplished in this way for the prosperity of our Zion."

During Ruter's administration, the student body increased from 80 to 130, and the senior class from 5 to 16. These five seniors received the first bachelor of arts degrees granted by a chartered Methodist college.[11]

Not only was Augusta the first chartered Methodist school of collegiate rank in the United States; it also had a strong faculty. John P. Durbin, who began his studies under Ruter, was professor of ancient languages. Durbin later became editor of the *New York Advocate* and president of Dickinson College. J. P. Tomlinson, professor of mathematics and natural philosophy, served as president of Augusta from 1836 to 1849 and eventually led Ohio University. Henry B. Bascom, one of the most distinguished members of the Ohio Conference, had been president of Madison College in Uniontown before Ruter brought him to Augusta to teach moral science. Bascom subsequently edited the *Southern Methodist Quarterly Review* and was elected a bishop by the southern Methodists. Ruter himself was given the title of president and professor of oriental languages and belle lettres. With these strong educators, he sought to make Augusta a "nursery not only of learning but also of morals and religion."[12]

In May, 1832, while attending the General Conference in Philadelphia, Ruter "felt an earnest desire to be given up exclusively to the work of the ministry." Shortly after returning to Augusta, he submitted his resignation as president. "No honors, no emoluments seemed of value compared with the great duties of preaching the gospel of Christ. My resignation was dictated by these views, and some objects connected with the welfare of my family." In August Ruter was transferred to the Pittsburgh Conference and appointed to Smithfield Church in Pittsburgh.

During this period (1832–34), Ruter and Charles Elliot persuaded the Pittsburgh Conference to adopt a rigorous supplement to the regular course of study for young ministers (initiated by the General Conference in 1816). In addition to more demanding studies in biblical, historical, and theological areas, their reading list included works in geography, zoology, botany, chemistry, moral and political philosophy, and logic.[13] In his advice to young ministers, Ruter declared: "In order to acquire that knowledge and wisdom which are necessary to enable you to sustain with propriety, honor and usefulness, the character of a minister of the Gospel, it will be proper to spend much of your time in reading and study. Much depends on a proper selection of useful books."[14]

Within two years the church once again called upon Ruter to take the helm of a college. In 1833 the Pittsburgh Conference assumed control of Allegheny College, a Presbyterian school which had been founded at Meadville in 1815. Although the school owned an attractive three-story brick building and had collected the largest library west of the Allegheny Mountains, it had never attracted more than twelve students at a time nor had it established the necessary patronage. Since the college was competing with two other Presbyterian schools in the state and carrying a debt of several thousand dollars, the Allegheny College trustees eagerly sought a new owner.

Having deciding to take over the college at Meadville, the Pittsburgh Conference nominated Martin Ruter to be the school president. Ruter was fully aware of the problems of Allegheny College and reluctant to accept the nomination.

> I not only had no desire to enter again upon college duties, but I earnestly desired, at least in reference to this college, to be excused from undertaking them. My brethren thought differently and urged on me the importance to the church . . . of securing the advantages of a good college for the benefit of our people and the community. I therefore consented to take charge of this college for a season.[15]

To publicize the re-opening of Allegheny College as a Methodist institution. Ruter prepared an extensive prospectus emphasizing that the school would be thoroughly Christian but not sectarian. The trustees would still include "literary gentlemen of different religious persuasions." The new president also obtained an $8,000 grant from the Pennsylvania Legislature, to be paid over a four-year period on the condition that friends of the school would match that amount. Apparently on Ruter's recommendation, the trustees approved a system of manual labor, which would enable students to earn part of their college expenses by farming an acre of land or by working for a local business. The program proved to be popular and attracted numerous young people who could not have attained an education otherwise. On the strength of these changes, Allegheny College began the year 1833 with 40 students and ended the year with 120.[16]

In his first baccalaureate address at Allegheny, delivered September 25, 1834, Ruter summarized his views on education:

> Though your pupilage now closes, you scarcely can consider your education as finished. So far from this, it can only be said that you are now prepared to cultivate the sciences by your own skill. The treasures of learning have been spread before you and you have perceived that there is an immensity in their resources. The foundation of literary honors and eminent usefulness must be laid in the morning of our days, but the superstructure must not be neglected afterwards. No one was ever born a scholar, nor is it possible to become one without mental discipline. Those who have astonished mankind by their powers, have accomplished their work not so much by the superiority of natural talents, as by patient attention and perserving industry. The votaries of learning should not only add to their acquirements, but aim at improving the arts and sciences themselves. Shall we be told that after so many improve-

ments, no room remains for others? This was the cry of the indolent prior to the days of Bacon, Locke, Newton, Herschel, and others. But it is not true. Rivers may dry up, fountains may fail, but the sources of useful knowledge can never be exhausted.[17]

From the beginning Ruter had planned to remain at Allegheny College for "perhaps two or three years, until the College shall have acquired a degree of prosperity and permanency sufficient to secure its usefulness." By 1836 he believed this status had been attained. While attending the General Conference in Cincinnati in May, 1836, Ruter discovered his ultimate goal. Reports of Texas independence from Mexico reached the city and stirred the hearts of the delegates. For Ruter, news of the victory at San Jacinto sounded a clear call. "I offered myself as a missionary to Texas. . . . It appeared to me a mission of the utmost importance to the inhabitants of Texas and to the Church; and I felt a strong desire to be useful in that distant land."[18] After the conference, he returned to his duties at Allegheny to wait for the bishops' advice on when he should leave for Texas. Word finally came of his appointment as "Superintendent of the mission to Texas," and in July, 1837, Ruter "took an affectionate leave of the trustees, faculty, and students," who had gathered in a great throng on the banks of French Creek. Ruter and his family traveled by flatboat to Indiana, where his wife and children were to stay while he established the mission in Texas. Delayed by "the rage of Yellow Fever at Nachez, Vicksburg & New Orleans" until frost could allay the epidemic, Ruter finally crossed the Red River into East Texas in late November, 1837. Three weeks later he arrived in Houston, where as superintendent of the Texas mission he discussed with the leaders of the republic his plans for establishing a college in Texas. "My labors," Ruter explained, "will be directed to forming societies and circuits, establishing schools, and making arrangements for a college or university."[19] In a letter to the missionary society in New York he wrote: "It has appeared to me that we ought, as soon as practicable, to establish in this Republic a well endowed University and several subordinate schools of different gradations. In two or three places, subscriptions have been taken for buildings; and to provide permanent funds, we propose obtaining donations of land."[20]

Before he could bring his dreams to reality, Ruter died on May 16, 1838, apparently of typhoid fever complicated by pneumonia.[21] Details of his educational plans can be sifted from the writings of his close friends, such as Lydia Ann McHenry, herself a leader in Texas Methodism. She credited Ruter with originating "the idea of establishing such an institution of learning in Texas as should qualify the youth of the country for filling stations of honor and usefulness. . . . He went so far as to draw up several articles of a charter to be presented to the next Congress."[22] David Ayres, a layman who spent many hours with Ruter as both guide and friend, also described the educator's proposal:

> Dr. Ruter's grand plan was to establish a good school, of the ordinary kind, in every settlement, and to lay the foundation for one Central University for all Texas. His plan for the latter was, to establish an Academy, or High School, in a central location, and concentrate the attention and interest of the growing Methodist Church in Texas on it, until it should be gradually developed into a University. . . . The location he had chosen for this University for all Texas, after a careful and patient examination of the country, was only six miles south of the present [1857] site of Chappell Hill."[23]

Despite Ruter's untimely death, his vision awakened the determination of his colleagues. On February 1, 1840, Rutersville College—the first college to begin operation in the Republic of Texas—opened its doors with sixty-three students and three faculty members. The work which began then is now carried on by the successor to Rutersville, Southwestern University, in Georgetown, Texas—continuing the tradition begun by Martin Ruter, pioneer Methodist educator.[24]

NOTES

1. Quoted in Mrs. S. R. Campbell. "Martin Ruter," *Biographical Sketches of Eminent Itinerant Ministers,* Thomas O. Summers, ed. (Nashville: Methodist Episcopal Church, South, 1859), 322. Hereafter cited as Summers.

2. *General Minutes,* 1 (1773–1813), 249, 264.

3. *Minutes,* 285, 331, 355, 377, 402, 433, 462; and Summers, *Biographical Sketches,* 322–23.

4. Ernest Ashton Smith, *Martin Ruter* (Cincinnati: Methodist Book Concern, 1915), 330–32; and Ruter Papers, Bridwell Library, Southern Methodist University.

5. John O. Gross, *Martin Ruter: Pioneer in Methodist Education* (Nashville: Board of Education of the Methodist Church, 1956), 18–20; and Summers, *Biographical Sketches,* 324.

6. Gross, *Martin Ruter: Pioneer,* 19–21; and Smith, *Martin Ruter,* 44–47.

7. See Ruter's letter to Levi Bartlett, 12 Mar. 1819. Ruter Papers, Bridwell Library, Southern Methodist University.

8. Gross, *Martin Ruter: Pioneer,* 23.

9. Summers, *Biographical Sketches,* 336; his unpublished work includes "Translation of and Critical Remarks Upon Various Portions of Holy Scriptures" and "Letters to a Young Minister," holographs, Methodist Publishing House Library, Nashville, Tennessee.

10. Summers, *Biographical Sketches,* 325.

11. Gross, *Martin Ruter: Pioneer,* 28–29; and Smith, *Martin Ruter,* 47–57.

12. *Zion's Herald,* 5 Mar. 1828.

13. Pittsburgh *Conference Journal,* 23 Aug. 1834, as quoted in Robert D. Clark, *The Life of Matthew Simpson* (New York: Macmillan, 1956), 43.

14. "Letters to a Young Minister," holograph, Methodist Publishing House Library, Nashville, Tennessee.

15. Summers, *Biographical Sketches,* 326–27.

16. Smith, *Martin Ruter,* 83–91.

17. Quoted in Gross, *Martin Ruter: Pioneer,* 14.

18. Summers, *Biographical Sketches,* 328; and *General Minutes,* 2 (1829–39), 473.

19. Quoted in Summers, *Biographical Sketches,* 348.

20. Ruter to Nathan Bangs, 29 Jan. 1838, as printed in the *New York Christian Advocate & Journal,* 6 Apr. 1838.

21. Dr. A. P. Manley to Mrs. Ruth Ruter, 17 May 1838. Ruter Papers, Bridwell Library, Southern Methodist University. Manley's diagnosis was: "a pulmonary affection in which the liver & bowels were also largely involved—brought on by cold, etc."

22. Quoted in Summers, *Biographical Sketches,* 358.

23. David Ayres, "Early Methodism in Texas," *Texas Christian Advocate,* 13 Aug. 1857. The eventual location—chosen by the "Rutersville Company"—was in central Fayette County, six miles northeast of LaGrange (roughly half-way between Austin and Houston).

24. Ralph Wood Jones, *Southwestern University: 1840–1961* (Austin: Jenkins Publishing Co., 1973).

15

Andrew Sledd
(1870–1939)

by Arthur W. Wainwright

I F ANDREW SLEDD had written his autobiogrpahy, he would have entitled it *Memories of a Southern Schoolmaster*.[1] Although that title looks forbidding, it would have been accurate. As a high school principal, a member of college and seminary faculties, and a university president, he spent most of his life in educational work. But he was not just a teacher and a university administrator. His influence extended beyond the confines of the academic world and impinged on the life of church and society, where he readily entered into conflict and sometimes emerged with scars.

He was born on November 7, 1870, in Lynchburg, Virginia. The son of Robert Newton Sledd, a leading minister in the Virginia Conference of the Methodist Episcopal Church, South (MECS), he was educated at Randolph-Macon College, Virginia, and in 1892 became a high school principal in Arkadelphia, Arkansas. He returned to Randolph-Macon to complete his B.A. and M.A. and served as an instructor for a year at Randolph-Macon Academy in Bedford, Virginia. In 1896 he obtained an M.A. in Greek from Harvard and after holding the post of teaching fellow at Vanderbilt was appointed in 1898 to the position of professor of Latin at Emory College, which was situated at Oxford, Georgia, near Covington and about thirty miles from Atlanta. In 1899 he married Annie Florence Candler, the daughter of Bishop Warren Akin Candler, who had formerly been president of the college. The couple had nine children, one of whom was stillborn.[2]

Sledd's career at Emory came to an abrupt end when he was plunged into controversy over an article he had written. One of the scandals of American life at that time was the practice of lynching. Georgia had its

ANDREW SLEDD

Photo by Elaine Ellerbee of a painting by Donald Blake of Andrew Sledd courtesy of Candler School of Theology Library.

share of these atrocities. A notorious case was that of Sam Hose, a black who in 1899 was hunted down as a suspect for the murder of a white farmer and the rape of the farmer's wife. Hose, who was named as guilty of both crimes by the wife herself, was savagely mutilated and burned to death by a mob near Newnan, Georgia. Special excursion trains were run to provide an audience for the ghastly event, and the charred remains of the victim were carried away as souvenirs. It was in reaction to this and other lynchings that Sledd wrote an article entitled "The Negro: Another View," which was published by the *Atlantic Monthly* in July, 1902.[3]

The position maintained by Sledd was not extremely liberal by the standards of a later age. In one respect it looks reactionary. Although he admitted the possibility of a change in the distant future, he affirmed without hesitation that "now the negro is an inferior race." But he did not content himself with the expression of this kind of sentiment; and when he proceeded to assert that "the negro has inalienable rights," he ran into trouble. He pointed out that many individual blacks were superior in education, manners, and morals to individual whites. Yet whites treated blacks like animals, and the most terrible scandal of all was lynching, which was readily condoned by many of the white population. "Freedom," he wrote, "does not, indeed, imply social, intellectual, or moral equality; but its very essence is the equality of the fundamental rights of human creatures before God and the law."[4]

Sledd's article was read in Georgia, and the caldron boiled over when a letter from Mrs. W. H. (Rebecca Latimer) Felton was printed in the *Atlanta Constitution*. Through her championship of women's rights and other causes Felton was known as a reformer. But she had no love for the black race; and, having read his article, she had no love for Andrew Sledd. The South, she believed, had been misrepresented and insulted by him. She herself had unashamedly advocated lynching as a punishment for rapists. In her opinion, Sledd's brand of liberalism would endanger the safety of white women. She turned against him all her talents as a verbal sharpshooter. He was a "snivelling inkslinger." If he lived in the South, he would be wise "for his health's sake" to move elsewhere. "He may yet be thankful," she warned, "to get off without an extra application of tar and feathers." She pronounced against him her decree of banishment: "Pass him on! Keep him moving! He does not belong in this part of the country."[5]

A chorus of approval greeted the tirade which Felton had unleashed. "Professor Sledd," declared the *Atlanta Journal*,[6] "so misrepresents the people of Georgia and of the south in connection with their attitude to the negro race, as to seem to destroy his usefulness for the future as a member of the faculty of any institution seeking to educate and train the sons of southern white men." Words were soon translated into deeds. A group of youths burned two figures in effigy in the courthouse square of Covington. One figure was supposed to be a black man; the other figure, embracing him, represented Andrew Sledd.[7] Popular anger mounted against Sledd, and pressure was brought upon him to resign his post. Within a week of the publication of Felton's letter he had tendered his resignation to James E. Dickey, the recently appointed president of Emory College.[8]

Dickey did nothing to deter him from his intention to leave. Sledd himself was sick of the affair and ready to move. To his father-in-law, Bishop Candler, he wrote, "I want to get away; I feel alien and wronged." Candler, although his previous relationship with Sledd had been far from smooth, was incensed by the treatment his son-in-law and by consequence his daughter had received. He delivered a pained rebuke to Dickey: "You let the enemies of the college lynch a capable professor and banish my child from Georgia."[9]

Sledd had other supporters besides the bishop. His colleagues on the faculty at Emory asked the trustees to grant him a thousand dollars to tide him over the uncertain months ahead. Various leaders of the MECS declared their sympathy for him in letters to Bishop Candler. Some northern journals spoke out in favor of Sledd. "Prof. Andrew Sledd's virtual dismissal from Emory College," said the *New York Evening Post,* "is a disgrace shared by Georgia and the Southern college world." His fame even spread across the ocean, and the secretary of a group of British Quakers wrote to him for information about his article.[10]

Rebecca Felton had long been a foe of Bishop Candler, and although she professed ignorance of Sledd's background, the bishop was not convinced. Writing to President Kilgo of Trinity College during the heat of the crisis, he said, "Old Mrs. Felton as you know has borne me a grudge for years"; and Bishop Elijah E. Hoss told Candler, "Old Sister Felton, I understand, started the row. More than likely she did it because she wanted to hit you over Professor Sledd's shoulders." Candler was afraid of being accused of nepotism and made no public statement about the case.[11] But in 1903 he himself was the author of an article in condemnation of lynching.[12] The initiative taken by Sledd was bearing fruit.

In another quarter the events at Emory did not go unheeded. Trinity College, the forerunner of Duke University, handled a similar crisis with greater dexterity. In 1903 one of its faculty, John Spencer Bassett, had committed the offense of claiming that Booker T. Washington, a black, was, apart from Robert E. Lee, the greatest southerner born in the past hundred years. The president of Trinity, Candler's friend John C. Kilgo, together with the entire college faculty, rallied around the beleaguered professor when the clamor arose for his dismissal; and Bassett kept his job.[13] Kilgo's reaction contrasted sharply with that of Dickey in the Sledd crisis at Emory.

After his departure from Emory, Sledd went to do graduate study at Yale, from which he received a Ph.D. in Latin in 1903. The same year he was appointed professor of Greek at Southern University, Greensboro, Alabama. A year later he became the first president of the new University of Florida, which under his administration moved from Lake City to Gainesville. It was not an easy move because it aroused the hostility of business interests in Lake City and involved the absorption of other institutions into the state university. Even though it was the product of a merger, the University of Florida had an initial enrollment of only 102 students and fifteen faculty.[14] Sledd was under pressure to increase the number of students but was more concerned about improving academic standards. According to his own account, this concern was the cause of his undoing. "In 1909," he wrote, "despite the unanimous and cordial support of the Board of Control of the institution, I was forced to resign the presidency. The charge against me was that the attendance upon the institution did not increase with sufficient rapidity under my administration."[15]

For the second time in seven years he had left an academic position under duress. He did not remain unoccupied but was appointed pastor of First Methodist Church, Jacksonville, Florida.[16] The academic world soon opened its doors to him again. In 1910 he was chosen for the presidency of Southern University, where he had served for a year as professor. The university was a Methodist foundation, which later merged with Birmingham College to form Birmingham-Southern College. Sledd tried without great success to improve its struggling financial condition. He was remarkably effective in building up a strong faculty, but lack of money prevented him from keeping them all. He maintained firm discipline and paid attention to the athletic program. Although he himself had attained a high reputation as a baseball player during his student days, he opposed intercollegiate athletics because they distracted the participants from their studies.[17]

His four years in the presidency of Southern University brought to an end the first part of his career, in which he had been involved in the teaching of classics and in academic administration. His writings during that part of his life show that education was second only to eternal salvation in his list of priorities and was a prize to be attained through rigorous discipline. He wrote:

> An education is, and of right ought, to be, a costly thing—costly, not only in money, but in time and toil, in determined, persevering, long-continued effort, and in the resolute and continued sacrifice of ease and pleasure of body,

and of all the lower inclinations, aspirations and desires. Aside from the welfare of the immortal soul, it is the pearl of the greatest price, and to win it a
man must not only sell all that he hath but must give himself also, freely and
fully, in the purchase price.[18]

According to Sledd, the supreme concern of a church-related college
should be the new birth of its students and their subsequent progress in
the Christian life. The curriculum should be designed with this concern
in mind, and a central place should be given to instruction in the Bible
and ethics. "If young people," he declared, "are to come to know Christ
or continue to be Christians, they must know about Christ and his teach-
ings, the principles and practice of the religion to which they give themselves."[19]

A high academic standard for both students and faculty was a goal
that Sledd consistently sought to reach. In church-related colleges, he
insisted, the search for that goal must not conflict with the church's basic
purpose; teachers in those colleges should give acceptance to the
church's beliefs.[20] Academic freedom was a cause that he vigorously
supported; and in that cause he wrote a defense of his former colleague,
Enoch Marvin Banks, who had been dismissed from the University of
Florida after comparing Jefferson Davis unfavorably with Abraham Lincoln and making a similar comparison of the South with the North in the
Civil War.[21] But in Sledd's opinion there were limits to academic freedom
in a church college; faculty members who disagreed with the church's
principles should resign their positions.[22] "The sense of the supreme
obligation of righteousness," he affirmed, "must dominate the institution and determine its institutional policy and tone. Such a condition
can only be reached when the authorities of the institution, including its
teaching force, know Christ and love him with the passion of a super-
human loyalty."[23]

The second part of Sledd's career began in 1914 when he resigned his
presidency of Southern University to become professor of Greek and
New Testament literature at the newly founded Candler School of Theology. The MECS had decided to establish Emory University in Atlanta.
Bishop Candler was the university's chancellor, and its chief benefactor
was his brother, Asa Griggs Candler, the president of Coca-Cola.
Emory's theology school was named after the bishop. The family relationship with the bishop did not hinder Sledd's appointment, but, in
any case, with his advanced degrees in classics he was the best qualified
academically of the school's original faculty.

He was also the best qualified by temperament to undertake one of
the more hazardous tasks of academic politics. It was he who led the
successful move to oust Plato T. Durham from the deanship of the Can-

dler School of Theology. Durham, who had received adverse criticism as an administrator, resigned in 1919 but remained as a professor in the seminary.[24]

During the 1920s Sledd and some of his colleagues were given a hard time by advocates of biblical literalism. In 1921 the force of this opposition had been felt at Southern Methodist University in Dallas when John A. Rice was driven from his Old Testament professorship because of a book in which he accepted critical theories about the Pentateuch.[25] The faculty of the Candler School of Theology also came under fire. Word spread around the churches and conferences that some of the faculty members were unsound in their views about the Bible. Franklin N. Parker, who was Durham's successor as dean, rallied to the defense of his colleagues. In a statement issued in 1922 he claimed that they were all "firm believers in evangelical Christianity." "I know of no man," he asserted, "who doubts the inspiration of the scriptures or questions the fact of divine revelation, though some of them probably differ as to whether inspiration is verbal or general."[26]

Parker's statement was diplomatically phrased but did not halt the attack on the seminary. Thomas H. Lipscomb had been dismissed from his position as professor of English Bible at Emory College, which by this time had moved from Oxford, Georgia, to the Atlanta campus. Lipscomb, who had become a pastor in Mississippi, believed that he had been treated unfairly at Emory because of his conservative theology. He published a pamphlet in censure of the opinions of various Methodist leaders. He mentioned by name several of the faculty of Emory University and directed a sustained attack on Sledd. He charged him with "questioning the authority of Paul, Isaiah, or any other inspired writer except what he accepted from the lips of Jesus," and accused him of claiming that nothing was "established and certain in theology or in any other branch of knowledge."[27]

Lipscomb sent his pamphlet to the members of the church's 1922 General Conference. Bishop Candler was displeased with the tract. "In my judgment," he told Lipscomb, "it has hindered rather than helped the cause which you professed a desire to promote."[28] The conference took no action in the matter, but its journal printed two telegrams from Emory students in support of their professors.[29] Opposition to the faculty continued. Lipscomb's charges were reported by the *Southern Methodist*, an antimodernist publication, which complained that the bishops had appointed Sledd to a committee entrusted with the task of supervising the curriculum of Methodist centers of higher education. Bishop Candler received letters critical of both college and seminary faculty at Emory. When he tried to divert attention to the liberalism of northern institutions, he was told, "But first clean up your Georgia university."[30]

The criticisms went on for several years. In 1926 T. E. Davenport, a Georgia minister, told the bishop, "I have come in contact with some of the students at Emory who say that much of the hour devoted to Bible study by some professors is taken up teaching the doubts and not the facts of the Bible."[31] In spite of these rumblings of opposition, all the members of the seminary faculty remained in their appointments.

Within Emory College the course of events was different. In the second half of the 1920s John Knox and Ernest Cadman Colwell, both of whom were advocates of the higher criticism, had to give up their positions as Bible teachers in the college. Although objection was raised to a stand taken by Knox against labor conditions in local cotton mills, he was aware that complaints by parents and alumni about his biblical views were also a factor which led to his departure from Emory. Colwell has clearly ascribed his own dismissal to his views about the Bible.[32] By contrast the seminary faculty held its ground. Those who were the chief targets of opposition had more seniority than Knox and Colwell. Moreover, Bishop Candler, who had resigned the office of university chancellor in 1922, continued to wield great influence in the seminary. Though he himself was theologically conservative, he was reluctant to turn against the professors whom he had appointed to its faculty. If ever he wavered in hs loyalty to them, there was always the family tie with Sledd. It is reported that when Candler once asked Dean Parker to remove Wyatt A. Smart from the faculty, the dean replied, "Very well, Bishop, if we get rid of Smart, I shall insist that we include your son-in-law, Sledd. These men are peas from the same pod!"[33] Both Smart and Sledd stayed on as professors.

Another factor helped the seminary faculty. The professors who were most suspect were popular with many people in the church. Smart, Durham, and Sledd were in demand as preachers and speakers. E. B. Chappell, editor of Sunday school publications, wrote to Candler after hearing two sermons by Sledd at Lake Junaluska, "He may be a little awry in regard to some matters of Biblical criticism, but in my opinion he is the greatest preacher in Southern Methodism."[34] With support of this kind the faculty was hard to dislodge.

An issue that improved Sledd's image with some of the more conservative of the southern Methodists but tarnished it in the eyes of liberal friends was his reaction to the proposed merger with northern Methodism. He played a vigorous part in the debate, which went on from 1924 until 1926, when the plan under discussion was rejected by the southern church. Sledd was fiercely loyal to his native South and was convinced that the plan would produce a church dominated by northerners. His Old Testament colleague, W. A. Shelton, was an ardent champion of the scheme; and in a pamphlet written in opposition to

Shelton's views, Sledd argued that the time was not yet ripe for this particular plan. He was not opposed to unification in principle but regarded the scheme as inadequate. He believed that it neglected the problem of race, on which he held basically the same views as in 1902; and he felt that it failed to alleviate the tensions between North and South.[35]

Sledd took an active part in civic affairs while he was at the school of theology. For many years he was a member of the board of education in Decatur, Georgia, the city where he lived. From 1920 until 1936 he served as the board's secretary and treasurer, and the duties of these offices took up a considerable part of his time.

Although he did not make any great or original contribution to biblical scholarship, he was capable of writing with learning on points of detail.[36] But the three books which he published while he was at the seminary were intended for laypeople. Two of them, *St. Mark's Life of Jesus* and *His Witnesses, A Study of the Book of Acts,* are in the nature of popular commentaries, clearly and attractively written. The other volume, *The Bibles of the Churches,* is a history of the process by which the books of the Bible came to be recognized as Scripture. He presents the material in a lively style, giving a thoroughly readable account of a topic that could easily become wearisome. These three volumes, like the Sunday school notes which he wrote for the *Adult Student,* are evidence of his ability to use his scholarship in the service of laypeople.

He was appointed in 1930 to the committee for revising the American Standard Version of the New Testament. The committee was eventually responsible for the Revised Standard Version. Sledd strongly emphasized the importance of giving priority to accuracy in translation and believed that too much weight was being given to liturgical and stylistic considerations. This disagreement about policy led to his resignation from the project in 1937.[37]

His most important contribution to the church and the educational world was as a seminary teacher. In the South he was a pioneer in making known the methods of higher criticism. A high proportion of his students had been brought up as biblical literalists. They were profoundly disturbed to find a seminary professor who rejected the traditional authorship of many of the New Testament writings, including John's Gospel and Epistles. His views were not as radical as those of some other scholars. For example, in lectures given in the early 1920s he accepted the traditional view of the authorship of Mark's and Luke's Gospels and the Acts of the Apostles. He claimed that Colossians was the work of Paul and, although he admitted a degree of uncertainty, inclined to the view that Paul wrote Ephesians and Second Thessalonians.[38] But his views were radical enough to give him notoriety in southern Methodism.

In spite of the shock of their first encounter with his teaching, the obvious integrity of his faith convinced many of his students that his approach to the Bible was consistent with genuine Christianity. He was responsible for teaching courses in rhetoric and speech as well as New Testament, and in this way was able to demonstrate his concern for the regular work of the ministry. His insistence on academic rigor did not blind him to the practical aims of theological education.

He was in a key position to exert influence over future leaders and used his opportunities well. He was active in developing the seminary curriculum and was responsible for overseeing the library. But he was specially remembered for his work as a teacher. One of his students was Nolan B. Harmon, who became editor of Abingdon Press, where he was involved in the production of the *Interpreter's Bible*. Harmon, who was later elected bishop, describes Sledd as "an excellent, incisive teacher," who challenged many of his presuppositions. "Dr. Andrew Sledd, something of an iconoclast," he writes, "had a big hand in unsettling my fundamental convictions as I went on to read the New Testament with him."[39]

Sledd had a memorable impact on students who were to make their mark as New Testament scholars. One of them was Ernest Cadman Colwell, who was appointed president of the University of Chicago and later of the School of Theology at Claremont. Colwell, who became a leading expert in the text and language of the New Testament, had shown no enthusiasm for Greek as a college student. After his entry into the Candler School of Theology his attitude changed. "Student gossip," he wrote, "made it clear that the best teacher in the school was Andrew Sledd." He found Sledd to be "an incredibly efficient teacher," who stimulated his interest in Greek and encouraged him to proceed to advanced studies.[40]

Another of Sledd's pupils, John Knox, became professor of biblical studies at Union Theological Seminary, New York, and established himself as one of the leading New Testament scholars in America. His encounter with Sledd strengthened his interest in the subject. "It is not surprising," he observed, "that after my college major in the classics I should find my interest centering in New Testament studies, particularly since instruction in them was of so superior a kind." Knox had been brought up with a literalist approach to the Bible, and the issues raised by Sledd thrust him into a spiritual crisis. Sledd's own example of faith led to a resolution of that crisis. "Dr. Sledd himself," wrote Knox, "manifestly had, in his own experience, so firm and so vital an assurance of 'things unseen,' and this without any such external authority as the Bible's mere words, that my previous assumptions could not fail to be challenged."[41]

One of the students most influenced by Sledd was Albert E. Barnett, who taught at Scarritt College and eventually followed in his teacher's footsteps as professor of New Testament at the Candler School of Theology. Barnett was a devoted admirer of Sledd. He spoke of his clarity and objectivity in the classroom: "With great deliberation that let the class almost see his mind at work, he would marshal the data under interpretation, never using his position to obscure views that countered his own, seeking rather to induce students to use their own critical faculties. At the same time, anyone who wanted to know what he thought had only to ask." This passion for order and precision did not make Sledd insensitive to spiritual concerns in the classroom; and in the pulpit he was often carried away by great emotion. "He created the sense of God's presence in wonder working power," wrote Barnett, "because that power had registered in his own life and he made it available through his preaching and teaching."[42]

During Sledd's twenty-five years at the seminary a great number of future pastors, teachers, and church administrators studied under him. Some of his pupils became teachers overseas, like Marvin H. Harper in India and John M. Norris in Korea and Argentina.[43] Others, like F. Darcy Bone and John Q. Schisler, were active in Sunday school publications. As these and many other students passed through the seminary, they learned from the challenge and inspiration offered by Sledd.

His effectiveness as a teacher was partly the result of his command of the subject and his clarity of presentation. It was also the outcome of his own personal faith, which was evident as he interpreted the Scriptures. He regarded the Bible as "the unfolding record of a great redemptive movement that still flows on to its realization in the Kingdom of God." When he spoke of "the sense of a Presence that has never been withdrawn and of a Love that has never wearied," he was speaking from his own experience. For him the Scriptures only reached their "true Christian value" when they brought men and women into the presence of Christ.[44]

An athletic man who regularly walked two miles in each direction between his home and the seminary, Sledd continued to be a full-time faculty member until his sudden death of a heart attack on March 16, 1939. The years he labored brought him conflict and setbacks. There was the clash with Rebecca Felton and the disagreement at the University of Florida. There was the controversy about higher criticism. He had problems with his personal finances and suffered tragedy in the death of his teen-age son Andrew.[45] But the years brought him great achievement. His impact was widespread and lasting. Adherence to principle was his strength. Always a controversial man, he spoke his mind fearlessly, whether he was dealing with lynching or academic standards or church unification or biblical criticism. His work as a teacher was accomplished with dedication and success. His influence extended through his students to wide areas of the church's life. He introduced a generation of pastors, educators, and other leaders to new ways of looking at the Bible. He also showed them that the Bible, even when it was seen from unfamiliar angles, was an essential source of nourishment for Christian faith.[46]

NOTES

1. Albert E. Barnett, *Andrew Sledd: His Life and Work* (n.p., n.d.), 3.

2. The surviving children were Frances, Andrew, Warren, Robert, Marvin, James, and the twins Antoinette and Florence.

3. Andrew Sledd, "The Negro: Another View," *Atlantic Monthly* 90 (July 1902): 65–73. For Sam Hose see *Atlanta Constitution*, 24 Apr. 1899, pp. 1,2, and *Atlanta Journal*, 24 Apr. 1899, pp. 1, 3.

4. Sledd, "The Negro," 66, 67, 72. Sledd's father had previously written an article which upheld similar basic principles but did not attack racial injustice with the same vehemence. See R. N. Sledd, "A Southern View of the Race Question," *Quarterly Review of the Methodist Episcopal Church, South* 8 (July 1890): 327–44.

5. Mrs. W. H. Felton, "The Negro, as Discussed by Mr. Andrew Sledd," *Atlanta Constitution*, 3 Aug. 1902, Section 3, p. 4. For her attitude to lynching see *Atlanta Constitution*, 23 Apr. 1899, p. 18, and John E. Talmadge, *Rebecca Latimer Felton: Nine Stormy Decades* (Athens, Georgia: University of Georgia Press, 1960), 113–18.

6. *Atlanta Journal*, 4 Aug. 1902, p. 6.

7. *Atlanta Constitution*, 7 Aug. 1902, p. 4.

8. Minutes of the executive committee, board of trustees of Emory College, 12 Aug. 1902, in Minutes of the Board of Trustees of Emory College, 6 June 1903 (Special Collections, Woodruff Library, Emory University).

9. Sarah Antioinette (Nettie) Candler to her mother (Mary E. Curtright), c. 1900–1902 (?), Andrew Sledd to Warren A. Candler, 27 Aug. 1902, Candler to James E. Dickey, 13 Dec. 1902 (Warren Akin Candler Papers, Special Collections, Woodruff Library, Emory University). Compare Raymond H. Firth, "The Life of Andrew Sledd," B.D. thesis, Emory University, 1940, 7–13; Mark K. Bauman, *Warren Akin Candler: The Conservative as Idealist* (Metuchen, N.J., and London: Scarecrow Press, 1981), 156–57.

10. Minutes, executive committee, 3 Sept. 1902; in Emory trustees minutes, 6 June 1903. E. E. Hendrix to Candler, 27 Aug. 1902, R. J. Bigham to Candler, 24 Aug. 1902, W. C. Lovett to Candler, 1 Sept. 1902 (?), E. E. Hoss to Candler, 25 Sept. 1902, J. D. Hammond to Candler, 14 Feb. 1903 (Candler Papers). *New York Evening Post*, 19 Aug. 1902. See also Henry Y. Warnock, "Andrew Sledd, Southern Methodists, and the Negro: A Case History," *Journal of Southern History* 31 (August 1965), 264–65. Sledd to Candler, 8 Nov. 1902 (Candler Papers).

11. Candler to J. C. Kilgo, 13 Aug. 1902 (John Carlisle Kilgo Papers, Duke University Archives, copy in Candler Papers).

12. Warren A. Candler, "Must Put Down the Mob or Be Put Down by It," *Atlanta Constitution,* 9 Sept. 1903, p. 6.

13. Virginius Dabney, *Liberalism in the South* (Chapel Hill: University of North Carolina Press, 1932), 339–41.

14. Barnett, *Andrew Sledd,* 5–6; *The University Record of the University of Florida,* vol. 26, series 1, no. 5, March 1931, 204.

15. Andrew Sledd, "The Dismissal of Professor Banks," *Independent,* 25 May 1911, p. 1113.

16. Barnett, *Andrew Sledd,* 6.

17. Joseph H. Parks and Oliver C. Weaver, Jr., *Birmingham-Southern College 1856–1956* (Nashville: Parthenon Press, 1957), 103–19.

18. Andrew Sledd, *A Southern Methodist College* (Atlanta: n.p., 1901 [?]), 11.

19. Andrew Sledd, "Religious Training in Church Colleges," *Nashville Christian Advocate* 21 (July 1911): 10.

20. Sledd, *A Southern Methodist College,* 18–19.

21. Sledd, "The Dismissal of Professor Banks," 1113–14.

22. Sledd, *A Southern Methodist College,* 18.

23. Sledd, "Religious Training in Church Colleges," 10.

24. Barnett, *Andrew Sledd,* 9; Boone M. Bowen, *The Candler School of Theology— Sixty Years of Service* (Atlanta: Candler School of Theology, 1974), 31.

25. Robert Watson Sledge, *Hands on the Ark: The Struggle for Change in the Methodist Episcopal Church, South, 1914–1939* (Lake Junaluska, N.C.: Commission on Archives and History, United Methodist Church, 1975), 144–46.

26. Parker to Candler, 1 Apr. 1922 (Candler Papers).

27. Thomas H. Lipscomb, *The Content of "Christian Education," An Arraignment and an Exposition* (n.p., 1922), 5, 12; Lipscomb to Candler, 17 May 1922 (Candler Papers).

28. Candler to Lipscomb, 25 May 1922 (Candler Papers).

29. *Journal of the Nineteenth General Conference of the Methodist Episcopal Church, South* (Nashville: Publishing House, Methodist Episcopal Church, South, 1922), (16 May 1922): 151–52.

30. *Southern Methodist* (August 1922): 2, 3. N. G. Augustus to Candler, 24 Nov. 1922 (Candler Papers).

31. Davenport to Candler, September 1926 (Candler Papers).

32. John Knox, *Never Far from Home* (Waco, Tex.: Word Books, 1975), 55. Ernest Cadman Colwell, *Adam and the Sun* (n.p., n.d.), 14–15. Bauman, *Warren Akin Candler*, 230–31.

33. Bowen, *The Candler School of Theology*, 36.

34. Chappell to Candler, 15 Aug. 1922 (Candler Papers).

35. Andrew Sledd, *Proof or Propaganda? An Open Letter to the Rev. Dr. W. A. Shelton on Unification. A Reply to his Paper, "It is 'Up to You'"* (n.p., 1924[?]). Compare Andrew Sledd, *Bishop Moore's Interpretation of the Plan of Unification* (n.p., 1925[?]).

36. Andrew Sledd, "The Interpretation of Luke 17:21," *Expository Times* 50 (February 1939): 235–37.

37. Barnett, *Andrew Sledd*, 17.

38. This information is based on lecture notes taken by Marvin H. Harper.

39. Harmon, *Ninety Years and Counting* (Nashville: Upper Room, 1983), 41–42.

40. Colwell, *Adam and the Sun*, 17–18.

41. Knox, *Never Far from Home*, 42–43.

42. Barnett, *Andrew Sledd*, 15, 17–18.

43. Afterwards Harper taught at the Candler School of Thelogy, and Norris at Union Theological Seminary, New York.

44. Andrew Sledd, *The Bibles of the Churches* (Nashville: Cokesbury Press, 1931), 7, 8, 219–20.

45. Barnett, *Andrew Sledd*, 14–15.

46. This essay was originally to have been written by Dr. James W. May, emeritus professor of liturgics and American church history at the Candler School of Theology. Dr. May had to withdraw from the project because of illness, and the author is greatly indebted to him for help and suggestions. Thanks are also due to Earl D. C. Brewer, Marvin H. Harper, John Knox, John M. Norris, Marvin B. Sledd, Warren C. Sledd, Mrs. Jane Ellen Speers, and various others who have provided information. Further research into the life and work of Andrew Sledd is being done by the Rev. Terry Matthews of Duke University.

16

Isabella Thoburn
(1840–1901)

by Carolyn De Swarte Gifford

IN THE EARLY decades of the twentieth century when higher education for women in India was no longer seen as an innovation, its
supporters enjoyed recalling the story of a female missionary who suggested to a Brahman that she teach his wife to read. The Brahman responded with amused disbelief and scorn. "Women have no brains to
learn," he sneered. "You can try to teach my wife, and if you succeed, I
will bring round my cow and you may attempt to teach her."[1] During the
nineteenth century most of the Eastern world, as well as much of the
West, shared the Brahman's view that women were unteachable. Trying
to educate them would be a waste of time. Even worse, allowing women
access to knowledge would upset a social order based on the superiority
and dominance of males.

Isabella Thoburn did not agree with the notion that it was useless to
teach women. Convinced that God meant her to consecrate her life to
educating the women of India, she labored over thirty years to make her
vision of the new Indian Christian women a reality. In the process of
realizing her vision, she founded Lucknow Woman's College, the first
Christian institution of higher education for women in Asia. Her life and
work epitomize the struggle to overcome deeply ingrained prejudices
against women's learning. But more importantly, they reveal her joy in
awakening her students to the value of intellectual knowledge and the
opportunity of Christian service to their sisters in India.

Thoburn herself chose the motto of Lucknow Woman's College: "We
receive to give." It was the ideal by which she lived and thus the one she
modeled for her students, inspiring them by example to seek ways of
helping more women become educated. For Thoburn and many other

ISABELLA THOBURN

Photo courtesy of United Methodist Commission on Archives and History.

women church leaders of her time, the education of women was an integral part of their Christian faith. They firmly believed that Christianity lifted women from imprisonment in ignorance and freed them for positions of responsibility and leadership in a new social order based on equality.

Isabella Thoburn was born March 29, 1840, into a Methodist farm family living near Saint Clairsville in eastern Ohio. She received her early education in a district school and then attended nearby Wheeling Female Seminary. During her late teens and early twenties, she taught in an Ohio country school and spent a year studying art at the Cincinnati School of Design. She returned to teaching and administrative duties in both public and private, Methodist-related schools from the Civil War until the late 1860s. In 1859, at the age of nineteen, she became a member of the Methodist Episcopal Church (MEC).

That same year, Thoburn's brother James was sent to India as a Methodist missionary. Seven years later, James Thoburn wrote his sister about his work in the Indian mission field and his conviction that "so long as the womanhood of the Church was left in ignorance . . . there could be no vigorous future to the coming Christian community."[2] Almost as an afterthought, he invited his sister to join him and begin a boarding school for girls. To his astonishment she replied promptly that she would accept his invitation as soon as a way could be found for her to get there.   ·

While Isabella Thoburn awaited an opportunity to become a missionary to India, other women of the MEC were being made aware of a special ministry which they described as an aspect of "woman's work for woman." Missionaries returning to the United States on furlough told of the existence of millions of Indian women to whom both the saving Word of the gospel and the freeing possibility of education were denied. They called for a few brave women to go to the aid of their Indian sisters, and for many more women who would provide financial support for this new and challenging woman's work for woman. In response to such appeals, Methodist women in Boston formed the Woman's Foreign Missionary Society (W.F.M.S.) in March, 1869.

At the first public meeting of the W.F.M.S. two months later, Isabella Thoburn was introduced as a potential candidate for the mission field if funds could be found to send her. Knowing that they had less than three hundred dollars in their treasury, those attending the meeting remained silent. Finally one spoke: "Shall we lose her [Thoburn]," she asked, "because we have not the needed money in our hands? No, rather, let us walk the streets of Boston in our calico robes, and save the expense of more costly apparel. Mrs. President, I move the appointment of Miss Thoburn as our missionary to India."[3] The motion was carried, and less than a year later, Thoburn arrived at Lucknow in the Oudh district of the North India Conference of the MEC where her brother James had just been appointed presiding elder.

She immediately began her educational task, gathering a group of young girls to meet for classes in a rented room in the Lucknow bazaar. By 1871 the number of students had increased to the point where the W.F.M.S. purchased Lal Bagh (Ruby Garden), a property large enough to house a boarding school as well as a day school for girls. Lal Bagh also functioned as the headquarters for W.F.M.S. activities and missionary meetings in the North India Conference. During the last third of the nineteenth century, Lucknow was developing into a strong spiritual center of Christianity in North India, and the conference was steadily enlarging its membership. Statistics reported in *Heathen Woman's Friend*, the journal of the W.F.M.S., attest to this rapid numerical growth. In 1860 the conference consisted of two preachers and five communicants; by 1890 there were 200 preachers and 9,782 communicants. In 1860 the Oudh district numbered 20 Methodists; by 1890 there were 2,200. Methodist-sponsored educational institutions also reflected the growing community. In 1860, 41 students were enrolled; by 1890, 17,241 students attended Methodist schools.[4]

The last set of statistics, however, reveals more than the mere increase in size of the Methodist community in North India. It indicates a rising demand that the mission conference provide education as well as engage in evangelism in its constituency.[5] Isabella Thoburn's educational activities can best be understood in this context. In fact, she played a significant role in creating the context through her continual insistence on the need for and the legitimacy of the church's educational mission, and in particular its responsibility for the education of young women. An 1883 report of W.F.M.S. work in North India shows results of Thoburn's push for girls' schools: that year there were 1,873 girls in city schools the W.F.M.S. supported, 270 of them at Lucknow.[6]

Thoburn's school at Lucknow, offering classes through the high school level, fast acquired a reputation for excellence. The July, 1885, issue of *Heathen Woman's Friend* mentions with pride that the government inspector of schools in North India considered the Lal Bagh school, with one possible exception, the best Anglo-vernacular school he had ever seen, and without doubt the finest in the region.[7] In 1885 the annual education report of the British government in India announced that Lal Bagh took highest place among native girls schools of Upper India. Its students were beginning to sit for university entrance exams and matriculate at government-sponsored universities. "If the school continues to pass such candidates," the report states, "it will have to be classed as a college."[8]

Lal Bagh's principal, Isabella Thoburn, had also recognized the increasing desire for college education among her students. The January, 1886, *Heathen Woman's Friend* contains her initial appeal for funds to begin the first Christian woman's college in India. In the article she reviews the current situation in Indian education and describes her inability to place her students in institutions of higher education with strong Christian ideals and influence. She concludes that the only possible solution to her students' dilemma is for the W.F.M.S. to found a Christian woman's college. She prefaces her plea for funds with a concise statement of the aim of the college she hopes to establish:

> We need strong-minded women at the top, in order to lift up the great mass of ignorance below, and there is not a [Christian] woman's college in all the Empire. Shall we not have the first at Lucknow? Many of you who read this can spare $5,000 as easily as your Indian sister can her 500 rupees and I send my plea to you with strong hope that you will appreciate at its true value this new project, and send over money to help us.[9]

Thoburn's "new project" was actually the culmination of nearly two decades of struggle to persuade both Indian society and the mission community the women's education was an effort worth the investment of personnel, time, and money. Although Hindu and Muslim cultures in North India had strong, centuries-old traditions of educating boys, neither culture placed a correspondingly high value on the education of girls. The sneering Brahman who compared his wife's intellectual capacity to that of his cow should not be seen as a caricature of a high-caste Hindu male. His attitude was that of the overwhelming majority of the Indian population, both male and female, who believed that women were incapable of serious study.

An Indian woman's role and status in her culture were defined by her relationship to men. She was a daughter, a wife, or a mother—preferably a mother of sons, but never a person in her own right. Her duty was to serve the men to whom she was related, a duty which left little time for schooling. A woman's well-being depended upon how favorably her male relatives treated her, giving her great incentive for pleasing the males in her life. A woman without a male protector—father, husband, son, or son-in-law—was in dire straits, as evidenced by the custom of *sati* or "widow-burning" as missionaries termed it. Women who had lost their husbands and were without other male protectors often threw themselves on their husbands' funeral pyres, with the encouragement of Indian society which knew well the desperate situation widows faced alone. Although British officials, Christian missionaries, and some Hindu leaders had attempted to put a stop to this practice by legal action, it was not uncommon during Thoburn's time.

Also common for Muslims and upper-caste Hindus was women's seclusion in a separate area of an extended-family household. The only
males permitted into the *zenana* (women's quarters) were relatives. As
the exclusive property of their husbands, wives could not even be
looked upon by men who were not extended family members. The seclusion of women, called *purdah nashin* (literally, "sitting behind a
screen"), shocked the missionary community, particularly the women,
who were accustomed as Westerners to participating to some extent in
public life. Shortly after Thoburn arrived in Lucknow, she sent a letter
back to the United States addressed to "The Young Ladies of Our Colleges and Seminaries." In it, she likened the secluded status of many
Indian women to

> being kept in a state of perpetual childhood, [a] childhood in ignorance, but
> not in innocence or happiness. . . . I think of you often . . . and of your bright,
> hopeful lives, in comparison with limited privileges and dark prospects of
> these girls around me. You have every incentive and opportunity to cultivate
> your minds—they are shut away from all means of improvement . . . their
> world is bounded by the walls of the *zenana*.[10]

For Thoburn, the great tragedy of the seclusion of women was that they
would never be given an opportunity to develop their minds fully
through education. Thus they would remain "in a childhood of ignorance" no matter what their chronological age.

Both she and her brother James believed that the custom of *purdah
nashin* must be abandoned; that, indeed, Indian society's entire view of
the position of women must be fundamentally altered. According to the
Thoburns, such a change would be accomplished only by Indian's conversion to Christianity, a "social Christianity" which would bring about
not merely individual conversions but a radical restructuring of society
to reflect Christian values and ideals.[11] James Thoburn's vision of
woman's place in the new Indian Christian society was somewhat more
limited than that of his sister. He saw educated women presiding over
Christian homes. Isabella Thoburn dreamed of a far broader role for
women as leaders in the wider world—educators, doctors, nurses, evangelists—filling responsible roles in society. Her school would prepare its
students for these roles.

As one might expect, missionary efforts to effect fundamental
changes in Indian culture met with great resistance. Hindus and Muslims not only resisted becoming Christians. They also opposed attempts
to educate women, and they immediately perceived a connection between the education of women and conversions to Christianity. By the
late 1860s missionary wives had gained entry into the *zenanas* where

their husbands could not go. Once inside, they taught women and girls to read using the Bible as a primer, and began to train native "Bible women" to continue the work of literacy and evangelism. Just as Thoburn began her first missionary term, a widely discussed incident occurred in which a Bible woman converted to Christianity along with her two daughters. The three women had left their home, and one son-in-law initiated a court battle in order to force the women to renounce their Christian faith and return to their husbands' custody as "possessions." He won the case, with the result that all three women reconverted to Islam and acknowledged their husbands' ownership of their persons. Local authorities immediately closed down the *zenana* school the women had taught. With rumors of another conversion in Calcutta, more than 700 miles away, *zenana* teaching was forbidden in the area around Lucknow and only gradually allowed to recommence.[12]

Amid rumors and hostility, the missionary community was understandably uneasy about its insecure relationship to the Indian society it hoped to convert. It also faced problems of limited and constantly changing personnel and inadequate funding. The situation necessitated continual discussion among missionaries about how best to employ their small resources. Such discussion often centered on the question of education versus evangelism, and Thoburn's plans for girls' schooling became one focus of controversy over how money should be spent and personnel assigned. Would it not be wise, some asked, to postpone the development of higher education for women while the mission concentrated its energy on evangelism?

Tension surfaced from another area of disagreement as well. There was dissension within the missionary community over the role of women in the enterprise. Were women to serve simply as wives, helpmeets to their husbands who would actually plan the goals and strategies of mission activity? Or were women to assume new duties and participate more fully in the direction of mission work? Men were already discovering that women could minister to their Indian sisters by entering the *zenanas*, however precarious that ministry might be. Special evangelistic and teaching roles for women meant that men must relinquish some of their traditional authority, and American men, like their Indian counterparts, were not often willing to do that. If husbands were nervous about their wives' taking control of certain aspects of ministry, they had even more misgivings about the prospect of single female missionaries. James Thoburn reports with apparent surprise male missionary rumblings on the subject even before his sister arrived in India as one of the first two single woman missionaries sent by the W.F.M.S. "The brethren of the mission were by no means sure that they wanted a contingent of young women to be added to the permanent working force in the field."[13]

Controversy over the roles of women continued, becoming refocused around the issue of education for girls and young women. Many in the mission community gave it low priority. They had to be convinced, just as Indian society did, that there was worth in an educated womanhood. Women's higher education was still a much-debated subject back home in the United States. The first coeducational colleges and universities had been established only fifty years before Isabella Thoburn proposed to start her Christian college for women in India. Women's colleges had existed for slightly more than two decades. Americans were still dubious about whether their daughters had as much intelligence as their sons, and arguments raged over whether a young woman's health would be ruined if she tried to pursue the same course of study which her brother followed. In 1882 during a speech before a large mission conference, Thoburn reported that progress was finally being made in overcoming her colleagues' prejudices against women's education.

> Ten years ago missionaries who were preparing boys for the university degrees insisted that their sisters would be spoiled if taught English. Less than half of ten years ago I have myself turned a blackboard to the wall to hide a geometrical diagram, when visitors were announced who would be grieved, if not shocked, at what they considered wholly out of place in a girls' school. When the girls had learned their Euclid and had matriculated, and had brought up the whole tone of the [high] school, lifting the ambition of its pupils from idleness and dress to work and study, observers were convinced, and it was no longer necessary to avoid argument by concealing the unfinished work of the [high] school classes.[14]

Although she had some reason for optimism, opposition to her plan for extending opportunities for education beyond high school level was still strong several years later. In a leaflet she had prepared for circulation in the U.S. during her second furlough (1886–90), she noted the creation of rising expectations for further education among her high school students: "We have taught them that, though women, they have minds that are capable of receiving education and that require it." Then she posed a crucial question: "Shall we now teach them that they require less, and are less capable than their brothers?"[15] For Thoburn the answer was clearly no, and she pressed ahead toward her goal of establishing a Christian woman's college, one which would be a center of higher education in North India. Her school would prepare young women to pass the fine arts exam (taken at the end of the second year of college) and eventually to receive a B.A. degree. By the mid-nineties, Thoburn saw the need for teachers who could instruct students in the latest Western pedagogical trends, and she began a normal school course. Graduates of the B.A. program were encouraged to go for advanced degrees at medical and nursing schools.

Thoburn's vision of her college extended beyond a challenging intellectual environment. She wished to produce an institution which would provide her students with a thorough grounding in Christian ideas and action so that as graduates of Lucknow Woman's College they could be models of the Christian life and leaders in a new Christian India. One of the social customs Thoburn felt must disappear was the caste system, deeply entrenched in traditional Hindu society. She knew that it would take time and patience to break down caste and racial divisions since they pervaded every aspect of daily life as well as receiving sanction in Indian religious, legal, and social institutions. Yet she believed that, as Christians, she and her teachers and students could not maintain such divisions.

Creating a college without accommodation to caste distinctions would be no easy task. Missionaries who ran schools, hospitals, and dispensaries had to deal constantly with the necessity of providing separate wings for members of different castes and with making sure that food prepared for one caste did not come into contact with a member of another, lower caste. Bringing young women in different castes together and adding Eurasians, Europeans, and Americans to this cultural mixture would be a difficult undertaking. But Thoburn had already been doing so for many years at Lucknow boarding school. She went about her work in a quiet but firm manner, showing by her own example that caste divisions could be broken down. She treated her students, indeed everyone, as persons of equal worth to whom she gave unlimited love and attention. Caste status simply did not matter to her since she felt that it would not have mattered to Jesus.

Thoburn was well aware that she asked a great deal of both students and teachers by suggesting that they place themselves in a situation where caste distinctions would be ignored. "To do it we must dare something and renounce something. To work for and with all classes of people, we must be one with all, and belong to no class ourselves, which will sometimes mean that we must become low-caste."[16] They would find it easier, she thought, to move beyond the world of rigid caste separations if they lived in a residential college rather than commuting daily from their homes in which caste rules were strictly enforced. Thus Thoburn strongly encouraged her students to board at Lucknow where they would be under the supervision and influence of Christian teachers—both Indian and American—who were dedicated to breaking down caste barriers.

The new Christian India which the Thoburns and other missionaries envisioned would take its place in the larger world-community of both Eastern and Western countries. Its leaders would need to be truly multilingual, able to speak and write fluently in more than one Indian language as well as in English. As a matter of sheer practicality, Thoburn's students had to become bilingual, taking required courses in Indian languages in order to pass government exams at various levels. All other required government exams were administered in English, so students had to master that language. As usual, however, Thoburn's rationale for bilingual education went beyond the merely practical. She wished to instill in her students a respect for what was unique and beautiful in Indian culture as expressed in its languages and literature. In contrast to some Westernized Indian students who spoke and wrote only in English and evidenced contempt for everything Indian, Thoburn's students were taught to love India and make service to their country a vocation.[17] Yet mastery of English was vitally important to her because it was often the only language common to people from the many different regions of India, as well as the key to communication with Britons and Americans. A well-educated Indian woman was required to express herself in both the vernacular and English. One who wished to spread Christianity must be further able to translate into various Indian tongues the gospel message often learned initially in English. Isabella Thoburn fervently hoped that Indian graduates of her school would become effective native missionaries. In order to do this they must be capable of speaking about their faith in more than one language.

Thoburn had great dreams for the higher education of women, but she did not establish Lucknow Woman's College without struggle. From the day the school opened on July 12, 1886, it was plagued with financial problems. It also received criticism from segments of the missionary community and from some W.F.M.S. members. Thoburn was forced for health reasons to take a furlough just as the college was getting started. She was in the United States from 1886–90 in the crucial beginning stage, and the absence of her vigorous leadership was apparent. Direction of the institution fell to several different women, none of Thoburn's stature, until she returned to take over in 1890. While she was away there were few applicants for admission to the college; for several years, in fact, there were none at all. Missionary colleagues seriously questioned whether there really was need for a woman's college. On her return, Thoburn insisted that there was, and increased enrollment during the 1890s bore out her conviction. By 1894 there were fifteen young women enrolled and several excellent teachers, both Indian and American, who had been recruited by Thoburn. Her staff was hand-picked to embody Christian idealism and missionary spirit as well as to exemplify a love of intellectual knowledge.

In recognition of the high standard of education developed during a decade, the college was granted a charter by the British government in India in 1896. That same year the first B.A. candidate was ready to take exams given at the University of Allahabad, the institution to which Thoburn's college was related. Lucknow Woman's College was developing on a firm academic footing, but its financial troubles were not over.

Thoburn served as the chief fund-raiser for her institution as well as being its administrator and one of its professors. For many years *Heathen Woman's Friend* was filled with reports of the growth of the college, almost invariably including an appeal for funds. It was not difficult to persuade women in the United States to send money designated for scholarships. But that was not what the college needed or what Thoburn wanted. She wished her students to pay their own way as a means of getting them to place a high value on their education. Furthermore, money was desperately needed for "bricks and mortar"—maintenance, new buildings, and repairs to existing structures—along with faculty salaries. Thoburn suggested various methods for raising money, from endowing a professor's chair to forming missionary societies among college girls in America whose goal would be to help support a sister institution in India. In an 1897 letter to a leader of the W.F.M.S., Thoburn states her case more bluntly than usual:

> I need money very much [for the college], if only it would come without limitations. If I had thirty dollars I could get the matting I need so much for the college dormitories, or twenty other things that will face me as soon as I go home. I left an order for a bookcase when I left that is to be paid for from Lilly's fund, but I have no fund for dining room and bed room. These things are not interesting, but they are very essential.[18]

Finally the college's shaky financial situation led the North India Conference to send Isabella Thoburn on another furlough, this time for the sole purpose of fund-raising. Accompanied by Lilavati Singh, one of her ablest teachers, Thoburn toured the United States, speaking to annual conferences, mission groups, and individual churches about supporting Lucknow Woman's College.

Despite all of their financial worries, Thoburn and her staff managed to provide students with a sound education geared toward enabling them to think for themselves. It was often difficult to change habits of rote memorization rooted in centuries of traditional Indian ways of learning, but Indian women were introduced to research methods, with the aid of encyclopedias and other reference books sent from the United States by W.F.M.S. branches. Women who had grown up in a culture which taught them to behave in a shy, deferential manner were formed into debate teams and learned how to defend opposing positions just as their American counterparts were doing. The college staff hoped that debates, elocution classes, literary contests, and calisthenics—an innovation for both Indian and American college women—would produce a generation of articulate, healthy Indian women.[19]

Thoburn died of cholera at age sixty-one on September 1, 1901, shortly after returning from her fund-raising tour. In 1903, Lucknow Woman's College was renamed Isabella Thoburn College to honor a great pioneer in higher education for women in Asia, and it continues today to prepare young Indian women for Christian leadership, under the direction of Dr. Kamala Edwards.[20] The college was not simply a memorial to one who was intent on founding a strong scholarly institution, although Thoburn always wished her college to strive for academic excellence. It was also a testimony to the profound respect and love that students, staff, and missionary colleagues bore for one who continually manifested through her life the Christian idealism in which she believed so strongly.

Her death occasioned an outpouring of tributes which reveal how integrally linked her faith and life were. They speak of a teaching style which was truly exemplary—worthy of being imitated—and which extended beyond the classroom to every facet of life in the college. Her personal concern for her students was boundless and her patience, inexhaustible. She was remembered for her fairness and impartiality, her quiet humor, her ability to inspire students toward their best efforts, and her instinctive understanding of all kinds of people. Many recalled her skilled and gentle nursing of sick students and staff, the Bible lessons she gave, and the Sunday afternoon prayer meetings she conducted.

Thoburn's exemplary life was grounded in her sense of consecration. Although she had worked with a spirit of dedication from the time she arrived in India, she made her consecration explicit during her second furlough by becoming a deaconess, joining with other women who sought to commit their entire lives to Christ-like service. It was this consecrated spirit of service which Thoburn hoped to instill in her students. Lilavati Singh wrote of listening to Thoburn tell stories of missionary heroes: "I remember her face fairly glowed when she said: 'If you once get the taste for this service, nothing else will satisfy you.'"[21] Through all of her years in India, Isabella Thoburn was the genuine embodiment of the motto she chose for her school: "We receive to give." Her gift to Methodist higher education was twofold: the founding of her institution for women and her exemplary life.

NOTES

1. James L. Barton, *Educational Missions* (New York: Student Volunteer Movement for Foreign Missions, 1913), 107. In this context the word *Brahman* means a member of the highest caste in Hinduism, a group traditionally responsible for priestly duties and possessing great status in Indian society.

2. James M. Thoburn, *Life of Isabella Thoburn* (Cincinnati: Jennings and Pye, 1903), 33.

3. Mary Sparkes Wheeler, *First Decade of the Woman's Foreign Missionary Society of the Methodist Episcopal Church: With Sketches of Its Missionaries* (New York: Phillips and Hunt, 1881), 46.

4. Rev. E. W. Parker, "Good Wishes From India for the College," *Heathen Woman's Friend* 21 (May 1890): 280.

5. See Barton, *Educational Missions*, for a thorough discussion of the rationale for and the results of educational missions as they were understood by the second decade of the twentieth century. Barton's conclusions about the place of the educational aspect of missionary work were first developed and tested by Isabella Thoburn and many others on the mission field during the five decades preceding this 1913 report. According to Barton, the secretary of the American Board of Commissioners for Foreign Missions, "educational missions . . . are but a single department of the university of the Kingdom of God, holding a place of large importance but inseparable from the institution as a whole." (p. 3) The goal of missions, bringing in the kingdom, would be accomplished not only by evangelism but also by introducing the results of modern Western science, particularly in the area of medicine; by bringing the benefits of Western industrialization to "industrially backward races"; by developing educational systems to combat illiteracy; and by fostering the growth of democratic institutions of government. Barton's assumption that the coming of the kingdom of God would mean the realization of modern Western civilization throughout the world was widely shared by the ecumenical mission community in the early twentieth century.

6. Rev. B. H. Badley, "City Schools for Girls, North India," *Heathen Woman's Friend* 16 (January 1885): 160.

7. "Gleanings, " *Heathen Woman's Friend* 17 (July 1885): 19.

8. Thoburn, *Life of Isabella Thoburn*, 181.

9. Isabella Thoburn, "A Woman's College for India," *Heathen Woman's Friend* 17 (March 1886): 210–11. By 1886 when Thoburn wrote this article, there was already an institution of higher education for women, Bethune College in Calcutta. It was not a Christian college, however. It had been established by the

Brahmo Samaj (Society of God), a movement founded in 1828 as a result of a Hindu renascence which continued throughout the nineteenth century and on into the twentieth. Mohandas K. Gandhi, for example, was strongly influenced by the ideas and leadership of this awakening. During the 1800s Hindu and Muslim intellectuals wrestled with the problem of remaining true to their own venerable traditions while responding to the challenges of modern Western culture which they encountered in the rule of the British and in the Christian missionary presence.

10. Isabella Thoburn, "To the Young Ladies in our Seminaries and Colleges," *Heathen Woman's Friend* 1 (May 1870): 89. See item three in "Gleanings," *Heathen Woman's Friend* 17 (July 1885): 19, for a description of the situation of Hindu women, especially widows.

11. See Thoburn, *Life of Isabella Thoburn*, 81; also Barton, *Educational Missions*, 107–28.

12. Badley, "City Schools for Girls," *Heathen Woman's Friend* 16 (January 1885): 159, and Isabella Thoburn, "Then and Now," *Heathen Woman's Friend* 26 (September 1894): 65.

13. Thoburn, *Life of Isabella Thoburn*, 34. See also p. 89, and Benton Thoburn Badley, ed., *Visions and Victories in Hindustan* (Madras, India: Methodist Publishing House, 1931), 583–86.

14. Thoburn, *Life of Isabella Thoburn*, 173.

15. Thoburn, *Life of Isabella Thoburn*, 190.

16. Thoburn, *Life of Isabella Thoburn*, 180. See also p. 105, and Isabella Thoburn, "Lucknow College Library," *Woman's Missionary Friend* 28 (March 1897): 244, for a description of the diverse racial and caste makeup of a class of fifteen students attending Lucknow Woman's College. *Woman's Missionary Friend* was a continuation of the W.F.M.S. journal, *Heathen Woman's Friend*. The name change occurred in January, 1896, apparently reflecting increasing sensitivity on the part of the W.F.M.S. leadership.

17. Lilavati Singh, "Recollections," in Thoburn, *Life of Isabella Thoburn*, 361.

18. Letter of Isabella Thoburn to Mrs. (J.T.) Gracey, 24 May 1897. Access 79–16, 1467–5–3: 29, General Commission on Archives and History, the United Methodist Church, Madison, N.J. Permission for quotation has been granted by the General Board of Global Ministries of the United Methodist Church.

19. Lilavati Singh, "Class Day at Lucknow College," *Woman's Missionary Friend* 33

(April 1901): 117–18. See also Florence L. Nichols, "College Education in India," *Woman's Missionary Friend* (April 1896): 110.

20. Ruth Dinkins Rowan, "Kamala Edwards Goes Home," *New World Outlook* 68 (September 1979): 37.

21. "Miss Singh's Recollections," in Thoburn, *Life of Isabella Thoburn,* 362.